The Lesbian and Gay Movements

Dilemmas in American Politics

Series Editor: **Craig A. Rimmerman,** *Hobart and William Smith Colleges*

If the answers to the problems facing U.S. democracy were easy, politicians would solve them, accept credit, and move on. But certain dilemmas have confronted the American political system continuously. They defy solution; they are endemic to the system. Some can best be described as institutional dilemmas: How can the Congress be both a representative body and a national decision-maker? How can the president communicate with more than 250 million citizens effectively? Why do we have a two-party system when many voters are disappointed with the choices presented to them? Others are policy dilemmas: How do we find compromises on issues that defy compromise, such as abortion policy? How do we incorporate racial and ethnic minorities or immigrant groups into American society, allowing them to reap the benefits of this land without losing their identity? How do we fund health care for our poorest or oldest citizens?

Dilemmas such as these are what propel students toward an interest in the study of U.S. government. Each book in the *Dilemmas in American Politics Series* addresses a "real world" problem, raising the issues that are of most concern to students. Each is structured to cover the historical and theoretical aspects of the dilemma but also to explore the dilemma from a practical point of view and to speculate about the future. The books are designed as supplements to introductory courses in American politics or as case studies to be used in upper-level courses. The link among them is the desire to make the real issues confronting the political world come alive in students' eyes.

BOOKS IN THIS SERIES

The Lesbian and Gay Movements: Assimilation or Liberation?, Second Edition
Craig A. Rimmerman

Inequality in America
Stephen Caliendo

"Can We All Get Along?": Racial and Ethnic Minorities in American Politics, Sixth Edition
Paula D. McClain and Joseph Stewart Jr.

The Democratic Dilemma of American Education: Out of Many, One?
Arnold Shober

Onward Christian Soldiers? The Religious Right in American Politics, Fourth Edition
Clyde Wilcox and Carin Larson

The New Citizenship: Unconventional Politics, Activism, and Service, Fourth Edition
Craig A. Rimmerman

Claiming the Mantle: How Presidential Nominations Are Won and Lost Before the Votes Are Cast
R. Lawrence Butler

Voting for Women: How the Public Evaluates Women Candidates
Kathleen A. Dolan

Two Parties—or More? The American Party System, Second Edition
John F. Bibby and L. Sandy Maisel

The Role of the Supreme Court in American Politics: The Least Dangerous Branch?
Richard L. Pacelle Jr.

Money Rules: Financing Elections in America
Anthony Gierzynski

The Accidental System: Health Care Policy in America
Michael D. Reagan

The Image-Is-Everything Presidency: Dilemma in American Leadership
Richard W. Waterman, Robert Wright, and Gilbert St. Clair

The Angry American: How Voter Rage Is Changing the Nation, Second Edition
Susan J. Tolchin

Remote and Controlled: Media Politics in a Cynical Age, Second Edition
Matthew Robert Kerbel

Making Americans, Remaking America: Immigration and Immigrant Policy
Louis DeSipio and Rodolfo de la Garza

From Rhetoric to Reform? Welfare Policy in American Politics
Anne Marie Cammisa

No Neutral Ground? Abortion Politics in an Age of Absolutes
Karen O'Connor

Payment Due: A Nation in Debt, a Generation in Trouble
Timothy J. Penny and Steven E. Schier

Bucking the Deficit: Economic Policymaking in the United States
G. Calvin Mackenzie and Saranna Thornton

The Lesbian and Gay Movements

Assimilation or Liberation?

SECOND EDITION

Craig A. Rimmerman
Hobart and William Smith Colleges

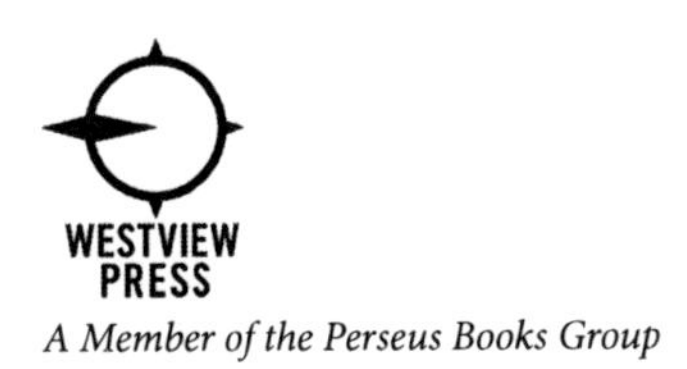

A Member of the Perseus Books Group

To those teachers, scholars, and activists who paved the way.

Westview Press was founded in 1975 in Boulder, Colorado, by notable publisher and intellectual Fred Praeger. Westview Press continues to publish scholarly titles and high-quality undergraduate-and graduate-level textbooks in core social science disciplines. With books developed, written, and edited with the needs of serious nonfiction readers, professors, and students in mind, Westview Press honors its long history of publishing books that matter.

Published by Westview Press,
A Member of the Perseus Books Group

Find us on the World Wide Web at www.westviewpress.com.

Library of Congress Cataloging-in-Publication Data
Rimmerman, Craig A.
The lesbian and gay movements : assimilation or liberation? / Craig A Rimmerman. -- Second Edition.
pages cm. — (Dilemmas in American politics)
ISBN 978-0-8133-4849-0 (paperback) — ISBN 978-0-8133-4850-6 (e-book) 1. Gay liberation movement—United States. 2. Gay rights—United States. 3. Homosexuality—Political aspects—United States. 4. Assimilation (Sociology) 5. United States—Social conditions. 6. United States—Politics and government. I. Title.

HQ76.8.U5R58 2014
323.3'2640973--dc23

2014011428

10 9 8 7 6 5 4 3 2 1

Contents

Illustrations

Preface

This book owes its existence to the wonderful 1992–1993 sabbatical year that I spent in Washington, DC, as an American Political Science Association Congressional Fellow. I lived at Dupont Circle, the heart of Washington's vibrant gay community, and I witnessed firsthand the excitement, hope, and anticipation of the Democrats' return to power in the 1992 presidential election. And then like so many people in DC's lesbian and gay community (and in the country writ large), I experienced immediate disappointment with President Clinton's handling of the gays-in-the-military fiasco. By day, I worked as a congressional fellow in the offices of Senator Tom Daschle (D-SD) and Representative Barbara Kennelly (D-CT), and I observed the early months of the Clinton presidency unfolding from the inside of Congress. And I met and socialized with lesbian and gay activists who embraced both the assimilationist and the liberationist perspectives that are at the core of this book's underlying dilemma.

Now some twenty years later, I revisit some of the important issues and questions that grew out of my time living and working in the nation's capital. How much progress have the lesbian and gay movements made over the years in achieving larger movement goals? And what are those goals? How have they changed over time? Which political organizing strategies are the most effective, and which are the least effective? What are our criteria for effectiveness? Why is there such virulent opposition to public policies that would support and explicitly value lesbians, gays, bisexuals, and those who are transgendered? And what would our society look like if we broadened our conception of citizenship to include sexual minorities?

The policy issues that are at the core of this book—HIV/AIDS, the military ban, and same-sex marriage—have been among the most contentious public policy issues of our time, and as such they are an excellent set of issues for exploring the tensions between the assimilationist and liberationist political organizing strategies, which is our central dilemma. Much has changed within each of these policy areas since the first edition was published in 2008. Indeed, many of these changes represent significant progress, as we will see, and are the result of hard organizing work on the part of the lesbian and gay movements over the course of many years. But much work still needs to be done, as we will also see. With these issues in mind, this book will be of interest to students and teachers of American politics, public policy, social movements, and interest groups, as well as activists working for these causes.

I have had the support and encouragement of so many people while writing this book. I especially wish to thank Westview's Dilemmas in American Politics editorial board, which encouraged me to "get this book done!" And a huge thanks to Ada Fung, Westview acquisitions editor, whose professionalism and gentle encouragement helped me complete this book in a timely way. Ada personifies the best qualities in an editor, especially the belief that an author has something of value to contribute to the world. I also acknowledge the excellent copyediting of Carrie Watterson and the work of Westview senior project editor, Amber Morris, who was instrumental in moving the manuscript toward publication.

I thank, as well, my students over many years (since 1986!) who have helped make Hobart and William Smith a wonderful place to teach. I won't be able to recognize all of them here, but I especially wanted to mention those who have been especially supportive of and inspirational to me over the years: Brian Allyn, Phil Anderson, Martha Belz, Richie Bonney, Lauren Borislow, Dan Boysen, Daniel Budmen, Peter Budmen, Coty Burgess, Geneva Calder, Caleb Campbell, Nate Campbell, Patrick Carroll, Ben Chaplin, Rose Cherubin, Matt Chin, David Cooke, Emma Daley, Owen Dodge, Jane Erickson, Lily Farnham, Brian Franz, Hilary Gove, Ross Green, Lou Guard, Julie Hembeck, Anna Hertline, Ross Hicks, Nick Hindle, Lucy Hoagland, Holly Huffine, Graham Hughes, Matt Hursh, Will Inbusch, Austin Kana, Kate Kana, Patrick Kana, Stephanie Kenific, Alex Kent, Sean Kipperman, Jenna Klicker, John Paul Langevin, Erin Laskey, Mike Lucas, Maggie Markham, Sarah Marlow, Emily Miller, Ryan Mullaney, Kaylyn O'Brien, Zach Oberfield, Jinelle Park, Arthur Piantedesoi, Molly Doris-Pierce, Chris Pope, Mary Posman, Keegan Prue, Inty Ramirez, Tyson Reuter, Rachael Rich, Emma Richardson, Justin Ristau, James B. Robinson, Lela Rosen, Molly Rosenthal, Lauren Samuelson, Harrison Schutzer, Danielle Shaw, Tyler Shepard, Michael Shore, Ben Sio, Jamie Peter Smith, Ryan Sollenne, Max Swagler, Sean Walker, Patrick White, Sam Williams, the late Courtney Wilson, and Ashley Yang.

Thank you, as well, to an array of people who have been so supportive of my work and kind to me over the years: Lesley Adams, Stewart Auyash, Betty Bayer, Val Bunce, Lynne Cohen, Pat Cool, Bryce Corrigan, Tom Drennen, Zillah Eisenstein, Rhian Ellis, Shawn Fitzgibbons, Maureen Flynn, Ronny Frishman, Mark Gearan, Jack Goldman, Chris Gunn, Hazel Dayton-Gunn, Marianna Grigorov-Norberg, Gabe Heck, Susan Henking, Ron Herring, Liz Holmes, Mary Katzenstein, Dr. Adam Law, Steven Lee, Adam Levine, Derek Linton, Judith McKinney, Scott McKinney, Dunbar Moodie, Ilene Nicholas, David Ost, Eric Patterson, Don Spector, Laura Sposato, Kelly Switzer, Rich Szanyi, the late Deborah Tall, Ben Trumble, David Weiss, Clyde Wilcox, Stacia Zabusky, and Patty Zimmermann.

I thank, too, the entire Hobart and William Smith library staff, especially Jennifer Nace, who has ordered many materials pertaining to the second edition of this book and Vince Boisselle, Joseph Chmura, Maggie Gladden, Sara Greenleaf, Michael Hunter, and Dan Mulvey, for their continued support. I am appreciative that the Hobart and William Smith Faculty Research and Awards Committee provided ongoing support for this and related projects.

And I am so grateful to the lesbian and gay activists who very generously agreed to sit down with me to talk about many of the book's core ideas. I conducted interviews beginning in 1992, and they spanned across the United States: from Boston, New York, Los Angeles, and Philadelphia to Portland, Oregon, and Washington, DC. I am inspired daily by the courage and commitment of the many teachers, scholars, and activists who paved the way. It is to them that I dedicate this book.

Ithaca, New York
February 2014

1

Introduction to the Core Dilemma

If we are to transform our state of virtual equality, evident in pervasive discrimination, ambivalent public opinion, and the persistence of the closet, we must begin with ourselves—both individually and as a movement. Coming out is the one step each gay, lesbian, or bisexual person can take to shatter virtual equality and move closer to the genuine equality with heterosexuals that is our birthright as moral human beings. Our challenge as a movement requires an examination of the strategies that have brought us to this troubling juncture.

—**Urvashi Vaid,** *Virtual Equality: The Mainstreaming of Gay and Lesbian Liberation*

Trying to find common ground for political mobilization among all these identities has become one of the most difficult tasks of what has come to be called the gay rights movement.

—**Robert Bailey,** *Gay Politics, Urban Politics: Identity and Economics in the Urban Setting*

Urvashi Vaid's and Robert Bailey's observations capture the challenges facing the contemporary lesbian and gay rights movements.[1] Vaid and Bailey point to the reality that all social movements, including the lesbian and gay movements, must constantly examine their broader political, social, and cultural approaches to change. The goal is to assess the difficulties and possibilities that have faced the movements over time with an eye toward what might be done in the future to expand the traditional notions of democracy and citizenship.

This is a particularly auspicious time to engage in this kind of critical examination, given the increasing cultural visibility of lesbians, gays, bisexuals, and those who are transgendered, reflected in an array of popular television shows, including *Glee, Shameless, Mad Men, Downton Abbey, Modern Family, The L Word, Queer as Folk, Six Feet Under, Will and Grace, The Sopranos, Rescue Me, Nip/Tuck, Buffy the Vampire Slayer, Oz, NYPD Blue,* and *The Shield,* to name a few. And when a moving, mainstream Hollywood film, *Brokeback Mountain*, receives considerable critical praise from reviewers and enthusiastic attention by the moviegoing public, one recognizes the sea change that has taken place since even the mid-1990s. But what does this visibility really mean for people's daily lives? In recent years we have seen increased public tolerance and support for people coming out of the closet. Indeed, Margaret Talbot has written in the *New Yorker* that "the more gay friends, family members, and co-workers straight people know they have, and the more gay celebrities they are aware of, the harder it is for society to deny rights on the basis of some specious presumption of otherness" (Talbot 2013, 21). The students I teach now are more likely to be supportive of their "out" peers than others were even ten years ago. And courses related to the lesbian and gay movements across academic disciplines are often among the most popular offerings on college campuses. This undoubtedly reflects the political organizing and education of earlier eras and the salience of these complicated and challenging issues to young people's lives.

At the same time, the lesbian and gay movements have achieved tangible accomplishments establishing open communities of lesbians and gay men in urban areas throughout the United States. In addition, openly gay men and lesbians have been successful in the electoral arena, from city councils to state legislatures to the US Congress. Indeed, Tammy Baldwin (D-WI) is the first openly lesbian or gay member of the United States Senate, elected in 2012. Community organizations and businesses target the interests of the lesbian and gay movements. And some progress has been made through the legal system, most notably in the Supreme Court's 2003 *Lawrence v. Texas* decision that ruled state sodomy laws unconstitutional. As the constitutional historian Michael Klarman has accurately pointed out, "fifty years ago, every state criminalized same-sex sodomy; today it is a constitutional right." And Klarman correctly celebrates progress that the movements have made in fighting employment discrimination as well: "Thirty years ago, not a single state barred discrimination based on sexual orientation in employment or public accommodations; today more than twenty states have enacted such laws" (Klarman 2013, 218).

College and professional sports are beginning to mirror changes in society writ large. In 2013, Robbie Rogers, an outstanding professional soccer player, publicly identified himself as gay and, within several months, signed a professional contract with the LA Galaxy, as an out, proud gay man. Brittney Griner, a women's college basketball star at Baylor University, came out of the closet to little fanfare and signed a professional contract to play with the Phoenix Mercury of the WNBA. Jason Collins, a journeyman center who had played for five NBA teams and was still an active player, came out on *Sports Illustrated*'s website on April 29, 2013, followed by a cover story in the May 6, 2013, issue of the magazine. Collins's coming out story was greeted with considerable fanfare as he became the first male athlete from one of the four major professional sports (baseball, basketball, football, hockey) to do so. On Sunday, February 23, 2014, Collins became the first openly gay professional player, after signing a ten-day contract with the NBA's New Jersey Nets earlier in the day. He debuted that evening when the Nets played the Lakers in Los Angeles. Neither the NFL, MLB, or NHL had ever had an openly gay athlete prior to Collins's debut. Collins's groundbreaking act and the New Jersey Nets' willingness to afford Collins the opportunity, will undoubtedly inspire other professional athletes to come out while active participants in their respective sports.

Indeed, in February 2014, in an act of tremendous courage, University of Missouri defensive lineman and graduating senior, Michael Sam, announced that he is gay in interviews with *ESPN* and the *New York Times.* Sam had previously come out to his entire college football team in August 2013 and received tremendous support from his coaches and teammates. His announcement came roughly two months before the NFL draft and led to widespread speculation that it would continue to pave the way for other gay, lesbian, bisexual, and transgender athletes in professional sports.

But for all of the so-called progress, lesbians and gay men remain second-class citizens in vital ways. For example, though in May 2013 the Boy Scouts of America ended its long-term policy of preventing openly gay youths from participating in any of its organizational activities, this major policy change, effective in January 2014, was passed only after considerable acrimony and internal organizational debate. Although this development was viewed as evidence of progress by some in the lesbian and gay movements, the policy was undercut by the inability of the organization to address "the even more divisive question of whether to allow openly gay adults and leaders" (Eckholm 2013, A1). In doing so, the Boy Scouts of America reinforced the worst assumptions of out adults who are in organizational leadership positions.

In addition, there is considerable societal disagreement over an array of interrelated issues, including same-sex marriage, adoption of children by same-sex couples, and ordination of lesbian and gay people into the clergy (Olson, Djupe, and Cadge, 2011, 189). Out lesbians, gays, and bisexuals occupy less than one-tenth of 1 percent of all elected offices in this country (Sherrill 1996, 469); very few transgendered people have been elected to public office. In most states, lesbians and gay men are forbidden to marry, to teach in many public schools, to adopt children, and to provide foster care. If evicted from their homes, expelled from their schools, fired from their jobs, or refused public lodging, they usually are not able to seek legal redress. The topic of homosexuality is often deemed inappropriate for discussion in public schools, including in sex education courses. Many public school libraries refuse to carry some of the many books that address the issue in important ways. Lesbians and gays are often reviled by the church and barred from membership in the clergy. They are the victims of hate crimes and targets of verbal abuse, and the possibility still exists that they will be beaten, threatened, attacked, or killed for simply loving another human being. Their parents reject them, and many gay youth have either attempted or contemplated suicide. Indeed, political scientist Mark Hertzog concludes that "no other group of persons in American society today, having been convicted of no crime, is subject to the number and severity of legally imposed disabilities as are persons of same-sex orientation" (1996, 6).

What does all of this mean for how the contemporary lesbian and gay movements conceive of their political organizing strategies, especially given the determination by the Christian Right to use lesbian and gay issues, such as same-sex marriage, as wedge issues in elections at all levels of government? Should policy and cultural change reflect a top-down model, or should it be inspired by grassroots organizing in local communities throughout the United States? And should the goal be a more assimilationist, rights-based approach to political and social change, or should movement activists embrace a more liberationist, revolutionary model, one that might embrace a full range of progressive causes? This last question is the central dilemma of this book, given how the assimilationist and liberationist approaches have been integral to the lesbian and gay movements' organizing over the past sixty years.

Throughout their relatively short history, the lesbian and gay movements in the United States have endured searing conflicts over which strategy to embrace. This book explores this dilemma in both contemporary and historical contexts within a broader social-movement theoretical setting. The assimilationist approach typically embraces a rights-based perspective, works within the broader framework of pluralist democracy—one situated within classical liberalism—and fights for a seat at the table. In doing so, the assimilationists celebrate the "work within the system," or "let us in," insider approach to political activism, rather than the "let us show you a new way of conceiving the world" strategy associated with lesbian and gay liberation. Assimilationists are more likely to accept that change will have to be incremental and to understand that slow, gradual progress is built into the very structure of the US framework of government.

A second approach, the liberationist perspective, favors more radical cultural change, change that is transformational in nature and often arises outside the formal structures of the US political system. Liberationists argue that there is a considerable gap between access and power and that it is not enough to simply have a seat at the table. For many liberationists, what is required is a shift in emphasis from a purely political strategy

FIGURE 1.1 Social and Political Movements Compared

Social Movements	*Political Movements*
Ideology	Lifestyle
Multiple Leaders	Single Leader Entrepreneur
Social and Political Spheres	Political Spheres Only
Have-Nots	Haves
Social Group Identity	Diverse Social Groups
Group Consciousness	Issue Positions

Source: Baer and Bositis 1993, 166. Reprinted by permission of Pearson Education, Inc., Upper Saddle River, New Jersey.

to one that embraces both structural political and cultural change, often through "outsider" political strategies. The notion of sexual citizenship embraced by liberationist activists and theorists is much more broadly conceived, as sociologist Steven Seidman describes: "buoyed by their gains, and pressured by liberationists, the gay movement is slowly, if unevenly, expanding its political scope to fighting for full social equality—in the state, in schools, health-care systems, businesses, churches, and families" (2002, 24). Political theorist Shane Phelan claims that liberationists often "attempt to subvert the hierarchies of the hegemonic order, pointing out the gaps and contradictions in that order, thus removing the privilege of innocence from the dominant group" (2001, 32). As I will demonstrate, the assimilationist and liberationist strategies are not mutually exclusive.

To better explicate the book's central dilemma, I will couch my analysis within the broader context of social-movement theory. First, it is necessary to understand how social movements differ from political parties, interest groups, and protests. They have three distinguishing features: they grow out of "a mass base of individuals, groups, and organizations, linked by social interaction," they "organize around a mix of political and cultural goals," and they "rely on a shared collective identity that is the basis of mobilization and participation" (Wald 2000, 5). Political scientist Sidney Tarrow extends this definition, stating that social movements involve "mounting collective challenges, drawing on common purposes, building solidarity and sustaining collective action" (1994, 3). They are also decentralized and comprise an array of organizations. They are often confused with political movements, but there are key differences between them, as Figure 1.1 demonstrates.

Unlike political movements, which tend to represent middle-class interests, social movements tend to represent those at the margins of American society, as defined by class, race, gender, or sexual orientation. Political movements are often defined through a single leader and her or his organization, whereas social movements are generally much more decentralized and sometimes have no real leader per se. Finally, social movements develop a comprehensive ideology, whereas political movements most often focus on narrow objectives such as handgun control or the nuclear freeze. Often, social movements push for political change at the same time they seek structural change in the social, cultural, economic, and private spheres (Baer and Bositis 1993). At their core, social movements inspire participatory democracy.

> [Social movements] raise expectations that people can and should be involved in the decision-making process in all aspects of public life. They convert festering social problems into social issues and put them on the political agenda. They provide a role for everyone who wants to participate in the public process of addressing critical social problems and engaging official power holders in a response to grassroots citizen demands for change. In addition, by encouraging widespread participation in the social change process, over time social movements tend to develop more creative, democratic, and appropriate solutions. (Moyer et al. 2001, 10)

The lesbian and gay movements certainly meet the criteria for an existing social movement. Lesbians, gays, bisexuals, and transgendered people have persistently occupied a place at the margins of society.

The vulnerability of groups at the margins of US society permits elites to create serious obstacles to political participation and control of the political agenda (Scott 1990, 72). In response to their structural and cultural marginalization, groups outside the mainstream identify strategies that they perceive will meet their needs while challenging structures that constrain their life choices. These strategies commonly include developing alternative resources, constructing different ideological frameworks, and creating oppositional organizations and institutions. Such structures are most often "grounded in the indigenous or communal relationships of marginal groups" (C. Cohen 1999, 48). This is especially true for the lesbian and gay movements.

From the vantage point of marginalized groups, then, social movements are vehicles for organization, education, and resistance. They are often galvanized when they perceive "changes in political opportunities that give rise to new waves of movements and shape their unfolding." Successful social movements build on political opportunities by seizing and expanding them, thus turning them into collective action (Tarrow 1994, 7). I will examine how well the lesbian and gay movements have done so by studying the intersection between the assimilationist and liberationist strategies over time. We will see that social-movement politics are conflictual, messy, and complicated; they defy easy generalizations and their behavior often eludes simple explanations.

Chapter 2 places the development of the lesbian and gay movements within their proper historical context. Particular attention is devoted to the development of the assimilationist and liberationist approaches over the past sixty years by examining the creation and goals of the Mattachine Society and the Daughters of Bilitis in the 1950s, the rise of the homophile movement in the 1950s and 1960s, and the connections between that movement and the movements growing out of the Stonewall Rebellion of 1969.

The assimilationist-accommodationist strategy prevailed within the broader movements until Stonewall. Despite their accomplishments, Stonewall threw mainstream homophile organizations on the defensive, as newly energized lesbian and gay activists, many of them veterans of the various movements of the 1960s, demanded a new style of political organizing and leadership. This more confrontational liberationist approach embraced militancy and the unconventional politics associated with the antiwar, women's liberation, and civil rights movements. The modern gay liberation movement was soon born, built on some of the same ideas that undergirded the original Mattachine Society envisioned by Harry Hay and his cofounders almost twenty years earlier. For those who embraced gay liberation, a rights-based strategy was far too limited. The goal should be to remake, not merely reform, society. Chapter 2 explores these conflicts within the broader movements throughout the 1970s and 1980s, which were dominated by the rise of a conservative insurgency in society at large. The response of the Christian Right to the movements' gains in the 1970s and early 1980s is also examined in considerable detail.

Chapter 3 explores the tensions between those activists who embraced an insider assimilationist strategy and those who demanded an outsider liberationist strategy to political and social change, as reflected in broader movements' responses to public AIDS policy. As we explore this tension, we will devote considerable attention to the way AIDS activism in the 1980s, 1990s, and the early twenty-first century altered the landscape of lesbian and gay politics, mobilizing an array of newly politicized activists in the midst of a devastating global epidemic. ACT UP, Queer Nation, and the Lesbian Avengers are all organizations that developed at the height of the AIDS crisis and demanded a liberationist organizing strategy. The role of the Treatment Action Group (TAG), which typically embraced insider assimilationist political strategies, will also be explained. As one would expect, the chapter discusses the responses of Presidents Reagan, Bush, and Clinton and Congress over time to HIV/AIDS policy and broader movements' demands, as well as how the movements have intersected with the Christian Right. Finally, the chapter examines in considerable detail the debates over the "degaying" and "regaying" of AIDS in the 1990s, debates that provide a window to the contemporary landscape of lesbian and gay politics. This will all set a context for the discussion of the George W. Bush and Barack Obama presidencies and how those administrations have addressed HIV/AIDS policy. A major goal of Chapter 3 is to assess the circumstances under which the assimilationist and liberationist strategies were effective, as well as the Christian Right response of using the threat of AIDS as a part of its successful grassroots fund-raising.

At the heart of recent social-movement theory is the belief that expanding political opportunities help determine the overall strength of a social movement. With the election of President Clinton in November 1992, many members of the lesbian and gay movements perceived, after twelve long years of Republican control of the White House, the opportunity for forceful presidential leadership that would be much more supportive of sexual minorities' interests. This is the broad context in which the military-ban issue appeared on the policy agenda soon after Clinton was elected. Chapter 4 assesses the original circumstances under which Clinton proposed to overturn the ban, how he attempted to do so once he became president, and why he fell short of his goal. It interrogates the role of the lesbian and gay movements in interacting with the Clinton administration, Congress, and the Christian Right during the 1993 debate. It explores broader movements' strategies and the debates between those who argued vigorously for overturning the ban (the assimilationist perspective) and those who argued that the movements need to transcend narrow rights goals and instead pursue broader political, social, and economic change (the liberationist perspective). The implementation of the "Don't Ask, Don't Tell" policy is also assessed in light of the lesbian and gay movements' goals and political strategies. The chapter concludes with a discussion of the circumstances under which President Obama and Congress overturned the ban on lesbians and gays in the military and what the new policy means for lesbians, gays, bisexuals, and transgender people who are or will be serving in the military.

The campaign for same-sex marriage has depended on the courts for much of its success. It was inspired not through consensus among activists but by a relatively small coterie of lawyers. Today the campaign is rooted in litigation, though it has now garnered the support of most major national lesbian and gay organizations, including the Lambda Legal Defense and Education Fund, National Gay and Lesbian Task Force, and Human Rights Campaign. It has clearly become one of the leading issues of the mainstream assimilationist lesbian and gay movements. Chapter 5 will discuss how the issue has developed over time, with particular attention to the June 2013 Supreme Court decisions in *United States v. Windsor* and *Hollingsworth v. Perry*.

There are, however, vocal critics of same-sex marriage within the lesbian and gay movements. The arguments associated with the liberationist critique will be outlined in detail. These conflicts within the broader lesbian and gay movements are placed within a discussion of debates over the Defense of Marriage Act (DOMA; codified into law in the fall of 1996). In addition, considerable attention will be devoted to same-sex-marriage policies and political organizing on the part of supporters and opponents at the state level, with specific attention devoted to Hawaii, Vermont, and Massachusetts. The goal is to see the conflicts and tensions between the assimilationist and liberationist perspectives as played out within the context of a contentious public policy issue.

Chapter 6 explores the movements' futures. As the analysis presented in this book will reveal, the goal of equal rights is the centerpiece of the contemporary lesbian and gay rights movements' strategies. This rights-based approach has dominated mainstream movement thinking from the early years of the homophile movement to the debate over AIDS, the military ban, and same-sex marriage today. As we will see, a narrow rights-based perspective, rooted in identity politics, is largely unquestioned and unchallenged by mainstream contemporary lesbian and gay movements, especially those that dominate politics and public policy at the national level. It has led to heightened cultural visibility but also to what Urvashi Vaid calls "virtual equality."

This final chapter assesses the limitations of embracing either an assimilationist or a liberationist strategy exclusively. Instead, it argues that both approaches have worked in important and complementary ways throughout the movements' histories and are not mutually exclusive. In addition, both the assimilationist and the liberationist strategies are necessary for the future, as the movements attempt to navigate the aftermath of the George W. Bush and Barack Obama presidencies and a still vigorous Christian Right movement at the national, state, and local levels. In the end, then, the dilemma presented throughout this book can be resolved by pursuing a dual organizing strategy, one that builds on the strengths of the assimilationist and liberationist strategies and one that recognizes the limitations of each approach to political and social change.

2

The Assimilationist and Liberationist Strategies in Historical Context

Harvey Milk, the first openly gay politician to be elected to public office in the previous decade, had said, "Coming-out is the most political thing you can do." It turned out that he was right. And as more and more gay men and lesbians came out to their families and friends—not because they had to, but because they wanted to—Americans realized that they knew someone gay or lesbian. And our world irrevocably changed.

—**Gene Robinson,** *God Believes in Love: Straight Talk about Gay Marriage*

The emergence of gay liberation would not have been possible but for the long, lonely organizing efforts of the Mattachine Society and the Daughters of Bilitis and, indeed, of the pioneers to whom they looked for inspiration.

—**Nicholas Edsall,** *Toward Stonewall: Homosexuality and Society in the Western World*

How have the assimilationist and liberationist strategies developed over time? That is the prevailing question underlying this chapter, which places the development of the lesbian and gay movements within their necessary historical context. Like so many of the social movements that came of age during the 1960s and 1970s, the activism of lesbians and gays in this period was rooted in the events of previous eras. Popular lore has it that the contemporary lesbian and gay movements began with the Stonewall Rebellion of 1969. Historian George Chauncey (1994) has written of the extensive gay network that developed in the streets, apartments, saloons, and cafeterias of New York City in the late nineteenth and early twentieth centuries. When, as a part of the virulent New York City crackdown of the 1930s, lesbians and gays were legally prohibited from gathering in any state-licensed public place, they fought for their rights in courageous ways—a precursor to the organized political resistance of the Daughters of Bilitis and Mattachine Society of the 1950s. Allan Berubé's pathbreaking work (1990) on lesbians and gays in the military during World War II found that the discriminatory and unjust treatment afforded them did not lead to an organized resistance movement per se, but it did inspire many lesbians and gay men to develop an all-important group identity. David K. Johnson's illuminating work (2004) on federal policies during the Cold War era in response to the so-called lavender menace provides concrete examples of individual and collective courage and resistance on the part of people who later organized for full citizen rights. John D'Emilio's important historical work (1983) chronicles the early years of the Mattachine Society, and Marcia Gallo's incisive work (2006) does the same for the Daughters of Bilitis, organizations that developed at the height of the McCarthy era, in the 1950s. And Barry Adam's study (1995) of the lesbian and gay movements focuses considerable attention on the rise of the homophile movement in the United States during the 1950s and the connections between that movement and the movements growing out of the Stonewall Rebellion of

1969. Indeed, as Alex Ross has aptly pointed out, public exposure in the pre-Stonewall era "required considerable courage" (Ross 2012, 47). These themes will be explored throughout this chapter by making connections between the contemporary lesbian and gay movements and the organizing that preceded them.

The tensions between the assimilationist and liberationist perspectives are also developed in historical context. Much of the work of the contemporary national lesbian and gay organizations has relied on an insider assimilationist strategy, one that strives for access to those in power and is rooted in an interest-group and legislative-lobbying approach to political change. It is an approach centered on civil rights, legal reform, political access, visibility, and legitimation that reinforces the existing political and economic framework associated with classical liberalism. For those who embrace a liberationist approach, however, the assimilationist perspective is far too narrow. As Urvashi Vaid has argued, the assimilationist perspective is far too rooted in "virtual equality—a state of conditional equality based more on the appearance of acceptance of straight America than on genuine civic parity" (1995, xvi). Liberationists challenge "virtual equality" and emphasize the goals of cultural acceptance, social transformation, understanding, and liberation (106).

David Eisenbach, a scholar of the movements, believes that all of the organizing activity over the past fifty years or so "has had remarkable political effects" that resonate in the present. What is his evidence for this claim? Looking back to the 2004 presidential election, Eisenbach notes that "the news media focused on the gay marriage controversy and the debate over the Federal marriage amendment, but the presidential candidates themselves displayed a notable consensus in favor of gay rights" (Eisenbach 2006, vi). And this was true of the candidates for the Democratic Party nomination—Wesley Clark, Howard Dean, John Edwards, Dick Gephardt, Dennis Kucinich, and Joe Lieberman—who all supported key elements of the contemporary assimilationist gay-rights agenda, including an increase in funding for HIV/AIDS research and services, the recognition of domestic partnerships, and sexual-orientation nondiscrimination laws. Three of the candidates supported same-sex marriage, but four opposed it, including John Kerry. Assimilationists would argue that all of this represents considerable progress, but liberationists would likely expect more concrete accomplishments that challenge the prevailing order of heteronormativity. As we will see, there are reasons for these differences in approach to political and social change and in the way they have developed over time.

One of the central goals of the early lesbian and gay movements in the United States was to improve the media depiction of homosexuality. Indeed, before the development of the modern lesbian and gay rights movement that began in the 1950s, "the media commonly depicted homosexuals as insane deviants and sexual predators." With that in mind, movement activists recognized the importance of altering the media's portrayal of homosexuality to present a more positive image, which was especially important as more people began to come out of the closet. The hope was that positive press coverage would lead to the public recognizing that homosexuality was not a threat and that this, in turn, would lead to much greater "political and legal progress" (Eisenbach 2006, vii).

The Birth of the Homophile Movement and the Foundations of Contemporary Politics

The homophile movement arose within the context of a prevailing ideology that regarded lesbians and gays "as perverts, psychopaths, deviates, and the like." Lesbians and gays internalized these negative labels, which ultimately became stereotypes. As John D'Emilio points out, "Whether seen from the vantage of religion, medicine, or the law, the homosexual or lesbian was a flawed individual, not a victim of injustice. For many, the gay world was reduced to a setting where they shared an affliction" (1983, 53).

In its early manifestations, the homophile movement embraced liberationist principles through the Mattachine Society. In 1951 Communist Party activist Harry Hay, then working at the Los Angeles People's Education Center as a music teacher, along with his co-organizers Rudi Gernreich, Bob Hull, Dale Jennings, and Chuck Rowland, built the Mattachine Society on communist principles of organizing and social change (Adam 1995, 67–68), a model that would soon lead to considerable controversy within the organization. Mattachine's founding statement of Missions and Purposes articulated the intended purposes of the new organization:

- "To unify" those homosexuals "isolated from their own kind"
- "To educate" homosexuals and heterosexuals toward "an ethical homosexual culture . . . paralleling the emerging cultures of our fellow-minorities—the Negro, Mexican, and Jewish Peoples"
- "To lead"; the "more . . . socially conscious homosexuals provide leadership to the whole mass of social deviates"
- To assist "our people who are victimized daily as a result of our oppression" (68)

As the above principles suggest, the organizers wished to galvanize a large gay constituency, one that was cohesive and capable of militant activity (D'Emilio 1983, 63).

Mattachine emerged as the first effective gay political organization in the United States, one that in its early years devoted itself to challenging and repealing repressive legislation and altering public opinion. Out of a Mattachine discussion group emerged *One,* the first publicly distributed American homophile magazine. According to historians Lillian Faderman and Stuart Timmons, "against heavy odds in the midst of the reactionary McCarthy era, ONE made a considerable impact nationally, appearing on newsstands in several US cities and selling about 5,000 copies a month, many of which passed through multiple hands" (2006, 116). The US Post Office placed a ban on *One* in 1954 but was overruled in 1958 by the Supreme Court, which stated that the ban violated free-speech protections guaranteed by the First Amendment (Adam 1995, 68). This incident serves as a sobering reminder of the repressive nature of the times.

But the Mattachine Society was not immune to serious criticism. In 1953 the organizational structure and militant ideology of the Mattachine Society was challenged by rank-and-file members. A Los Angeles *Daily Mirror* columnist had identified the lawyer for the organization as Frank Snyder, who had been an uncooperative witness before the House Un-American Activities Committee. Given the repressive political and cultural climate associated with the McCarthy era, it is no surprise that rank-and-file Mattachine members grew increasingly concerned with the organization's possible association with communism (Hunt 1999, 129).

The ultimate split between the organization's founders and its newer members reflected serious disagreements over assimilation and liberation, conflicts that have plagued the movements over the years. The Mattachine founders envisioned a separate homosexual culture, whereas other members worried that such a strategy would only increase the hostile social climate. Instead, they called for integration into mainstream society (D'Emilio 1983, 81). In the end, Harry Hay was expelled from the Mattachine Society in 1953, at the height of the McCarthy era, because of his Communist Party background and his unwavering support for more radical principles.

Hay's successors—Hal Call, Marilyn Reiger, and David Finn—and Phyllis Lyon and Del Martin, two lesbian activists who founded the Daughters of Bilitis in 1955, all embraced an assimilationist and accommodationist approach to political and social change. In practice, this meant the two groups sought to open a productive dialogue with an array of professionals or "experts" who had expressed views concerning homosexuality. Their strategy was to present themselves as reasonable, well-adjusted people, hoping that these heterosexual arbiters of public opinion would rethink their assumptions regarding homosexuality. This approach, rooted in dialogue, emphasized conformity and attempted to minimize any differences between heterosexuality and homosexuality. The activists hoped to de-emphasize sex, because the act of sex itself was the source of so much anger and fear directed at homosexuals. Ultimately, the architects of this assimilationist, accommodationist strategy hoped to reduce social hostility as a necessary precursor to the changes desired in both law and public policy (D'Emilio 1983, 109). They attempted to frame issues in ways that would accomplish this important goal.

The Daughters of Bilitis, San Francisco's second homophile organization, was founded by Lyon, Martin, and others in 1955. The organizers had no previous knowledge of the Mattachine Society. Their goal was to provide women an alternative to the bars in the form of a social club (Armstrong 2002, 37). They organized a network of local chapters beginning in 1958. Just two years later, and continuing for ten years, "they sponsored public biennial conventions on issues of importance to lesbians and gay men." Slowly, but surely, the organization began to lift "the veil of secrecy that surrounded lesbians' daily lives in mid-twentieth century America." Their newsletter played an integral role in this process. Indeed, "the first Daughters thought that their new group would provide a nice place for lesbians to meet; soon they added a newsletter that grew into an internationally known magazine" (Gallo 2006, xxi). From the outset, the organization supported women who were trying to raise children alone or with a partner. Although the Daughters of Bilitis (DOB) eschewed much of the Mattachine Society's ideology and tactics, they agreed that publishing a newspaper was important and began distributing their own, the *Ladder,* in 1956. This paper came out regularly between 1956 and 1971 and garnered the DOB national attention. The *Ladder* addressed a number of issues over the years, but a major theme was "dealing with issues of housing, school, being out, and dealing with hostile relatives and neighbors" (Bronski 2013, ix). The Mattachine Society, the Daughters of Bilitis, and *One* and the *Ladder* were the central organized elements of the homophile movement until the 1969 Stonewall Riots. Both organizations, in their later stages, embraced public education as their primary assimilationist goal "because they believed that the source of prejudice is ignorance or a misinformed view of homosexuals as different and dangerous" (Seidman 2002, 175).

The assimilationist, accommodationist strategy prevailed within the broader movement until the 1969 Stonewall Rebellion. During that time the movement as a whole gained little ground and, in fact, experienced some significant setbacks. For example, a medical model of homosexuality gained currency in this period, one that equated homosexuality with mental illness. This made it even more difficult for lesbians and gays to come out of the closet and to enter mainstream American life. But there were challenges to the more mainstream homophile, assimilationist strategy by such activists as Barbara Gittings and Franklin Kameny. Gittings and Kameny began openly embracing unconventional politics and picketing for basic rights and human dignity. Kameny expressed the ideological foundations of the 1960s homophile movement by arguing that homosexuals did not suffer from mental illness, constituted 10 percent of the population at large, did not need medical experts to speak on their behalf, and had a right to live their lives free from discrimination (Clendinen and Nagourney 1999, 114). Several years later he commented on the appropriate use of various political tactics in light of the Stonewall Rebellion: "I don't believe in picketing until you've tried negotiation and gotten nowhere and then tried picketing and gotten nowhere, then . . . I'm perfectly willing to go along to the next step—which is probably some sort of confrontation that possibly mildly oversteps the bounds of the law. If that doesn't serve, I'm willing to draw the line further, although I do draw the line at violence" (Teal 1995, 73–74). Kameny's endorsement of a more radical political strategy was inspired by the African American civil rights movement. And Kameny was not the only one inspired by a rise in civil rights militancy. Indeed, as early as 1966, lesbian and gay activists adopted a symbol of the civil rights movement—a black and white lapel button with an equals sign on a lavender background, signaling their desire for more daring avenues to effect change. Kameny's endorsement of a more radical political strategy reflects some of the tensions that would soon be felt within the homophile movement as it came under increased criticism and scrutiny from more radically minded lesbian and gay activists who called for liberatory change in light of Stonewall. Such tensions have continued to pervade the movements.

At the time of Stonewall, the situation for lesbians, gay men, bisexuals, and transgender individuals was much different than it is today. For example, homosexual sex was illegal in all states except Illinois at the end of the 1960s. There were no laws on the book at *any* level of government that protected lesbians, gay men, bisexuals, or transgender individuals from being denied housing or being fired from their jobs. In addition, no openly lesbian or gay politicians participated in politics anywhere in the United States. No political party had a gay caucus at that time. And there were few role models for young people who were struggling with their sexual orientation, as there were no openly gay or lesbian public school teachers, lawyers, doctors, or police officers. Unlike today, there were no television shows that had any identifiable lesbian or gay characters. Hollywood painted a particularly ugly view of gay life; most often, gay characters in movies killed other people or killed themselves (Carter 2004, 1–2). Those activists who were growing increasingly uncomfortable with more traditional forms of political organizing pointed to the lack of progress as evidence that a more radical, liberationist vision needed to be articulated.

But, by the time of Stonewall, the lesbian and gay movements could also point to concrete accomplishments. The Supreme Court had affirmed the legality of lesbian and gay publications. A number of state court rulings afforded gay bars more security, and the homophile movement had won constraints on police harassment of lesbians and gays in New York and San Francisco. In employment discrimination cases, the federal court provided the first victories. A dialogue was established with members of the scientific community regarding whether homosexuality should be classified as a mental illness. The movements had begun to shift to occasional media visibility, largely as a result of the transition to public protest. At the time of the Stonewall Riots, there were perhaps some fifty lesbian and gay organizations nationwide. Finally, and perhaps most important, the notion that lesbians and gays were a persecuted minority had infiltrated not only the lesbian and gay subculture but also the larger society (D'Emilio 1992, 238–239).

Despite these accomplishments, the mainstream homophile organizations were thrown on the defensive in the wake of Stonewall. Lesbian and gay activists, newly energized by their work in the various social and political movements of the 1960s, demanded a new style of political organizing and leadership. This more confrontational, liberationist approach embraced the unconventional politics associated with the antiwar, women's liberation, and civil rights movements. What was the connection between the latter and the lesbian and gay movements? Grant Gallup, a priest who was active in the African American civil rights movement, makes the connection well: "Many of us who went south to work with Dr. King in the sixties were gay. A lot of gay people who could not come out for their own liberation could invest the same energies in the liberation of black people" (Kaiser 1997, 136). And veteran civil rights activist John Lewis makes important connections between the Mississippi Freedom Summer of 1964 and the movements that followed:

> The atmosphere of openness and breaking down barriers that we developed that summer extended far beyond issues of race. It extended into everything from sexuality to gender roles, from communal living to identification with working classes. And they live on today. I have no doubt that the Mississippi Freedom Summer Project, in the end, led to the liberating of America, the opening up of our society. The peace movement, the women's movement, the gay movement—they all have roots that can be traced back to Mississippi in the summer of '64. (Lewis and D'Orso 1998, 273)

Lewis's observation reminds us of the important legacy that the African American civil rights movement left for other rights-based movements that developed throughout the decade of the 1960s.

Yet the rights-based strategy associated with the civil rights, women's, and homophile movements came under increased scrutiny and criticism in light of Stonewall. The modern gay liberation movement was soon born, built on some of the same ideas that undergirded the original Mattachine Society almost twenty years earlier. For those who embraced gay liberation, a rights-based strategy was far too limited. In their view, the goal should be to remake society, not merely reform it (Loughery 1998, 323).

The Stonewall Rebellion and Beyond

One way of thinking about the larger meaning of the Stonewall Rebellion is that "political movements are not born fully formed; they require numerous acts of small-scale resistance." As we have already seen, there were many small-scale acts of organizing, courage, and resistance in various forms prior to Stonewall. Scholar David Allyn believes that "without the prior activism, Stonewall might never have occurred, or rather, it might never have been turned into a symbolic event of major importance" (2000, 155). Michael Klarman points out that "Stonewall seemed to crystallize the incipient gay activism of the 1960s. . . . Within a year, gay liberation groups had formed on college campuses and in cities throughout the country" (2013, 17). The Stonewall Rebellion not only escalated the call for a more activist posture within the lesbian and gay civil rights movement but also fractured the movement into two distinct ideological strategic camps. On June 27–28, 1969, scores of gay men, lesbians, and transvestites who frequented a bar called the Stonewall Inn in New York City found themselves in a dramatic confrontation with the police, during a raid of the establishment. The raid itself was not newsworthy, as the police routinely harassed gay men, lesbians, and transvestites wherever they gathered, but the fact that they fought back this time was. The so-called Stonewall Riot, which lasted on and off for six days, quickly threw the more mainstream organizations associated with the homophile movement on the defensive and led to the widely accepted conclusion that "these riots are widely credited with being the motivating force in the transformation of the gay political movement" (Carter 2004, 1). And Stonewall eventually led to broad policy changes as well. As historian Phil Tiemeyer accurately points out, "The fights to abolish the sickness model of homosexuality, to eradicate sodomy laws, and to eliminate the exclusion of gays and lesbians from public life—including the workplace—had more momentum after Stonewall than ever before" (Tiemeyer 2013, 82).

It is in this broad context that the Gay Liberation Front (GLF) was founded in late 1969. Soon thereafter, similarly militant organizations were created in other countries, including Australia, Belgium, Britain, Canada, France, and the Netherlands, which is a testimony to the consequences of the Stonewall Rebellion for the international lesbian and gay rights movements. Toby Marotta captures the essence of the US organization in its first few weeks of existence: "radicals and revolutionaries shared the conviction that since every dimension of the existing system was bankrupt, a total transformation of society was desirable, and that to effect change, it was necessary to unite all oppressed minorities into a broad-based movement" (Loughery 1998, 324).

As it attempted to build the coalitions necessary for this movement, the GLF championed a broad New Left program. It attacked the consumer culture, militarism, racism, sexism, and homophobia. In challenging the latter, the GLF devoted considerable energy to how lesbians and gays were represented in the larger culture through language. With this in mind, the more widespread but clinical term *homosexual* was replaced by *gay*, pride became an important feature of liberation consciousness, and coming out was a crucial element of the liberatory experience (Loughery 1998, 321).

Within one year of the group's founding in New York, GLF organizations were born throughout the United States, including in Atlanta, Boston, Chicago, Iowa City, Los Angeles, Milwaukee, Portland, San Francisco, Seattle, and Washington, DC. College students organized many local groups on their campuses (Loughery 1998, 325). Meetings were run according to participatory principles, and hierarchy was eschewed as much as possible. Thanks to the courage and hard work of lesbian and gay activists around the country, an impressive amount of organizing was done in a short period of time, confirming the liberationist message about the importance of coalition building and historical context.

The euphoria and sense of unity that accompanied the birth of the GLF were short lived, as the post-Stonewall lesbian and gay movements faced the internal conflicts that beset many political and social movements in the late 1960s and early 1970s. There was considerable disagreement within the broader organization over its purpose (should it focus only on gay liberation, or should it be part of a larger political movement for progressive change?), its organizational structure, and the role of women and minorities. Disagreements over the treatment of women led to searing conflicts over sexism within the organization itself. In her memoir, *Tales of the Lavender Menace,* Karla Jay reveals the sexism she faced:

> Despite the push toward a gynandrous center, the sexism of some of the men was—for me, at least—the biggest obstacle toward immediately and completely immersing myself in GLF. A number of the men were more oppressive to women than any heterosexual guy I had known. A few of the men looked at me with such unveiled contempt that I started to give credence to the old adage that some men were gay because they hated or feared women. I'm sure that these guys would have preferred for the women to leave so that the GLF would become an all-men's group, sort of like a political bathhouse, where they could get naked with one another. If we were going to be there, however, a few men thought we might as well make ourselves useful by baking some cookies and making coffee. Some of the other women and I were constantly correcting men who called us "girls." "I'm a woman, not a 'girl.' How would [you] like me to call you 'boy'?" we'd remind them over and over. (1999, 82)

These disagreements undermined the overall effectiveness of the GLF and ultimately led to its destruction. But the lesbian and gay rights movements as a whole did not die out; they merely moved in a more assimilationist direction. As we have already seen, both before and after Stonewall, the movements were always much broader than one group. When the GLF fractured, another, less radical organization called the Gay Activists Alliance (GAA) became more prominent in shaping the larger movements' strategies.

Formed by Jim Owles and Marty Robinson in New York City in December 1969, the GAA attempted to focus on the single issue of gay rights, without the issue fragmentation and anarchic organizational style that had characterized the GLF. After initially joining the GLF, Owles and Robinson increasingly became disenchanted with the organization's inability to plan effectively and to temper revolutionary New Left doctrine in an effort to address the daily discrimination faced by lesbians and gays (Adam 1995, 86). They were particularly concerned with the GLF's affiliation with other elements of the political Left, including the Black Panthers and the antiwar movement. To the critics of the GLF, such affiliations "drained energy from the homosexual rights cause," and some of the affiliated groups were also clearly antigay (Hunt 1999, 81).

The GAA membership thought that meaningful reform would occur only if lesbians and gays organized politically and exercised their political muscle to force positive change. Their involvement in electoral politics set the stage for a strategy that has come to dominate the contemporary mainstream lesbian and gay movements. Candidates for election were questioned extensively concerning their views regarding issues of interest to lesbians and gays.

The GAA also embraced direct action in the form of "zaps," that is, carefully orchestrated disruptions of public meetings, on city streets, and in offices. Protesters often use satirical humor as a way to capture attention (Cruikshank 1992, 77). Arthur Evans, a veteran gay activist, remembers zaps as "little theatrical productions. The other side came across as looking really oafish, stupid, and boring and people on our side were exciting and wonderful and theatrical and inspiring and sexy and energetic" (Hirshman 2012, 120). Such nonviolent civil disobedience captured occasional media attention, disrupted the normal patterns of people's lives, and set the stage for the kind of political organizing associated with the AIDS Coalition to Unleash Power (ACT UP) in the late 1980s (as we will see in Chapter 3). In this way, the GAA's tactics were much closer to the GLF's than the Mattachine Society and Daughters of Bilitis pickets at the White House in the 1960s. Five demands were at the heart of GAA politics:

1. The repeal of New York State's sodomy and solicitation laws

2. An end to police entrapment of gay men

3. An end to police harassment of gay bars and an investigation into corruption in the New York State Liquor Authority

4. A law protecting gays and lesbians against discrimination in employment

5. An end to the bonding company practice of denying bonds to gays and lesbians (which excluded them from jobs requiring bonding) (Hunt 1999, 82)

The early GAA statement "What Is GAA?" stressed the organization's commitment "to a militant but nonviolent civil rights struggle and a membership open to all who share this approach and objective." Bob Kohler, a veteran GLF organizer, responded to the more assimilationist GAA approach by calling it "well-mannered conformist shit." In contrast, Kay Tobin, one of just a handful of women involved in the early years of the GAA's existence, claimed that it was "an exciting place for a range of us who weren't out-and-out revolutionaries" (Loughery 1998, 329). Most acknowledge that the GAA was even less responsive to women and people of color than the GLF had been. GAA members were charged with tokenism when it came to dealing with issues of race and feminism (331). Michael Schiavi, a historian of this period, accurately points out that "recurring fights indicated the deeper chasms in communication between GAA's men and women. Men had little interest in abortion or child care, while women resented organizational time spent on police harassment in public-sex forums like the piers and trucks along the Hudson" (2011, 101).

One major accomplishment of the GAA is that it established institutional structures that proved to be more long lasting than those created by the GLF. Indeed, many of these institutional structures have been embraced by an array of lesbian and gay organizations operating at the national level today (see Appendix 3). Indeed, "GAA's single-issue politic had a much greater impact than GLF on mainstream gay political organizing" (Bronski 2011, 212).The GAA ceased formal operations in 1974, soon after its community center suffered a catastrophic fire, but many of the organization's activists founded the National Gay Task Force, which today is the National Gay and Lesbian Task Force (Hunt 1999, 82).

William Eskridge describes the long-term effects of the Stonewall Rebellion: "literally overnight, the Stonewall riots transformed the *homophile reform movement* of several dozen homosexuals into a *gay liberation movement* populated by thousands of lesbians, gay men, and bisexuals who formed hundreds of organizations demanding radical changes in the way people were treated by the state" (1999, 99; emphasis in the original). The movement introduced four key ideas into the existing homophile movement that remain relevant even now. First, the crucial personal and political statement of coming out is integral to movement politics today. Second, a more visible lesbian and gay presence challenges traditional notions of the family, gender roles, and sexism. Third, Stonewall and its aftermath created a lesbian and gay counterculture (one that included bisexuals and transgender individuals), which helped to establish lesbian and gay identity, thus providing a foundation for the identity-politics strain in the movements today. (This counterculture has been assailed by conservatives, and the progressive Left has taken issue with identity politics.) Finally, the politics of the late 1960s and early 1970s emphasized that the lesbian and gay movements could not be divorced from movements addressing broader economic concerns, gender, and race. A mere rights-based agenda was far too narrow. The principle remains as controversial now as it was when the GLF introduced it to the existing homophile movement almost thirty years ago. Should the movements embrace a single-issue politics or attempt to build coalitions with other aggrieved groups to foster more progressive social change? This issue continues to tear at the fabric of the movements and is an important question underlying the assimilationist and liberationist perspectives critically.

The 1970s and the Challenge of the Christian Right

Perhaps the greatest policy success of the early 1970s was the 1973–1974 decision of the American Psychiatric Association (APA) to remove homosexuality from the *Diagnostic and Statistical Manual,* its official list of mental disorders. This decision did not come about because a group of doctors suddenly changed their views; it followed an aggressive and sustained campaign by lesbian and gay activists (Loughery 1998, 345). To bring about this important policy change, the movements used a combination of insider and outsider strategies with considerable skill and effectiveness. These involved a "louder watchdog presence at psychiatric conferences, behind-the-scenes lobbying, alliances with friendly and influential members of the APA, contact with regional psychiatric societies, the presentation of alternative papers, and a parade of 'healthy homosexuals.'" Most important, in the words of Ronald Gold, activists had learned to recognize "when to scream and when not to. It's an art. It's the art of politics" (346). Urvashi Vaid correctly emphasizes the importance of the APA's major policy change: "the American Psychiatric Association's removal of homosexuality from the list of mental disorders paved the way for legal and social attitudes to change" (2012, 180). Some ten years later, in the midst of the AIDS crisis, the ability to understand when insider and outsider politics might be most effective proved crucial to the maturing lesbian and gay movements. The "grassroots politics of knowledge" that the movements developed in their struggle with the APA had consequences for later challenges to the federal government's policies on AIDS research (Escoffier 1980, 139), as we will see in Chapter 3.

But the movements' accomplishments in the arena of psychiatry and beyond were viewed with increasing concern by those who feared any challenge to the primacy of heterosexuality in all institutions of American society. The Christian Right and other antigay conservatives consistently identified homosexuality as evidence of moral degeneracy in society as a whole. Therefore, they reacted to movement gains with hostility and a commitment to organizing their own grassroots constituency to undo these victories. Indeed, the constitutional historian Michael Klarman believes that "resistance to gay rights activism played an important role in the mobilization of the religious right in the late 1970s" (Klarman 2013, 26). During the 1970s, largely as a result of the Christian Right's effective mobilization, the lesbian and gay movements suffered major setbacks both locally and nationally. Six antigay referenda appeared in 1977 and 1978 alone.

One of the most effective spokespersons for the Christian Right position was Anita Bryant, a celebrity singer and the second runner-up in the 1959 Miss America contest who helped to galvanize conservative opposition to lesbian and gay rights in 1977 with her Save Our Children campaign based in Dade County, Florida. The goal of this campaign was "to convince voters that tolerance of homosexuality threatened society" (Eisenbach 2006, 279). In her first public statement endorsing the Save Our Children campaign, Bryant proclaimed:

> I don't hate homosexuals! But as a mother I must protect my children from their evil influence. Defending the rights of my children and yours. Militant homosexuals want their sexual behavior and preference to be considered respectable and accepted by society. They want to recruit your children and teach them the virtue of becoming a homosexual. . . . I don't hate homosexuals. I love them enough to tell them the truth. . . . [We] must not give them the legal right to destroy the moral fiber of our families and our nation. (280)

As an evangelist singer, national promoter of Florida orange juice, and the mother of two children, Bryant was a perfect spokesperson for the Christian Right. Her successful fight to persuade voters to rescind a six-month-old Dade County civil rights ordinance garnered considerable national attention in the mainstream press (Alwood 1996, 167). In challenging the Dade County ordinance, Bryant made two arguments. First, she insisted that the new law "discriminates against my children's rights to grow up in a healthy, decent atmosphere" (Loughery 1998, 373). Second, she claimed that God had called her to fight against "preferential legislation" that endorsed a degraded "lifestyle" (127). Both of these arguments have been invoked by opponents of lesbian and gay rights over the years, but the latter was particularly important. One activist astutely concluded that "gay rights was in trouble, the day 'special rights' was born" (374).

The reactionary climate of the late 1970s was ripe for Bryant's campaign. The Save Our Children organization, which led the Dade County fight, represented a profile of anti–lesbian and gay forces, forces that would galvanize in response to AIDS, the integration of the military, and same-sex marriage, as we will see later in this book. It galvanized conservative religious leaders and politicians; the campaign itself was founded on fundamentalist church networks, and Bryant obtained active support from the National Association of Evangelicals, which represented "more than three million people from 60 denominations." The association's television programs, the *PTL Club, 700 Club,* and *The Old-Time Gospel Hour,* afforded Bryant a national platform and raised funds on her behalf. Moral Majority founder Jerry Falwell campaigned against the Dade County ordinance in person, and the direct-mail political lobby Christian Cause extended its organizing efforts into Jewish and Roman Catholic hierarchies. Opposition to the Dade County ordinance arose at the local level as well. For example, Miami's archbishop distributed a pastoral letter to local Roman Catholic churches, exhorting their congregations to vote against lesbian and gay civil rights. The president of the Miami Beach B'nai B'rith and twenty-eight rabbis publicly lent their support to Bryant's cause (Adam 1995, 110).

The civil rights ordinance resurfaced in 1998, when the Miami-Dade County commissioners voted seven to six to ban discrimination based on sexual orientation. Even the narrow margin of the victory could not detract later from the importance of this victory for the lesbian and gay movements. The 1977 repeal had attracted considerable press attention, and Anita Bryant was now a national figure. She capitalized on her victory by launching an anti–gay rights campaign throughout the United States. By June 1978 voters in Eugene, Oregon; St. Paul, Minnesota; and Wichita, Kansas, had also rescinded local ordinances that had protected the basic rights of lesbians and gays. Fundamentalist churches, with the financial support of the business community, constituted the foundation of the antigay movement. By 1978, then, the conservative opposition against lesbian and gay rights had solidified and gained momentum. But this did not mean that the opposition was invincible. The lesbian and gay movements proved that they could organize an effective response (Button, Rienzo, and Wald 1997, 69). One of their most successful organizing campaigns came in California in response to the Briggs initiative.

The day after the 1977 Miami vote, California state senator John Briggs, from conservative Orange County, announced his plans to introduce legislation that would prevent lesbians and gays from teaching in California's public schools. When it became obvious that the legislation had little chance of passing, Briggs altered his tactics and organized a campaign to have his proposal placed on the ballot as a statewide initiative (D'Emilio 1992, 89). Within eleven months of Bryant's victory, Briggs filed the half million signatures that he needed to introduce a voter referendum. In May 1978, Briggs had hoped that his teachers' initiative, his support for a second initiative that would expand the use of the death penalty in California, and his public association with Anita Bryant would help make him a strong candidate for governor (Clendinen and Nagourney 1999, 376). Briggs attempted to build on some of Bryant's organizing strategies. Although he lacked her connections to the Christian Right, he tried to appeal to the same forces in California—and nationally, with the help of Bryant's contributor list. But Briggs miscalculated severely. In the end, the voters in California overwhelmingly defeated his Proposition 6 by a margin of 58 to 42 percent. Lesbian and gay activists worked together in a display of solidarity that overcame gender divides to help defeat the amendment. On the same night, Seattle voters defeated an initiative that would have repealed its gay rights law by a margin of 63 to 37 percent (389). The decade of the 1970s approached its final year with two important and highly visible victories for the lesbian and gay rights movements.

The 1970s also witnessed an increase in anti–lesbian and gay violence, as "fag bashings" became more commonplace throughout the United States. Antigay violence attracted considerable public attention in 1978 when Dan White, a member of the San Francisco Board of Supervisors, climbed into an open city hall window and then shot and killed openly gay board member Harvey Milk and Mayor George Moscone, who had supported Milk and lesbian and gay rights more generally. This broader societal hostility that developed in the 1970s helped set the context for how many would react to gay men with the onset of AIDS in the summer of 1981 (and beyond) during conservative president Ronald Reagan's first year in office.

Conclusion

This chapter began by asking how the assimilationist and liberationist strategies have developed over time. In answering this question, we have placed the development of the lesbian and gay movements within their proper historical context. We have seen how tensions between the assimilationist and liberationist strategies have manifested themselves in the pre- and post-Stonewall eras. The 1969 Stonewall Rebellion was an important moment in the development of the lesbian and gay movements because mainstream homophile organizations were thrown on the defensive. The rights-based strategy associated with the civil rights, women's, and homophile movements came under increased scrutiny and criticism in light of the Stonewall uprising. What has come to be known as the modern gay liberation movement was born in the face of Stonewall, built on some of the same ideas that undergirded the original Mattachine Society almost twenty years earlier. But we cannot refer to the complicated forces that constitute lesbian, gay, bisexual, and transgender organizing as a single movement, given the complicated array of identities involved, as later chapters will make clear.

The lesbian and gay movements achieved a number of victories by the mid-1970s; among the most prominent was the APA's 1973–1974 decision to remove homosexuality from its Diagnostic and Statistical Manual list of mental disorders. This victory, as well as others, was the result of consistent and persistent political organizing. The Christian Right responded to these perceived gains by linking homosexuality with moral degeneracy in society writ large. This theme manifested itself in Anita Bryant's Save Our Children campaign and John Briggs's proposed amendment to prevent lesbian and gay teachers from teaching in California's public schools. The Christian Right's organizing efforts were an augury of the shape of things to come—in the 1980s in response to the onset of HIV/AIDS, in the 1990s in response to military integration, and in the early twenty-first century in response to same-sex marriage.

All of the organizing activity over the past fifty years or so on the part of the lesbian and gay movements and their opponents has had consequences for contemporary politics and policy surrounding sexual-diversity issues today. We examine this argument in the development of HIV/AIDS activism and policy in the next chapter.

3

The Conflict over HIV/AIDS Policy

We will never know how my generation of gay men would have evolved without AIDS.

—**Andrew Hollernan**

What is there left to say about this gruesome, senseless killer AIDS? Except that the wrong people are dying, those who gave themselves incautiously to experience, to life; the risk-takers, the inventive ones. The fearful ones who literally sat on their asses still sit.

—**Martin Duberman,** *Waiting to Land: A (Mostly) Political Memoir, 1985–2008*

Perhaps the greatest of gay people's many accomplishments in addressing AIDS has been the creation of a diverse community that nurtures its members to see themselves as distinctive for many reasons besides their sexuality alone.

—**John-Manuel Andriote,** *Victory Deferred: How AIDS Changed Gay Life in America*

In what ways did the onset of AIDS in the United States during the early 1980s affect the organizing and political strategies of the lesbian and gay movements? How have the movements intersected with the policy process over time as AIDS has developed in America and on a global scale? These are the two questions that organize this chapter. In answering them, we explore the tensions between those activists who embraced an insider assimilationist strategy and those who demanded an outsider liberationist strategy to political and social change, as reflected in the broader movements' responses to AIDS policy. As we explore this dynamic, we will devote considerable attention to the historical development of AIDS policy and AIDS activism in the United States. It is argued that AIDS changed the landscape of lesbian and gay politics, mobilizing an array of newly politicized activists in the midst of a staggering epidemic that has so far claimed and disrupted millions of lives in America and throughout the world. AIDS emerged over time, in the words of Linda Hirshman, as a "triple threat: as a disease it required the caring services conventionally found in the biological family; as a sexual disease it threatened the bedrock norm of privacy-based sexual freedom; and as an epidemic it could only be resisted with all the resources of a paternalistic state" (2012, 180). Direct-action organizations such as ACT UP, the Lesbian Avengers, and Queer Nation, which grew out of the many policy and political challenges posed by AIDS, demanded a liberationist organizing strategy. Other organizations, such as the Treatment Action Group, did vital AIDS policy work from within the policy process.

In examining the development of HIV/AIDS within an appropriate historical context, we will interrogate the intersection between the lesbian and gay movements and the national policy process with particular attention to the presidencies of Ronald Reagan, George H. W. Bush, Bill Clinton, George W. Bush, and Barack Obama. This is a particularly opportune time to do so, given that the thirtieth anniversary of AIDS occurred in June 2011. Numbers provide a sense of the devastating toll of AIDS in the

United States. As of December 2011, 1.2 million Americans were infected with HIV, and more than five hundred thousand had died of AIDS (Bolcer and Harmon, 2011). There was a surge of new infections between 2002 and 2003, adding a quarter of a million new cases. By 2006, it was clear that the United States had "the most severe HIV epidemic of any developed country" and that anyone could be at risk (Hunter 2006, x). But this was particularly true for African Americans, who were becoming HIV positive at a much greater rate than other segments of the population, and for gay men, who were also becoming HIV positive at an alarming rate. According to data released by the Centers for Disease Control and Prevention (CDC), as of February 2013, "gay men are sixty times more likely than heterosexual men, and 54 times more likely than all women, to be diagnosed with HIV. Gay men account for 48 percent of the more than one million people living with HIV in the U.S., an estimated 532,000 men" (Andriote 2012). In addition, one of five gay men in twenty-one major U.S. cities is HIV positive. "Nearly half of all infected gay/bi men don't know they are HIV positive. More than two-thirds of infected black men, and nearly eighty percent of HIV-positive young men aged eighteen to 24, are unaware that they have the virus. As of 2008, AIDS had killed an estimated 617,025 Americans—48 percent (296,222) of them gay and bisexual men, most in the prime of life" (Andriote 2012). The response of the lesbian and gay movements and the federal government to the development of AIDS policy over time needs to be situated within this broad framework.

Several overarching themes are explored in this chapter. First, it is important to recognize that some of the same lesbian and gay activists who engaged in radical forms of AIDS activism have also run for political office and have taken seats on government regulatory organizations, such as TAG (Goldstone 2003, 3). In this way, these activists have worked both within and outside of the policy process. Second, in trying to ascertain the response of policymakers at all levels of government, it is equally important to understand that, when AIDS was first recognized in the United States, the groups affected were already the objects of negative perceptions by many Americans and had little political power: sexually active gay men, intravenous drug users, people who suffered from hemophilia, and Haitian immigrants (Siplon 2002, 4). Third, the larger lesbian and gay communities and their straight supporters were able to respond more convincingly to the challenges of HIV/AIDS than other affected groups for a variety of reasons, not the least of which was the intensity of their political and social organizing that developed out of necessity over time. HIV-positive and HIV-negative lesbians and gay men came together to confront the challenges of AIDS in their communities by creating an array of service organizations, such as the Gay Men's Health Crisis in New York City and the Whitman Walker Institute in Washington, DC. They played an active role in policy formation and treatment in the face of government indifference (8). In doing so, they were aware that public health professionals and government officials could do considerable harm by adopting policies, such as mandatory testing, that were viewed as discriminatory in a highly charged conservative political climate. Fourth, an enduring tension developed between those who argue for increased resources for care and treatment and those who claim resources should be devoted to stopping the epidemic. Finally, this chapter explores how the Christian Right and other conservatives have responded to AIDS over time. A major goal of this chapter is to examine the circumstances under which the assimilationist and liberationist strategies were effective, as well as how the Christian Right responded to these various tactics by using the threat of AIDS as part of its successful fund-raising approach.

The Early History of AIDS in the United States

AIDS first appeared on the scene in the summer of 1981. The *New York Times* reported on July 3 that forty-one gay men were dying from a rare cancer, as well as infectious complications, that stemmed from the depression of the immune system, the cause of which was unexplainable at the time. By 1982 and 1983, the seriousness of the AIDS epidemic "was widely experienced by gay men, not only as a threat to new-found sexual freedoms, but to the broad social and political gains of the community as a whole" (Odets 1995, 121). Many of the initial patients had too many sexual partners in common to be a coincidence. As a result, "sex was quickly isolated as the most likely and perhaps primary means of transmission." The CDC in Atlanta, as the US government agency responsible for tracking the development and incidence of disease in the United States over time, used existing data regarding male sexual partners to conclude that "repeated exposure to a series of STDs could be leading to the breakdown of the immune system in afflicted individuals" (Bereznai 2006, 225). This information was then used as the foundation for early prevention efforts, and it helped to cement in the public's mind (not to mention in the minds of journalists, politicians, and many in the medical-service delivery process) that AIDS was a "gay disease." Indeed, in the early years the syndrome had two names—"AID for acquired immunodeficiency disease, and GRID for gay-related immunodeficiency" (Engel 2006, 6). The CDC formally identified it as acquired immune deficiency syndrome, or AIDS, in July 1982 (Colegrove 2011, 113). All of this had early policy ramifications as well as consequences for those who were stigmatized as being "at risk" of contracting HIV/AIDS. Researchers considered an array of explanations for the cause and dissemination of HIV/AIDS in the early years, but none appeared to be satisfactory (7). Within two years, however, on March 3, 1983, the CDC made an official announcement that four groups were particularly vulnerable to AIDS: "homosexual men who had multiple sexual partners, intravenous heroin injectors, Haitians who had immigrated into the United States in recent years, and hemophiliacs" (Siplon 2002, 6). Each of these groups reacted to this official CDC announcement in different ways. Christopher Bram offers a perceptive overview of the emerging AIDS crisis: "The virus had been present for several years before it began to sicken and kill. Even then it only slowly came into focus. It was some time before it had a name. And in a cruel moral twist, it was spread sexually, which meant it could be interpreted as punishment for sex" (2012, 213). And Sean Strub reminds us of the historical context for the transmission of HIV/AIDS among gay men in the 1980s: "Systematic oppression, a hostile culture, and self-hatred damaged gay men, and when the '70s presented a sexual liberation unimagined only a few years before, it resulted in sexual behaviors and environments that created the perfect storm for a sexually transmitted virus to spread rapidly." Strub also wisely connects the epidemic to the absence of knowledge about gay men's sexual health: "the lack of knowledge about gay men's sexual health and access to health care that respected gay sexuality compounded the problem" (Strub 2014, 115).

By 1984, there was little evidence that AIDS was spreading into the population at large, as fewer than 1,500 people had died from the disease. But the exponential growth pattern within the gay male community suggested an epidemic, one that would not peak anytime soon. With this in mind, gay community advocates demanded that the National Institutes of Health (NIH) devote more funding to basic research. Activist Larry

Kramer was particularly vocal in his complaint that "in late 1983 that the agency was planning to commit only $5 million in funding to AIDS-related projects the following year out of a budget of over $4 billion, despite having already received grant requests for $55 million" (Engel 2006, 21–22). What understandably infuriated Kramer even further is that the NIH had already committed $8 million of its yearly budget to conducting such research, but the money had not yet been spent (22).

An array of mainstream politicians also accused the NIH of a laggard response to a growing crisis. Critics pointed out that previous outbreaks of Legionnaires' disease and the swine flu had received immediate attention from the federal government, and they argued that AIDS deserved the same. The National AIDS Vigil Commission, which included prominent political leaders Senators Edward Kennedy (D-MA) and Lowell Weicker (R-CT) and Mayors Dianne Feinstein (D-San Francisco) and Marion Barry (D-Washington, DC), marched on Washington, DC, in an effort to inspire greater federal government attention to AIDS (Engel 2006, 22). But AIDS struck at a terrible political time, one that witnessed the rise of a new fiscal and social conservatism with the election of Ronald Reagan and a more conservative Congress in 1980. In addition, Christian Right fundamentalists had accumulated greater power in American politics and policy. The growth of the Christian Right is epitomized by the rise of the Moral Majority, an organization rooted in religious fundamentalism and committed to grassroots mobilization of its constituency to elect conservative politicians at all levels of government. Galvanized by Reagan's election and the defeat of a number of liberal Democratic senators, the Moral Majority and other Christian Right groups sought to unseat members of Congress who opposed their conservative moral agenda.

AIDS Policy in the Reagan/Bush Years

The larger political culture quickly moved right as well. The Christian Right and other antigay conservatives identified homosexuality as evidence of moral degeneracy in society as a whole and AIDS as a punishment for homosexual behavior. The new conservatism scapegoated and stigmatized those with AIDS (Koop 1991, 198). It was widely reported as well that Christian Right groups such as the Moral Majority successfully blocked funding for AIDS educational programs and counseling and other services for people living with AIDS. Pat Buchanan, a former White

House aide, expressed a particularly ugly view of homosexuality and its connection to AIDS, when he proclaimed in 1983, "The poor homosexuals. They have declared war on nature and now nature is exacting an awful retribution." Norman Podhoretz, *Commentary* magazine editor, assailed AIDS funding efforts because he perceived that they were "giving social sanction to what can only be described as a brutish degradation." Phyllis Schlafly, executive director of the Eagle Forum, castigated the federal government and AIDS activists for failing to respond properly: "Why are young boys and men not warned that all who engage in homosexual activities can expect to become infected with AIDS? Why is AIDS presented by the media as a homosexuals' civil-rights problem instead of as a public health problem which the government can isolate and treat?" At various points in the epidemic, conservatives called for quarantining and tattooing people living with AIDS. For example, *National Review* editor William F. Buckley wrote in March 1986, "Everyone detected with AIDS should be tattooed in the upper forearm, to protect common-needle users, and on the buttocks, to prevent the victimization of other homosexuals" (Engel 2006, 70–71). And Jerry Falwell, the leader of the Moral Majority, was quoted as saying that AIDS "was the judgment of God. . . . You can't fly into the laws of God and God's nature without paying the price" (Clendinen and Nagourney 1999, 488).

It was against this political and cultural backdrop that the Reagan administration's lack of response to AIDS, especially in the early years, must be situated. The rise of the Christian Right and a general climate of conservatism were coupled with Reagan's 1980 presidential campaign and election. When AIDS was first reported in 1981, Reagan had just assumed office and was pursuing his conservative agenda by slashing social programs and cutting taxes, while at the same time embracing traditional moral values. Reagan famously proclaimed, "Government is not a solution to our problem. Government *is* the problem" in his 1981 inaugural address. With this political philosophy, "the Reagan administration moved quickly to downsize executive branch agencies, including the health agencies." Indeed, "one policy analyst at the time observed that the most striking gap in Reagan administration health policy was 'the absence of any positive agenda to address pressing problems in the health care sector'" (Harden 2012, 35). And even worse, his administration failed to "request an appropriation to fund AIDS research until May 1983—nearly two years after the official start of the epidemic—and in subsequent years the administration consistently attempted to cut already inadequate congressional appropriations to deal with the exploding crisis" (Gould 2009, 49). Reagan did not even mention the acronym *AIDS* publicly until 1987, when he spoke at the Third International AIDS Conference held in Washington, DC. And Edwin Meese, his attorney general, "had sanctioned [in 1986] firing anyone who co-workers merely perceived as having AIDS and causing them to fear contamination" (Duberman, 2009, 69). His administration did little to support medical research, expedite the testing and release of AIDS-related drugs, or promote AIDS education. Reagan's only concrete proposal as of 1987 was to call for widespread, routine testing. The death of his close friend Rock Hudson from AIDS in 1985 had no significant impact on Reagan's policies, although his biographer has said that he was deeply affected personally (Cannon 1991, 814). For Reagan and his advisers, AIDS was not a national problem; instead, it was a series of local problems to be dealt with by states and localities, not the federal government. This stance helped to fragment the limited governmental response early in the AIDS epidemic. Gary Bauer, a political and social conservative, was assigned with coordinating Reagan's response to AIDS. In doing so, he "tried to enact a three-pronged strategy to deal with AIDS: a national testing program that would detail exactly how many people had AIDS and where they lived; an education policy that emphasized personal, moral responsibility as the best way to enforce necessary behavior changes; and policies based on local community control because of its ability to enforce moral standards more effectively than the federal government and therefore comport better with conservative ideology" (Brier 2009, 7). Underlying Bauer's efforts was hostility toward homosexuality and celebration of abstinence and heterosexual marriage. Indeed, in a 1987 memo, "Bauer explained that the Department of Education needed to emphasize the idea that 'heterosexual sex within marriage is what most Americans, our laws and traditions consider the proper focus of human sexuality'" (87). Many members of the lesbian and gay movements and the larger public health community were understandably openly hostile to all elements of this three-pronged strategy, not to mention the negative assumptions about LGBT people that undergirded the strategy.

Reagan and his advisers perceived that AIDS presented serious political risks. As a presidential candidate, Reagan had promised to eliminate the role of the federal government in the already limited US welfare state, as well as to embrace social policies that promoted "family values." In the critical 1984–1985 years of the epidemic, Reagan thought of AIDS as if "it was measles and it would go away." Reagan's principal biographer, Lou Cannon, characterizes the president's response as "halting and ineffective" (Canon 1991, 814). It is not surprising, given his own morally conservative ideology and the strong conservative ethos of almost all of his appointees, that the administration had such a poor response to an emerging health crisis, particularly one that affected those at the margins of American society. For example, in the early 1980s, senior officials from the Department of Health and Human Services maintained publicly for political reasons that they had enough resources to address the AIDS crisis, while behind the scenes they pleaded for additional funding. The administration undercut federal efforts to confront AIDS in a meaningful way by refusing to spend the money Congress allocated for AIDS research (Rimmerman 2002, 88).

Reagan and his close political advisers also successfully prevented his surgeon general, Dr. C. Everett Koop, from discussing AIDS publicly until Reagan's second term. According to a mandate of Congress, the surgeon general's chief responsibility is to promote the health of the American people and to inform the public about the prevention of disease. In the Reagan administration, however, the surgeon general's role was to promote the administration's conservative social agenda, especially in regard to prolife and family issues. Thus, at a time when the surgeon general could have played an invaluable role in public health education, Koop was prevented from addressing AIDS publicly. Then, in February 1986, Reagan asked Koop to write a report on the AIDS epidemic. Koop had come to the attention of conservatives in the Reagan administration because of his leading role in the antiabortion movement. Reagan administration officials fully expected Koop to embrace conservative principles in his report on AIDS (Rimmerman 2002, 88). But "Koop nonetheless contradicted his conservative views on other subjects to take up the cudgel for a nondiscriminatory approach to the epidemic" (Baldwin 2005, 99). Koop argued that any successful AIDS policy strategy "required a commitment to rational science and Christianity as well as explicit discussions of sexual practice, drug use, and condom distribution" (Brier 2009, 81).

When the *Surgeon General's Report on Acquired Immune Deficiency Syndrome* was released to the public on October 22, 1986, it was a call for federal action in response to AIDS, and it underscored the importance of a comprehensive AIDS education strategy, beginning in grade school.

Koop advocated the widespread distribution of condoms and concluded that mandatory identification of people with HIV or any form of quarantine would be useless in addressing AIDS. As part of Koop's broad federal education strategy, the Public Health Service mailed AIDS information to 107 million American households. Koop's actions brought him into direct conflict with William Bennett, Reagan's secretary of education. Bennett opposed Koop's recommendations and called for compulsory HIV testing of foreigners applying for immigration visas, for marriage license applicants, for all hospital patients, and for prison inmates (Rimmerman 2002, 88–89). More broadly, Koop disappointed conservatives because "instead of producing a document that emphasized what was increasingly becoming a kind of conservative dogma about the need to push marriage over frank conversations about sex, Koop stressed his commitment to public health and accumulated a wide range of information about the epidemic" (Brier 2009, 88).

Not surprisingly, the Reagan administration did little to prohibit discrimination against people with HIV/AIDS. The administration placed responsibility for addressing AIDS discrimination issues on the states rather than on the federal government. In the face of federal inaction, some states and localities passed laws that prohibited HIV/AIDS discrimination, but many remained passive in the face of federal indifference. The situation remained unchanged until the Supreme Court, in its 1987 *School Board of Nassau County, Fla., v. Arline* decision, issued a broad ruling that was widely interpreted as protecting those with HIV/AIDS from discrimination in federal executive agencies, in federally assisted programs or activities, or by businesses with federal contracts (Rimmerman 2002, 89).

Reagan did appoint the Presidential Commission on the Human Immunodeficiency Virus Epidemic in the summer of 1987, chaired by Admiral James D. Watkins, to placate those who demanded a more consistent and sustained federal response to AIDS. Reagan meanwhile addressed the concerns of the Christian Right by appointing to the commission few scientists who had participated in AIDS research and few physicians who had actually treated people living with AIDS. In addition, the commission included outspoken opponents of AIDS education (Rimmerman 2002, 89).

In retrospect, it is clear that the commission was created to deflect attention from the administration's own inept policy response to AIDS. The Watkins Commission's final report did recommend a more sustained federal commitment to address AIDS, but this recommendation was largely ignored by both the Reagan and the Bush administrations. In fact, none of the commissions studying AIDS over the years has recommended a massive federal effort to confront AIDS at all levels of society. How might history view the Reagan approach to AIDS policy? Don Francis, a CDC official, gave one answer in his testimony before a congressional committee on March 16, 1987:

> Much of the HIV/AIDS epidemic was and continues to be preventable. But because of active obstruction of logical policy, active resistance to essential funding, and active interference with scientifically designed programs, the executive branch of this country has caused untold hardship, misery, and expense to the American public. Its effort with AIDS will stand as a huge scar in American history, a shame to our nation and an international disgrace. (Andriote 1999, 143–144)

Francis also argued that "an illness that at first threatened only gay men was the last issue the conservative Reagan administration wanted to spend government time or money to address" (Hirshman 2012, 174).

In what ways did the Bush presidency represent a point of departure from the Reagan administration's AIDS policies? As sitting vice president, George H. W. Bush had to balance his role as Reagan's adviser with his role as a presidential candidate in the 1988 election. As a candidate, Bush appealed to the Christian Right by endorsing policies that would publicly identify people who were HIV positive and that would require mandatory HIV tests when people applied for marriage licenses. On the campaign trail, Bush argued that HIV testing is more effective than spending money on treatment. After Bush's election in 1988, he continued most of the policies of the Reagan era. Bush did appear, however, to be more sensitive to the magnitude of the AIDS crisis.

The Bush administration continued Reagan's fiscal austerity with respect to AIDS. In addition, Bush embraced mandatory testing to prevent the spread of AIDS. Finally, his administration argued that local officials should design and implement AIDS educational strategies, although federal resources could be used to gather more AIDS information. His surgeon general, Dr. Antonia Novello, generally maintained a low profile on AIDS issues.

It was not until March 30, 1990, almost nine years after AIDS was first identified and more than a year into his presidency, that Bush gave his first speech on AIDS. He praised his administration's efforts in dealing with the AIDS crisis and asked the country to end discrimination against those infected with HIV. At the same time, Bush refused to eliminate a federal policy that placed restrictions on HIV-positive foreigners who wished to enter the United States. However, he did sign into law in 1990 the Ryan White Comprehensive AIDS Resource Emergency (CARE) Act, named for an Indiana boy who contracted AIDS from a contaminated blood transfusion and whose case received considerable media attention. The legislation was originally designed to provide federal assistance for urban areas that were hardest hit by AIDS, although he consistently opposed funding this legislation to the level its congressional supporters requested. The legislation was cosponsored by Orrin Hatch (R-UT) and Henry Waxman (D-CA) in the House of Representatives and Edward Kennedy (D-MA) in the Senate. It "provided substantial funds for a variety of purposes, including emergency assistance to the states and health services research." The Title I provision attracted the most attention, as it authorized "hundreds of millions of dollars to the worst-afflicted cities and metropolitan areas in the country. These 13 cities contained over 65 percent of all diagnosed AIDS cases in the country, and were facing dire shortfalls in funds for emergency medical care, public hospitals, private clinics, private hospital reimbursement, and emergency social services for AIDS patients and their families" (Engel 2006, 180). It has been recently described as "one of the most progressive pieces of social insurance in the past thirty years . . . which in principle guarantees that nobody dies of AIDS in America because they can't afford drugs" (Kim 2011, 6). The fact that Congress passed the Ryan White Act and that President Bush signed it into law reflected the slowly changing political climate, the dire lack of funding available to urban areas struggling with the AIDS crisis, and the important organizing work done by the lesbian and gay movements, who fought for consistent and increased funding from all levels of government. Given that AIDS in the United States was first recognized in large urban areas, especially Los Angeles, New York City, and San Francisco, it is not surprising that AIDS activists used the language of "urban disaster" to heighten public attention (Siplon 2002, 94–95). As we will see later in this chapter, disputes have arisen through the years over how resources provided under the Ryan White Act have been used. The debates over spending have accompanied reauthorization of the legislation in 1995–1996, 2000, and 2006.

Even President Bush began to recognize that his administration could not completely ignore the AIDS crisis. Besides signing the Ryan White Act, he called for the passage of antidiscrimination laws to protect those who had HIV/AIDS. In addition, he spoke of the need for greater compassion for those struck by AIDS and their families. And when he appointed Earvin "Magic" Johnson to the National Commission on AIDS (a carryover from the Reagan years), he received considerable credit, given Johnson's visibility in the world of professional basketball and the shock with which the nation reacted in the fall of 1991 to the news that he was HIV positive. But AIDS activists, as well as outspoken members of Congress such as Representatives Henry Waxman and Gerry Studds (D-MA), protested the administration's underfinanced and underdeveloped AIDS educational plan, while also deploring its failure to fund key federal AIDS initiatives directed at prevention, research, and treatment (Engel 2006, 189–191).

The chair of the National Commission on AIDS, June Osborn, criticized the president and his cabinet for failing to provide decisive leadership in "the national response" (Engel 2006, 191). And Magic Johnson resigned from the AIDS commission in frustration when it became apparent to him (and many others) that he was being exploited for his name and that President Bush had abdicated his own leadership responsibilities in confronting the AIDS crisis in meaningful ways.

Presidents often maintain a low profile with respect to newly identified public health hazards, perceiving them to offer limited political gain and many risks. The response of Presidents Ronald Reagan and George Bush to AIDS fits this pattern. In this case, both presidents were clearly uncomfortable with a major health problem that targeted those at the margins of American society—gay men and intravenous drug users residing largely in inner cities. Their views of the world simply did not allow for those most despised by society at large to receive their support. Indeed, many of those who assumed power in both administrations embraced political and personal beliefs hostile to gay men and lesbians. The prevailing conservative climate enabled the Reagan and Bush administrations' indifference toward AIDS (Rimmerman 2002, 87). But it also inspired the lesbian and gay movements to organize, as we will see in the next section of the chapter. Historian Martin Duberman points out that "by 1990, gay activism surrounding AIDS had galvanized the community, heightened visibility, and produced some measurable political progress that would have been unimaginable a decade earlier." More than fifty thousand people had died of AIDS by early 1990 "with more than double that number known to be affected by the virus" (2009, 69). Duberman captures the bleakness of the times well: "No successful treatment had yet emerged, and every effort to spread 'safe sex' information had been blocked by a frothing batch of conservatives insistent that any allocation of resources for prevention was the equivalent of actively promoting a vile, diseased sexuality" (69–70). It is within this hostile political and cultural environment that the lesbian and gay movements responded, often with fury and anger underlying passionate and committed organizing. But to understand that response, we must first place tensions within the movements in their proper historical context.

Response of the Lesbian and Gay Movements to the Reagan/Bush Years

The lesbian and gay movements endured serious divisions over the treatment of women in the late 1960s and 1970s. Profoundly influenced by the women's movement, lesbian separatists "rejected the gay rights movement as irredeemably misogynist and sexist." Capturing the spirit of the times, Jill Johnston wrote in 1975 that "lesbians are feminists, not homosexuals" (Gregory 2001, 159). The gap between men and women within the larger movements would continue well into the 1980s, with occasional interruptions, such as when lesbians and gay men joined forces to fight the 1978 California Briggs initiative. But when the AIDS crisis produced a tremendous antigay backlash in the 1980s, many lesbians and gay men recognized the importance of putting aside differences in the short term to respond to the heightened bigotry and prejudice that accompanied AIDS. It is no surprise, then, that one leading scholar of the movements would write that "although an AIDS movement and a gay and lesbian movement are conceptually distinct, in practice the boundary proved porous. . . . And AIDS, by arousing from apathy an economically privileged segment of the community, tapped resources that have allowed us to make the transition from a movement of only volunteers to one with an ever-growing number of full-time paid workers" (D'Emilio 2002, 76). Indeed, lesbians and gays who lived in smaller cities and towns in the 1980s established their first organizations with the creation of AIDS service groups; these organizations soon led to opportunities for political organizing. One major reason the lesbian and gay community chose to create their own service organizations is "because it did not want the government and public health professionals to do more, if 'more' meant crafting policies that it feared would be discriminatory and even punitive toward members of the community" (Siplon 2002, 8).

In the face of governmental indifference in the early years, the lesbian and gay movements had to offer their own responses to the emerging crisis. For example, a May 1983 brochure published by AIDS Project / LA offered several preventive measures that individuals could take. They included "eat a nutritionally balanced diet" as well as "reduce your number of sexual partners" (Bereznai 2006, 226). Community organizations located in major urban areas like AIDS Project / LA helped fill the void of the federal, state, and local government response to AIDS with resources for educational outreach and other social service programs.

The AIDS crisis also politicized an entire generation of lesbian and gay activists. The historian Michael Klarman captures this development well:

> Although AIDS proved devastating to the gay community and debilitating to the gay rights movement in the short term, it advanced the cause of gay rights over the longer term. For one thing, the epidemic forced tens of thousands of homosexuals out of the closet. In the words of one activist, "AIDS made it so we couldn't hide anymore." AIDS was a "call to action," which helped gay rights groups raise money and enlist new activists. Thousands of formerly apolitical gays and lesbians suddenly had a more direct stake in gay rights activism, and accordingly they volunteered to register voters and lobby policy makers. (2013, 39)

A veteran of ACT UP / Chicago identified the historical context for AIDS activism accurately: "People feared that the government would continue to allow massive numbers of gay men and others to die by not providing adequate funds for research, treatment, and social services—and that people with AIDS and gay people more generally might actually be rounded up" (Gould 2009, 11).

New organizations sprang up in communities throughout the United States, organizations that were created to care for the sick and to organize to increase attention to AIDS prevention, treatment, and the drug development process. And these organizations were staffed by lesbians and gay men as well as their straight supporters. Deborah Gould, a student of AIDS political organizing, has accurately pointed out that "lesbian participation is particularly notable because, in the years prior to AIDS, lesbians and gay men typically were not engaged in political activism together" (2009, 66). And another veteran of the movements, David Mixner, has concluded that "by the time the AIDS epidemic emerged, lesbians and gay men had learned to work closely together and many lesbians had emerged as leaders in the community. Women like Torie Osborn, Lori Jean, Elizabeth Birch, Hillary Rosen, Pat Denslow, Urvashi Vaid, Jean O'Leary and so many others became some of our community's greatest champions. All the while, they supported gay men in their struggle against HIV/AIDS. I can't believe we would be where we are today without their spectacular leadership" (2011, 143–144).

The issue of how to get those in power at all levels of government to respond to AIDS challenged the lesbian and gay movements in ways that they had never been challenged before. These failures of leadership at all levels of government forced lesbian and gay activists to confront two key dilemmas, articulated so well by Urvashi Vaid: "How were we going to get a response from an administration that did not care about us? And how were we going to motivate and mobilize a community that was largely in the closet and invisible?" (1995, 72–73). The lesbian and gay movements pursued several overlapping strategies in their response to AIDS: the "degaying" of AIDS, organizing for heightened visibility of the lesbian and gay movements, separating AIDS-specific reform from structural reform of the overall health-care system, and direct action in the form of unconventional politics (74). All of these strategies reflected a willingness to embrace both assimilationist and liberationist approaches to political, social, and cultural change, depending on the political moment and the historical circumstances. But, given the reality that people were increasingly getting sick and dying, the lesbian and gay movements were understandably focused on short-term goals, which included getting affordable drugs to those in need and providing AIDS outreach and education to stem the tide of infection. With this in mind, the organizing strategies often associated with the assimilationist perspective dominated the political discourse of the time, though, as we will see, groups such as ACT UP, Queer Nation, and the Lesbian Avengers all embraced liberationist strategies along the way.

The Degaying of AIDS

In the mid-1980s, AIDS leaders made a crucial decision to publicize the message that "AIDS is not a gay disease." The goal was to gain greater funding and public support and to convey the importance of AIDS prevention to all sectors of the population. The assumption was that the public and politicians would be more receptive to increased AIDS-related funding if gay men were not the targeted beneficiaries. That this strategy had to be used suggests how little progress had been made in combating the prejudice and hatred seemingly woven into the fabric of the larger culture. Thus, for roughly the next eight years, many AIDS groups de-emphasized lesbian and gay participation, denied that they were "gay organizations" per se, "and attempted to appeal to the general public by expunging gay references and sanitizing gay culture" (Rofes 1990, 11). A central goal was to capture the attention of straight society by stressing that heterosexuals—particularly women and children—were at risk of contracting HIV. In this way, AIDS activists embraced an assimilationist strategy, one that allowed nongay public-health officials to lobby on behalf of AIDS-specific issues while avoiding addressing lesbian-and gay-rights concerns (Rimmerman 2002, 97).

Heightened Cultural Visibility

A second consequence of the AIDS epidemic was to heighten the visibility of the lesbian and gay movements. To the extent that the media helped foster greater cultural change with respect to HIV/AIDS, it served as a means for integrating liberationist ideas into the developing AIDS movement in the United States. Media activism, which had characterized the movement since the 1950s, played an increasingly important role in the AIDS movements of the 1980s and 1990s (Vaid 1995, 79). Well before AIDS, lesbian and gay media were the principal outlets for information pertaining to lesbian, gay, bisexual, and transgender issues. They helped build community, and they were crucial arenas for political debate. The lesbian and gay media remained a vital information source even after the advent of AIDS. For example, in the early years of the epidemic, the *New York Native* provided some of the most forthright, accurate, and courageous reporting on AIDS. Dr. Lawrence Mass, then the paper's medical writer, authored the first news report and first feature article about AIDS, both of which appeared in the *Native* soon after the disease began striking gay men in early 1981. These were the first articles about AIDS to appear in the nonscientific press. Sadly, Mass was threatened with the loss of his job at the New York City Health Department for speaking out publicly about AIDS (Blasius and Phelan 1997, 574). The role of the *New York Native* and other lesbian and gay media sources cannot be ignored, especially given that the mainstream press largely shunned coverage of AIDS in the early years of the epidemic.

In the early years of the crisis, the mainstream press also ignored the grassroots organizations that were committed to education and prevention. For example, in 1982 the Gay Men's Health Crisis (GMHC)—the first grassroots AIDS service-related organization in the United States—was founded by Larry Kramer, Lawrence Mass, and others, including Alvin Friedman-Kien, who had diagnosed the first AIDS cases in New York and served as a faculty member at the New York University Medical Center. Upon the group's creation, Kramer targeted the mainstream media, hoping they would highlight the organization's AIDS prevention and educational efforts. But few showed any interest in the story at all. Claiming that they did not wish to contribute to a public panic over a yet-unnamed disease that still posed too many unanswered questions (Alwood 1996, 214–215), the media abdicated their important reporting and educational responsibilities. The GMHC, based in New York City, an epicenter of the AIDS crisis, performed an important education and organizing role at precisely the time when such efforts were desperately needed in the face of indifference at all levels of government. Kramer and his colleagues were particularly critical of New York City public health officials during Mayor Ed Koch's tenure for failing to offer comprehensive public education about AIDS, how transmission could be prevented, and how those living with HIV/AIDS could be supported with public health resources and also be treated with dignity and respect. Public health scholar James Colegrove of the AIDS policy response in New York City, points out, however, that "this accusation was exaggerated. While the Health Department had done little in the way of educating the lay public, it had been central to informing the city's health care workers about the new condition. . . . Nevertheless, the failure to produce mass educational messages for the lay public remained a serious weakness in the department's response to the new disease" (2011, 122).

The AIDS memorial-quilt project played a major role as well in raising public awareness of AIDS, yet it caused considerable controversy in the lesbian and gay movements. The October 11, 1987, March on Washington for Lesbian and Gay Rights was the occasion for the Names Project's first display of the quilt. March participants as well as the general public were reminded by the 1,920 panels, which covered the equivalent of two football fields, that AIDS had already claimed many lives. The timing of the quilt's appearance was deliberate: the 1988 presidential campaign was under way, and the quilt "provided a powerful symbol of the gay community's political struggle for equal rights and of the casualties of the simultaneous struggle for sexual liberation" (Andriote 1999, 365). But, much to the consternation of some activists, the opportunities for enhanced public education and greater movement visibility brought by the AIDS quilt did not begin to make up for the assimilationist strategy that undergirded the degaying of AIDS, which characterized the Names Project's way of representing the disease. One letter writer reported his frustration on visiting the quilt in Washington, DC:

> That evening the candlelight march was led by invited parents of people with AIDS as thousands of mostly gay people marched behind them in the silent arc of candles. While this gesture towards parents was certainly admirable and appropriate, it was unforgivable for the project not to show the same level of respect for the partners of people who had died of AIDS. Surely it is not too much to expect an overwhelmingly gay-run organization to strive to recognize gay relationships in a more sensitive manner than society has shown. (Rofes 1990, 12)

Other activists were frustrated by the inability of the Names Project to connect its organizing work to a larger political and cultural strategy, one that was associated with liberationist values and goals. For example, Urvashi Vaid argued that it "didn't do enough to politicize people" (Andriote 1999, 367). And Vaid commented further, "That George Bush, who did so little, could be quoted on the back of the Names Project book reveals the irony of the depoliticization of the AIDS movement" (1995, 78).

In the end, the lesbian and gay movements achieved mixed success in their attempts to achieve heightened visibility around the AIDS issue. The strategy was undermined by tensions over whether the assimilationist or liberationist approach to political, social, and cultural change should prevail.

AIDS-Specific Reform

As we have already seen, AIDS mobilized lesbians and gay men in communities throughout the United States and fostered the creation of new organizations at the national and local levels. The creation of these new organizations raised additional tensions over strategy and goals within the lesbian and gay movements. What should be the relationship between the newly created AIDS service organizations and the broader lesbian and gay movements? Should such organizations critique the prevailing health-care system, or should they merely focus on providing basic services in a time of crisis? It is certainly understandable why many, faced with scarce resources and a serious public health crisis, embraced a more "pragmatic" response. But this more narrowly focused, assimilationist approach has understandably been the target of considerable criticism from the liberationist point of view. The primary critique is that AIDS service organizations focused too much on accommodating themselves to the existing health-care system rather than linking health-care service delivery to class, race, and gender concerns.

The GMHC and the AIDS Action Council are prime examples of this liberationist critique. When Larry Kramer and others met in his Greenwich Village apartment in the summer of 1981 to discuss the onset of what eventually came to be known as AIDS, they decided that New York City needed an organization that was "founded by the gay community for the gay community." Over the years, the GMHC has provided counseling, education, and social services in support of those who are sick, and it has become thoroughly institutionalized. By the late 1990s, the organization had served more than seventy-five thousand clients annually, with a support staff of more than two hundred and nearly seven thousand volunteers. Over time, representatives of the GMHC have participated in AIDS-related meetings at all levels of government. Though founded as a local organization, the GMHC has had an important national presence, and it has embraced a quintessential conventional insider approach to political change (Rom 2000, 222). Specifically, the GMHC has largely avoided addressing larger structural inequalities in the health-care system.

This same approach has characterized the AIDS Action Council. Founded in 1984, the AIDS Action Council has been a leading national voice on AIDS, representing 3,200 of America's AIDS organizations and the millions of Americans they serve. The organization's mission statement asserts that "AIDS Action is the only organization solely dedicated to responsible federal policy for improved HIV/AIDS care and services, effective HIV prevention and vigorous medical research." A former director of the organization told me that "we realized that there had to be a nongay voice associated with the policy aspects of AIDS, and that is why the AIDS [Action] Council was created" (personal interview, February 19, 1997). In this way, the organization has played an integral role in reinforcing the assimilationist strategy. Like the GMHC, the AIDS Action Council has pursued conventional insider approaches to change. And as a former executive director of the organization acknowledged to me, there was considerable "conflict over short-term responses to AIDS and long-term political and policy planning" (personal interview, February 19, 1997). But it is also easy to understand why the AIDS Action Council pursued a mainstreaming, insider-politics, assimilationist strategy. Such a strategy led to tangible political accomplishments, including increased funding for AIDS and major legislation, in the form of the Ryan White CARE Act. This same strategy embraced a more narrowly focused political and cultural approach, one that would soon have to make room for unconventional outsider politics with the birth of ACT UP in 1987.

Direct Action and the Rise of Unconventional Politics

On October 14, 1987, Jesse Helms, a conservative member of the United States Senate (R-NC), responded on the Senate floor to a safe-sex comic book that had been written by the GMHC and distributed in New York City. Helms was outraged by the book, and, in protesting its content, he helped to usher in a national debate regarding the most effective ways to halt the spread of HIV. The GMHC had responded to Helms by informing him that the book was not supported by federal funds. Federal resources were used, instead, for workshops and educational sessions that were created to offer AIDS risk-reduction education. Helms voiced opposition to this workshop program in his Senate floor speech and ultimately concluded that "abstinence only" programs were the only ones worthy of federal government support. He offered a legislative amendment, Amendment 956, which, if passed, would have prevented the CDC from spending any federally authorized funds to "provide AIDS education, information, or prevention materials and activities that promote, encourage, or condone sexual activity outside a sexually monogamous marriage (including homosexual activities) or the use of intravenous drugs." What is most shocking about this affair is not Helms's rant or his amendment, but the fact that his proposal "drew almost no verbal opposition from his more liberal colleagues in the Senate." At the time, only Senators Lawton Chiles (D-FL) and Lowell Weicker (R-CT) challenged him on the floor. Weicker provided the stronger opposition by arguing that education and research were the only viable weapons in combating AIDS. He claimed that "any sort of an education process that excludes a part of the population, in particular a high-risk population, is not the education effort that the crisis deserves" (Siplon 2002, 67). In the end, Helms's amendment "was modified to only prohibit funding efforts that would seem to be promoting homosexuality" (68). But the damage was clearly done, and the incident reveals the power that social conservatives had in the national policy process at the time.

How did AIDS activists respond to such retrograde and pernicious policies during the deepening health crisis? Some responded with fury, embracing the unconventional outsider politics of the AIDS Coalition to Unleash Power, or ACT UP. Formed in March 1987 in New York City, ACT UP has been responsible "for producing some of the most important advances in AIDS research and some of the most crucial improvements in the lives of people with AIDS" (P. Cohen 1998, 1). The group's founding statement declares it a "diverse, non-partisan group united in anger and committed to direct action to end the AIDS crisis" (Reed 2005, 182). Larry Kramer provided the impetus for founding ACT UP with a 1987 speech at the Lesbian and Gay Community Services Center of New York. In this now infamous speech, Kramer challenged the lesbian and gay movements to organize, mobilize, and demand an effective AIDS-policy response. He informed the audience of gay men that two-thirds of them might be dead within five years. In his speech, Kramer asked, "Do we want to start a new organization devoted solely to political action?" Kramer's speech inspired another meeting at the Community Services Center several days later, which more than three hundred people attended. This event essentially signaled the birth of ACT UP. Thereafter, ACT UP / New York routinely drew more than eight hundred people to its weekly meetings. As the organization grew, it remained the largest and most influential of all of the chapters (Rimmerman 2002, 105). By early 1988, active chapters had spread to other cities throughout the country, including Boston, Chicago, Los Angeles, and San Francisco. At the beginning of 1990, ACT UP had spread across the globe, with more than a hundred chapters worldwide (Vaid 1995, 94–95). But as former Rhode Island ACT UP activist

Peter F. Cohen makes clear, "ACT UP / New York was originally *the* ACT UP—the first chapter, and historically the largest. Despite the eventual appearance of ACT UP chapters around the country, ACT UP / New York continued to provide leadership for the movement, especially in areas of national concern such as work concerning experimental drugs." In addition, ACT UP / New York received most of the media attention, perhaps because it "organized many of the demonstrations associated with the group as a whole," such as the 1989 "Stop the Church" protest in New York City's St. Patrick's Cathedral (1998, 3). The New York chapter also helped organize highly visible demonstrations in other communities throughout the United States.

ACT UP's original goal was to demand the release of experimental drugs. Underlying ACT UP's political strategy is a commitment to radical democracy and principles of participatory democratic theory. For example, no one member or group of members had the right to speak for ACT UP; this was a right reserved for all members. There were no elected leaders, no appointed spokespeople, and little formal structure to the organization (Rimmerman 2002, 105). ACT UP most often targeted six major institutions: advertising, the arts, the Catholic Church, corporations, government bureaucracies, and the mass media (Reed 2005, 182). Over the years, ACT UP has broadened its original purpose to embrace a number of specific practical goals. It has demanded that the US Food and Drug Administration (FDA) release AIDS drugs in a timely manner by shortening the drug testing and approval process, and it has insisted that private health insurance as well as Medicaid be forced to pay for experimental drug therapies. However, ACT UP members also "insisted that availability of new treatments would not be sufficient to guarantee all people with AIDS access to drugs." AIDS historian Jennifer Brier accurately points out that "ACT UP's mission needed to include a commitment to affordable treatment and universal health care, a point that proved prescient when set against the development of protease inhibitors (combination drug therapies) in 1996 and the inability to distribute them" (2009, 9). Ten years into the AIDS crisis, ACT UP understandably questioned why only one drug, the highly toxic azidothymidine (AZT), had been approved for treatment. ACT UP also demanded federally controlled and funded needle-exchange and condom-distribution programs as well as a serious sex-education program in primary and secondary schools created and monitored by the US Department of Education (Rimmerman

2002, 106–107). Steven Epstein has accurately observed that "few social movements are inclined to mix 'moral crusades' with 'practical crusades,'" which ACT UP did successfully (1996, 232). In addition, ACT UP demanded successfully that the CDC "expand the definition of AIDS to include infections and diseases commonly occurring in HIV-infected women and poor people" (Gould 2009, 5).

What makes ACT UP such an interesting organization to study is the fact that it has embraced both liberationist and assimilationist approaches to political, social, and cultural change. As one movement scholar has argued, ACT UP "has made self-conscious cultural struggle part of its core work," thus embracing a broad liberationist strategy for change (Reed 2005, 179). But it is also assimilationist to the extent that ACT UP chapters throughout the United States challenged the mainstream policy process to respond to the needs of people with AIDS in the short term. Linda Hirshman describes the challenges facing ACT UP well: "ACT UP, like all direct-action movements, was constantly navigating the line between being disruptive enough to be effective and too disruptive to be effective" (2012, 206). As we have already seen, the group is part of a long tradition of grassroots initiatives in the United States, especially the African American civil rights movement, that practiced unconventional politics to promote political, social, and cultural change.

Part of ACT UP's genius is its ability to creatively bridge these two approaches, "particularly through use of the visual and performing arts, in challenging the media's packaging of protest and trivialization of movements." It accomplished this goal "most effectively through the use of striking, aesthetically rich images, accompanied by witty, sound-bite-worthy slogans" (Hirshman 2012, 180). ACT UP embraced slogans such as "Silence = Death" and used political art to convey its message to the public. The organization was adept in securing media attention from the start and, as a result, was able to communicate greater awareness of AIDS issues to the lesbian and gay communities and to the larger society.

The media covered a number of ACT UP demonstrations, including its very first, held on Wall Street in New York on March 24, 1987 (Rimmerman 2002, 107). The target of this protest action was Burroughs Wellcome, the pharmaceutical company that was charging $10,000 for a one-year supply of AZT. At the time, people were optimistic that AZT was the drug that could finally help those with HIV/AIDS. As Patricia Siplon, a student of AIDS policy, points out, "It seemed to be a particularly cruel irony that the long-awaited treatment should be priced out of the reach of many people who sought it" (2002, 19). Other high-profile demonstrations included a 1987 protest at New York's Sloan-Kettering Hospital to demand an increase in the number of HIV drugs to be developed and made available. In 1988 more than a thousand ACT UP protesters surrounded the FDA's Rockville, Maryland, headquarters, "where their representatives met with agency officials and, remarkably, succeeded in getting the FDA's drug approval process foreshortened" (Duberman 2009, 70). In 1989, ACT UP activists demonstrated at AIDS hearings held by the US Civil Rights Commission to protest its inept response to AIDS. In the same year, ACT UP / New York's "Stop the Church" demonstration disrupted Roman Catholic cardinal John O'Connor's mass in Saint Patrick's Cathedral to protest his opposition to condom distribution. Also in 1989 several hundred ACT UP protesters disrupted the opening session of the June 1989 Fifth International Conference on AIDS held in Montreal, Canada. Jennifer Brier describes the meaning and scope of ACT UP's Montreal protests:

> Contingents from the New York chapter of ACT UP and Toronto's AIDS Action NOW! took over the podium to read the "Montreal Manifesto" to the audience of several thousand AIDS researchers. The manifesto's ten demands underscored the need for universal rights for all people living with AIDS. The first called for access to treatment for AIDS, a position that by 1989 had gained currency through ACT UP's activism targeting major pharmaceutical companies such as Burroughs Wellcome and the Food and Drug Administration. . . . The breadth and audacity of the Montreal Manifesto's demands illustrated the scope of AIDS activism in the late 1980s. Activists, protesting for the first time at an international AIDS conference, made several critical arguments that linked science and politics, all of which functioned as political critique of the status quo. (2009, 156–157)

In one further action that unavoidably caught the attention of the media, ACT UP members invaded the studio of the *MacNeil / Lehrer News-Hour* on January 22, 1991, chained themselves to Robert MacNeil's desk during a live broadcast, and flashed signs declaring "The AIDS Crisis Is Not Over" (Rimmerman 2002, 108).

Critics both within and outside of the lesbian and gay movements protested that some of these actions were too disruptive and counterproductive. "Stop the Church" and other demonstrations heightened an already existing tension within the movements, between those who favored more traditional assimilationist insider lobbying activities and those who embraced the radical direct action associated with ACT UP. As we have already seen in Chapter 2, these tensions have been prevalent throughout the development of the lesbian and gay movements. Stanley Aronowitz, a student of social movements, offered a perceptive view of ACT UP's approach, a perspective that gives us a deeper understanding of what motivated its creative response to political activism:

> ACT-UP's tacit strategy was to force on public officials, church, and business leaders their most horrific nightmare: exposure by means of actions that signify disrespect. By presenting itself as an "out-of-control" intransigent mélange of queers and misfits, it reveals a capacity to opt out of what is expected of a "responsible" civic organization: to play by the rules. From the perspective of the Establishment's code, to refuse these rules is to engage in the politics of *terror*. (1996, 131)

By 1992, there were divisions in ACT UP over strategy and tactics and over its treatment of women and minorities. Women in ACT UP considered forming their own caucus to ensure that women with AIDS were represented in AIDS political activism and ultimately in the policy process. Although men and women were both "infected with HIV in similar ways—through unprotected vaginal or anal intercourse or intravenous drug use," in the more advanced stages, full-blown AIDS in men "often caused KS, while women experienced bacterial pneumonia, pelvic inflammatory disease, and cervical cancer. This meant that even as the number of women with HIV increased during the 1980s, very few were actually diagnosed with AIDS and instead were categorized as having the less advanced ARC [AIDS Related Complex]" (Brier 2009, 172). The divisions within ACT UP helped to spawn spin-off organizations, such as Queer Nation and the Lesbian Avengers. Queer Nation appeared in June 1991 with a central goal of radicalizing the broader AIDS movement (and the lesbian and gay movements) by embracing confrontational politics and reclaiming the word *queer*. Perhaps the most controversial tactic promoted by Queer Nation members and supporters was "outing," a strategy designed to publicize and challenge closeted lesbians and gays in positions of power in American society.

Founded in the fall of 1992 by six lesbian friends and organizers—Maria Simo, Anne-Christine D'Adesky, Maxine Wolfe, Marie Honan, Ann Maguire, and Sara Schulman—the Lesbian Avengers also embraced unconventional politics as a response to a larger lesbian and gay movement that they perceived to be dominated by men who refused to address sexism in meaningful ways. The organization embraced tactics similar to those used by ACT UP in its effort to attract media attention. The Lesbian Avengers has become known for its Dyke Marches, the first of which was held as a part of the 1993 Gay and Lesbian March on Washington. In addition, it has done important grassroots organizing work in fighting referenda hostile to lesbians, gays, bisexuals, and transgender individuals by organizing in those states where such referenda are on the ballot (Rimmerman 2002, 109).

What distinguishes all of this unconventional political organizing is the determination of these organizers to reach well beyond their lesbian and gay white male constituencies. The goal was to reach those in power throughout American society as well as ordinary citizens whom organizers perceived could be persuaded that people who have been infected with HIV should not be the targets of discrimination and vitriol. In this way, the organizations mentioned here transcended narrowly focused assimilationist organizing strategies and integrated liberationist ways of thinking into their invaluable work. But the organizations would face more serious challenges with a so-called friend, President William Jefferson Clinton, residing in the White House.

AIDS Policy in the Clinton/Bush/Obama Years

The 1992 election of Bill Clinton promised great opportunities for the lesbian and gay movements, especially after twelve years of conservative Republican rule. Although some AIDS activists were suspicious of Clinton's commitment, the "shriller voices in the AIDS activist community were receding into the background, and a group of leaders was emerging who could mix more easily with the administration" (Levenson 2003, 131–132). After all, Clinton had promised during the campaign that he would appoint an "AIDS czar" who would coordinate AIDS policy from the White House. In addition, he claimed that he would provide more funding for AIDS research and education than his Republican predecessors. Indeed, soon after taking office, he requested that Health and Human

Services secretary Donna Shalala create an AIDS task force that would establish AIDS research and treatment priorities for the administration. He used the occasion of AIDS Awareness Day to outline his administration's approach to AIDS at Georgetown University (Engel 2006, 234–235). Furthermore, Clinton excoriated the Bush administration's policy of banning the immigration of HIV-positive foreigners to the United States, thus signaling a more progressive overall policy. At a more symbolic level, he chose Bob Hattoy, an openly gay man who had been diagnosed with AIDS, to speak at the summer 1992 Democratic National Convention in New York. Capturing the initial hopes of many AIDS activists, David Kirp wrote in the *Nation* during the summer of 1994, "Clinton at Georgetown, [Kristin] Gebbie on the stump, Shalala rejecting business as usual for AIDS—that kind of official rhetoric matters greatly" (234).

It was not mere rhetoric that caught the attention of AIDS activists. From the vantage point of the lesbian and gay movements, Clinton's policy approach to AIDS represented a significant improvement over the policies of Reagan and Bush. During the 1992 presidential campaign, Clinton offered a number of HIV/AIDS policy-related promises, including:

1. increasing AIDS funding significantly;
2. implementing controversial proposals emanating from the National Commission on AIDS, like needle exchange programs and explicit safe-sex education;
3. accelerating the FDA's drug-approval process;
4. expanding clinical drug trials for promising treatments;
5. admitting HIV-positive Haitians being held without medical care at Guantanamo Bay Naval Base into the United States (Gould 2009, 415).

Clinton also embraced full funding of the Ryan White CARE Act, thus giving further momentum to the importance of maintaining and funding the act over the long term. He created the National Task Force on AIDS Drug Development to examine how new drugs could be released to the market more quickly. Clinton's Department of Justice took action to address discrimination against people who were either HIV positive or diagnosed with AIDS. In June 1993, the Clinton administration announced that rules governing the eligibility of people infected with HIV for disability benefits would be relaxed considerably. Finally, Clinton's 1992 election meant that more federal money was allocated for AIDS research. For example, in fiscal year 1994, funding for AIDS research increased by 18 percent (Foreman 1994, 123).

But it did not take long for lesbian and gay movement activists to be disappointed. As we will see in Chapter 4, Clinton's unwillingness to fight for his campaign promise to overturn the ban on lesbians and gays in the military frustrated many. And AIDS activists and people living with AIDS were soon disappointed as well. Clinton received praise for discussing AIDS more than did his predecessors, but in the end he failed to initiate the kind of comprehensive plan that activists had expected.

His AIDS czar appointments (Kristin Gebbie, Patricia Fleming, and Sandy Thurman) were all deemed to be ineffectual, and soon the idea of the office itself came to be viewed as more symbolic than substantive. His appointment of Dr. Jocelyn Elders, an Arkansas physician and professor of pediatrics, as surgeon general received praise, especially after her outspoken endorsement of sex education and AIDS-prevention outreach. But following Republican victories in the 1994 congressional elections, Clinton forced Elders's resignation when she angered conservatives by appearing to call for the teaching of masturbation to schoolchildren; in fact, Elders had endorsed what were perceived by many as reasonable, comprehensive sex-education programs. Her original comments had been badly distorted by conservatives for political reasons, and President Clinton refused to support her, thus further antagonizing lesbian and gay activists (Rimmerman 1998b, 401–402). In June 1995, White House security officers wore blue rubber gloves to check the bags of gay elected officials who were visiting the White House. Soon thereafter, White House spokesperson Michael McCurry apologized for "an error of judgment" (Engel 2006, 234).

AIDS activists were again disappointed when Clinton failed to endorse a promised needle-exchange program to target injecting drug users. In adopting a cautious middle ground, the administration called for a federally funded study on needle exchange and then concluded that more research was needed before any needle-exchange policy could be proposed. This was particularly frustrating for AIDS activists, who cited existing studies suggesting that needle exchanges could save lives. In addition, Clinton responded to the demands of social conservatives by eliminating mandatory AIDS educational programs for federal workers. The overall Clinton record on HIV/AIDS policy proved to be mixed and apparently even disappointed him. After he left the White House, he created a foundation that addresses, among other issues, HIV/AIDS, the William J. Clinton Foundation, one that would be the focal point of his international policy work as a former president.

Clinton's AIDS policy record allowed his successor, President George W. Bush, to have room to maneuver between rewarding his Christian Right supporters by focusing on abstinence as a centerpiece of his domestic and foreign HIV/AIDS policies and his 2003 pledge to spend $15 billion to fight global AIDS over a ten-year period. But the prevailing AIDS policy theme of the Bush administration was abstinence-only coupled with efforts to undercut federal funding for safe-sex education for young Americans. In 2004, the administration established a website, aptly named 4parents.gov, as "a guide to help you and your pre-teen or mid-teen discuss important, yet difficult issues about healthy choices, abstinence, sex and relationships." Analyst Susan Hunter claims that "human rights and health groups reviewing the site were so appalled at what they found that 150 organizations asked that the U.S. Department of Health and Human Services . . . immediately take it off the Internet" (2006, 59). Esther Kaplan points out in her excellent book on the role of Christian fundamentalists in the George W. Bush White House that none of this should have been a surprise, given Bush's sorry record on HIV/AIDS as governor of Texas from 1994 to 2000. For example, Governor Bush never mentioned AIDS in any public address, despite the reality that "the state's AIDS cases surged to rank fourth in the nation." In addition, his appointment as Texas health commissioner openly opposed condom use because "it's not what God intended." And Bush himself viewed AIDS as such a low item on his policy agenda that "he refused to sign letters of support for AIDS grant applications" (Kaplan 2004, 168). As a presidential candidate during April 2000, Bush met with prominent gay Republicans in Austin. Carl Schmid, who attended the meeting and worked for the Log Cabin Republicans, said that "global AIDS wasn't on his agenda and it wasn't on ours" (169). A first draft of the 2000 Republican Party platform, which was largely written by Bush campaign officials, failed to even mention AIDS.

Just one month into the new administration, Bush's chief of staff, Andrew Card, announced that the White House office on AIDS would soon be eliminated. In response, protests were vigorous, and then–press secretary Ari Fleischer announced that Card's comment was "a mistake," though it soon became clear to AIDS activists that it was a "trial balloon," one meant to signal that AIDS policy would be shunted to the sidelines in the Bush White House. More evidence that the Bush administration was not interested in AIDS policy came in the months that passed before he appointed an AIDS czar, Scott Evertz, and the full year before he appointed his AIDS advisory council members. Scott Hitt, who had served as chair of the AIDS council under President Clinton, told Esther Kaplan, "I just don't get the sense that this administration is engaged" (Kaplan 2004, 169).

But in his 2003 State of the Union address, President Bush surprised many of his critics when he proposed a vigorous global program to fight AIDS. In justifying his plan, he said that "seldom has history offered a greater opportunity to do so much for so many. And to meet a severe and urgent crisis abroad, tonight I propose the Emergency Plan for AIDS Relief—a work of mercy beyond all current international efforts to help the people of Africa." In many ways, his plan was an outgrowth of the "compassionate conservative" philosophy that he first introduced in the 2000 presidential campaign to signal that he was a different kind of conservative when it came to social policy. His pledge would ultimately triple current US funding for global AIDS, "which was already more than double Clinton administration funding" (Behrman 2004, 307). Besides providing huge increases in global AIDS spending, however, the program's centerpiece is the primary approach of abstinence-only programs as prevention. Indeed, "the Bush administration has earmarked for abstinence education a third of all the money that it has given for AIDS prevention in the developing world" (Micklethwait and Wooldridge 2004, 149). The program received bipartisan support, as evidenced by Nicholas D. Kristof's September 2006 *New York Times* op-ed in which he claimed that "emphasis on testing could be incorporated into the extension of President Bush's fine program against AIDS, which will save some nine million lives and is up for renewal next year. That program, which provided huge increases in spending and will be Mr. Bush's best legacy, should be extended with even more money, while dropping its obsession with abstinence-only programs" (n.p.).

Critics such as Esther Kaplan, however, were scathing in their indictment of Bush's global AIDS plan:

> Rather than seek advice from the AIDS researchers, doctors, social workers, advocates, and people living with HIV who had set the AIDS agenda in the past, he would listen to pharmaceutical executives intent on preserving drug profits and to social conservatives whose abhorrence of gay and extramarital sex was matched only by their lack of AIDS expertise. Rather than promote public health solutions, he emphasized "personal responsibility." Rather than condoms, his mantra was abstinence and marriage. In Bush's hands, AIDS was born again—as a conservative issue. (2004, 169–170)

Kaplan and other critics have argued that Bush's focus on global AIDS allowed him to avoid addressing the many challenges of the domestic epidemic, which includes the rising rates of HIV infection among gay men, their partners, and IV drug users, many of whom live in urban America. Bush did little to recognize the significant increase in HIV infection among African Americans. And the administration was laggard in supporting full funding for the Ryan White CARE Act, which was targeted by social conservatives in the Republican-controlled House of Representatives during the first six years of the Bush presidency. In the end, his vision of compassionate conservatism was one that ignored the many challenges of funding for HIV/AIDS safe-sex education and policy initiatives at home.[1]

Barack Obama's 2008 election led to significant HIV/AIDS policy reforms at the federal level. In October 2009, Obama fulfilled a campaign promise by signing into law the repeal of the 1987 HIV Entry Ban, which had "prevented anyone with HIV from entering the U.S. for any reason." Waivers had previously been given to "opposite sex spouses of U.S. citizens," but "they were not granted to same-sex partners, so the burden of this policy fell disproportionately on gay men." Why was the ban so pernicious in its treatment of gay men? Sean Cahill offers two explanations. First, "the ban undermined public health by forcing HIV-positive visitors who risked entry to leave their medications at home." Second, the ban exacerbated the epidemic by preventing "many who were already here from getting tested, diagnosed, and treated." Obama's decision to repeal the ban was important because the United States had been previously associated with countries known for human rights abuses—Sudan, Yemen,

Singapore, and Egypt—that had also enforced a ban on HIV-positive visitors (Cahill 2010).

Obama addressed needle exchanges in his second major HIV/AIDS policy initiative in late 2009, repealing the ban "on using federal funds for syringe exchange" championed by former senator Jesse Helms in 1988. Helms's ban had ensured that federal funds could not be used to support the 185 syringe exchange programs operating throughout the United States. This significant policy change represents an important departure from previous administrations, and it occurred at a propitious time, given the fiscal crisis that has led to the cutbacks in state and local funding for syringe exchange program initiatives. As Sean Cahill accurately points out, "The repeal of the ban on the use of federal funds for syringe exchange will help this highly effective intervention to continue." Why is this important? Because "more than a third of AIDS cases in the U.S. are directly or indirectly associated with injection drug use, and more than a quarter million Americans have died from AIDS they contracted through sharing needles" (Cahill 2010).

One of Obama's most important HIV/AIDS policy reforms was his December 2009 "spending bill that completely eliminated [federal] funding for abstinence-only [programs] for the first time in nearly three decades. Since the Reagan years, the federal government has spent more than $2.5 billion on this approach." This represents a significant departure from the approach of previous administrations. Indeed, in October 2010, Obama embraced a sex-education campaign rooted in the "importance of educating teens about condoms in the age of HIV" (Cahill 2010). The $110 million campaign supports an array of programs, "including those that teach about the risks of specific sexual activities and the benefits of contraception and others that focus primarily on encouraging teens to delay sex" (Stein 2010, A3).

In addition, President Obama has reinvigorated the Office of National AIDS Policy (ONAP). The ONAP had been largely dormant under former president George W. Bush, as he pursued his global AIDS relief program and de-emphasized a domestic policy response to HIV/AIDS. Failing to appoint a director, Bush left the office essentially defunct from 2006 until he left office in January 2009. Under Obama, "ONAP has been hyperactive since openly gay health policy adviser, Jeffrey Crowley, was appointed director in February 2009." Obama, with ONAP leading the way, has developed "a national HIV/AIDS strategy that sets specific, measurable goals to reduce new infections, increase access to care, and reduce health disparities, particularly those affecting African Americans (half of new infections) and gay men (more than half of new infections)" (Cahill 2010). This is the United States' "first attempt in thirty years to create a coordinated plan to address the domestic epidemic." What is particularly noteworthy about Obama's national AIDS strategy is that the LGBT community is expected to engage in its own HIV/AIDS prevention work. The government's strategy document reinforces this point: "the burden of addressing the HIV epidemic among gay and bisexual men and transgender individuals does not rest with the government alone" (Andriote 2011, 435). In making this point, however, Obama and others in his administration recognize "that HIV/AIDS in America remains, as it has been for thirty years, a health crisis largely among gay and bisexual men of all skin tones and ethnicities." The document makes this point crystal clear by describing "the starkness and the enduring nature of the disparate impact on gay and bisexual men" (437).

But perhaps Barack Obama's most important contribution to the HIV/AIDS policy arena is his signing of his landmark health-care reform, the Patient Protection and Affordable Care Act (ACA), into law on March 23, 2010. This is the most comprehensive policy reform made to the American health-care system since Medicare and Medicaid were passed as key components of President Lyndon Baines Johnson's Great Society in 1965. Obama's health-care reform includes several elements that will undoubtedly improve the overall quality of health care for people living with HIV/AIDS. Most importantly, it will end health-care exclusions "based on pre-existing conditions. Eventually, it will end the waiting periods of up to a year for health insurance coverage for those with pre-existing conditions such as HIV—a time span that could prove deadly for someone newly diagnosed with AIDS. It will eliminate the Medicaid disability requirement, and it will increase access to Medicaid for millions of people" (Wortman, Francis, and Greenwald 2010, 44). It supports people living with HIV and especially older people in several ways. The law "would close the Medicare Part D treatment gap (colloquially called the 'doughnut hole') by 2020, making prescription medications more affordable for senior citizens and people with AIDS." In addition, it "prevents Medicare recipients who receive their HIV treatment through an AIDS Drug Assistance Program (ADAP) from being subject to additional prescription costs" (46). Finally, expanded access to health care might inspire some people struggling with

HIV to seek medical care, although it falls short of providing the universal access of a public option. This is a missed opportunity because "the promise of universal health care with no exclusions may lead more people to get tested for HIV" (Hofmann 2010, 9).

It is worth noting, however, that the implementation of the ACA could lead to unintended negative consequences for people living with HIV. For example, a controversial element of the new law is "the state-optional expansion of Medicaid eligibility and coverage. Not only is the actual buy-in of Medicaid eligibility up to each state's discretion, the exact components of services provided under the expansion are up for grabs as well, making any sort of prediction of medical coverage effects nearly impossible" (Armstrong 2013, 5). Why is this development important for people living with HIV/AIDS? Because "this expansion could potentially provide insurance coverage for some, but not all, services currently provided by the RWCA [Ryan White Care Act]," whose extension Obama signed into law in 2009. As a result, a concern is that "some individuals with HIV/AIDS will fall by the wayside in the transition and enrollment periods and will not have the ease of access that they once had" (2013, 5). This is just one of the many challenging dimensions of health-care policy reform facing those living with HIV/AIDS and their medical providers.

Response of the Lesbian and Gay Movements to the Clinton/Bush/Obama Years

The lesbian and gay movements witnessed an altered political landscape as AIDS entered its second decade in the United States and Republican dominance gave way to Democratic control of the White House and Congress. On the night of Clinton's November 3, 1992, victory, I celebrated with hundreds of lesbians and gays and their supporters at the Omni Shoreham Hotel in Washington, DC. When Clinton mentioned AIDS early in his election-night speech, the crowd erupted in a frenzy of excitement and joy. As I turned to survey the scene, I saw a man engulfed in tears, sobbing to his friend, "Maybe I will live after all."

Despite the hope and anticipation Clinton inspired in many (though not all) AIDS activists, the policy and human challenges were still there. People were still dying, the drug-approval process was slow and cumbersome, and AIDS organizations were strapped with an array of financial challenges. Against this backdrop, what political organizing strategies made most sense for the lesbian and gay movements in the Clinton era? Should a more narrowly focused assimilationist strategy be used to gain access to the Clinton White House and supportive members of Congress? Or should the movements embrace a more liberationist strategy to push for comprehensive medical care and demand that policy elites respond in forceful and radical ways to the deepening health crisis?

One of the most interesting organizations to develop in response to these important questions is the Treatment Action Group (TAG). Formed in 1992 by AIDS activists who were committed to a pragmatic assimilationist political strategy emphasizing the treatment of individuals with HIV/AIDS, TAG continues to be a pioneering organization addressing AIDS research and drug-development issues. The original founders came out of the disagreements that engulfed ACT UP / New York in the early 1990s and ACT UP's all-white, all-male Treatment and Data Committee. Duberman places the creation of TAG within its appropriate historical context: "The members of that committee, having increasingly mastered the arcana of current viral science, had become insiders, and were sharply accused by other members of the gay community with advocating primarily for people like themselves; antagonism and fractiousness became so intense by 1992, that the Data Committee broke away entirely from ACT-UP and set up as the Treatment Action Group" (Duberman 2009, 71). TAG founders embraced both assimilationist and liberationist strategies for political change. Unlike ACT UP, which had a democratic organizational structure, TAG accepted members by invitation only, and membership could be revoked by the board. In addition, TAG members received salaries, and the group accepted a $1 million check from the pharmaceutical company Burroughs Wellcome, the manufacturer of AZT, in the summer of 1992. TAG used this money to finance members' travels to AIDS conferences throughout the world, pay salaries, and lobby government officials (Rimmerman 2002, 110).

TAG's central goal has been to force the government to release promising AIDS drugs more quickly and to identify possible treatments for opportunistic infections (Burkett 1995, 339–340). It has done so by lobbying for improved clinical drug trials of protease inhibitors and other HIV drugs. In addition, it has called for a more coordinated AIDS research effort at the NIH by strengthening the Office of AIDS Research. TAG has been quite effective in lobbying government officials to address its organizational goals in a timely manner. However, considerable criticism was directed at TAG by some ACT UP members and other activists in the early years of its existence. Because the organization was perceived by some as small, elitist, and undemocratic, it was attacked for not fully representing the interests of the entire AIDS activist movement. These criticisms have largely dissipated in recent years, but they were unfortunate to the extent that they failed to recognize TAG's important contributions in forcing federal government officials to support more aggressive AIDS research. Sociologist Steven Epstein has identified the meaning of these and other conflicts for the larger AIDS movements:

> Gender and racial divisions, as well as debates over internal participatory mechanisms, insider/outsider strategies, and overall priorities and goals, are the kinds of issues that can tear apart any social movement. What particularly complicated the internal battles of the AIDS movement was the additional overlay of the politics of expertise. It was not simply that some people were working on the inside while others were outside—just as important, those who were on the inside were increasingly mastering specialized forms of knowledge with which their fellow activists on the outside did not come into contact. (1996, 292–293)

These conflicts were compounded by differences of class, gender, race, and education, all of which can divide any social movement, as Epstein suggests. Indeed, the release and development of protease inhibitors highlighted these divisions, even as they were extending some peoples' lives and improving the quality of some peoples' day-to-day existence. When they were introduced in the United States in the mid-1990s, "almost immediately, reports came in of how the new drugs were reducing the amount of HIV in infected individuals, sometimes to the 'undetectable' level, even as CD4 cell counts—essential to a healthy immune system—were correspondingly rising. But what also became quickly apparent was that the new drugs did not work at all for some people, and worked only briefly for others" (Duberman 2009, 199). In addition, the enormous cost of the drugs (up to $15,000 yearly) were prohibitive for many people without health insurance coverage or who fell through the cracks of the existing limited American health-care system. And finally, the drugs had considerable negative side effects for many of those who took them on a regular basis. These problems continue today even as some members of the lesbian and gay movements and the broader medical community celebrate "the end of AIDS."

Despite an array of challenges, including the medical and financial challenges associated with the release and development of protease inhibitors, from its inception ACT UP has had a considerable impact on AIDS-related public policy. The organization successfully used its nonviolent, direct-action approach to force the FDA to accelerate drug trials for AIDS and to consider ACT UP's "parallel track" proposal. Under this proposal, people with AIDS are given drugs before they complete the time-consuming and bureaucracy-ridden FDA approval process. ACT UP's protests also led Burroughs Wellcome to dramatically reduce the price of AZT. Other pharmaceutical companies have been shamed into cutting the prices of AIDS drugs. In addition, ACT UP forced the redefinition of AIDS to include women and to ensure that women with AIDS received disability benefits and were included in drug trials. ACT UP members have established needle-exchange programs, which are now widely credited with helping to reduce the rate of HIV infection among both injecting drug users and their sexual partners (Rimmerman 2002, 111).

By 1996, plagued with internal divisions over tactics and its relationship to the larger AIDS and lesbian and gay movements—and depleted by the deaths of many members—ACT UP still existed but was widely considered moribund. ACT UP suffered as well with the election of Bill Clinton: without a clear enemy in the White House, its efforts were undermined. Nonetheless, the organization's use of direct-action politics demonstrated the effectiveness of unconventional politics in challenging unresponsive policy elites. ACT UP's radicalism has also allowed other lesbian and gay organizations to seem much more moderate in their work on AIDS-related issues. A former executive director of the AIDS Action Council perceives that ACT UP has been quite successful in keeping "mainstream organizations from enjoying their seats at the table too much" and that "multiple political strategies have a tremendous effect" (personal interview, February 19, 1997).

In recent years, the few chapters that remain in major cities, including New York, San Francisco, and Washington, DC, have flourished by building creative new alliances, from work with the Rainforest Action Network to support for Green Party presidential candidate Ralph Nader. In early

2001, ACT UP members in San Francisco protested the thirty-nine pharmaceutical companies that sued the South African government for choosing to produce its own AIDS drugs. The Philadelphia ACT UP chapter has done excellent organizing work on behalf of increasing funding for the Ryan White CARE Act and for supporting President Bush's Emergency Plan for AIDS Relief on a global scale by demanding funding to match the rhetoric. As it has broadened its political strategy, some ACT UP chapters have embraced a liberationist social-justice agenda that transcends narrowly focused identity politics (Bull 1999, 18–19). The organization marked its twentieth anniversary on March 29, 2007, by marching on Wall Street to demand a single-payer comprehensive medical care plan. In this and other ways, ACT UP has made an invaluable contribution to saving people's lives in the face of governmental and societal indifference.

In addition to TAG, ACT UP has spawned two other AIDS activist and policy organizations, both of which embrace assimilationist and liberationist strategies in their campaigns on behalf of those with HIV/AIDS. Founded in 1990 as an outgrowth of ACT UP / New York, Housing Works has become a national model for providing housing, health care, and job training, coupled with vigorous advocacy, to those who are homeless and living with HIV/AIDS in New York City. Since its inception, Housing Works, a minority-controlled organization, has "housed and or provided supportive services to well over 15,000 individuals." In addition, "it created New York's first and most successful job training and placement program for homeless people with AIDS and HIV." In the years ahead, the organization promises to "create 1000 units of permanent new housing in New York City that is affordable to persons on public entitlements, persons on fixed incomes, and working persons." And it plans on "establishing a global network of grassroots activists committed to ending the twin epidemics of homelessness and HIV/AIDS" (http://www.housingworks.org, n.p.). In doing so, the organization combines a commitment to political activism with policy results.

A second organization inspired by ACT UP is Health Gap, which does most of its AIDS organizing and policy work in the global arena, fighting for the elimination of "barriers to global access to affordable, life-sustaining medicines for people living with HIV/AIDS as key to comprehensive strategy to confront and ultimately stop the AIDS pandemic." The group's efforts are centered on challenging "the pharmaceutical industry's excessive profits and expanding patient rights" (http://www.healthgap.org, n.p.). In doing so, it wishes to reform US and world trade policies so that affordable medicines are available on a global scale. Health Gap counts as its members US-based AIDS and human rights activists, people living with HIV/AIDS, public health experts, and fair-trade advocates, all of whom embrace assimilationist and liberationist approaches to political action and public policy, with an emphasis on global economic and social justice.

As AIDS reached its thirtieth anniversary in the United States in June 2011, the complexion of the disease and the public policy challenges had changed significantly. As analyst Jesse Archer explained, "Stories today focus on those living with the virus, many for 20 years or more. But we don't often hear about those over 40 who are newly positive. In 2011, the last year for which results are available, the CDC estimates that 19,757 Americans over age 40 were diagnosed with HIV" (2013, 44). A headline on the front page of the *Washington Blade* that appeared in 2006 captured this new reality: "Experts Debate the 'New' Face of AIDS: Gay Men, African Americans Hardest Hit by the Disease." Many Americans ignored the disease in the 1980s and early 1990s because they perceived it as largely a "gay disease." But by 2006, "many gay Americans seem to have joined their fellow citizens in not paying much attention to HIV/AIDS, thanks to the widespread belief that it is now an African disease." Phill Wilson, founder and chief executive officer of the Black AIDS Institute, claimed in late 2006 that "the whole universe of who is focusing on AIDS is getting smaller, and smaller, and smaller." And this comes at a time when the two groups most affected by HIV/AIDS in the United States are African Americans and gay men, "with both groups accounting for 49 percent of new HIV diagnoses in 2005, according to the Centers for Disease Control and Prevention" (Lee 2006a). One problem is that the major national LGBT rights organizations—the National Gay and Lesbian Task Force and Human Rights Campaign—have been distracted by other pressing concerns such as same-sex marriage and have continued the long-standing process of delegating the issue to HIV/AIDS-specific organizations such as the AIDS Action Council. John-Manuel Andriote has accurately pointed out that "the problem with this strategy is that, without advocacy from our most influential organizations—advocacy focused specifically on the needs of gay and bisexual men—the issues affecting those most in need are pushed to the margins of the GLBT legislative and political agenda" (2012, 28). In addition, the perception that AIDS is on the wane in this country is undermining the ability of the lesbian and gay movements to confront the many challenges of the epidemic. One such challenge is "the pernicious 1987 Helms Amendment . . . that continues to restrict federal support for the kind of targeted, explicit prevention messages public health experts have called for since 1986" (29). Another major challenge is the lack of public attention and policy maker interest with little publicity from the mainstream media or even the so-called gay media. And then there is the further "challenge of keeping a thirty-year old story new and relevant to young gay men in particular, while reminding older gay men that although the medical picture looks better for many with HIV, a positive antibody test result is still a death sentence for the overwhelming majority of people living with the virus in the world" (Andriote 2011, 387). How these challenges will be met remains to be seen. But they will undoubtedly require a combination of assimilationist and liberationist political strategies, coupled with insider and outsider politics of the kind that we have seen develop in the AIDS activist movement over time.

Conclusion

This chapter began with two key questions: In what ways did the onset of AIDS in the United States during the early 1980s affect the lesbian and gay movements' organizing and political strategies? And how have the movements intersected with the policy process over time as AIDS has developed in the United States and on a global scale? In answering these questions, we placed our analysis within its appropriate historical context. And we explored the tensions between those who embraced an insider assimilationist strategy and those who demanded an outsider liberationist strategy to political and social change, as reflected in the broader movements' responses to AIDS policy. The chapter has argued that AIDS changed the landscape of lesbian and gay politics by mobilizing an array of newly politicized activists. Their assimilationist and liberationist strategies developed out of movement organizing in the 1950s, 1960s, and 1970s, as we saw in the discussion of the rise of the lesbian and gay movements in Chapter 2. We have also seen that the Christian Right furthered its organizing agenda by using the threat of AIDS to mobilize its supporters and to raise money. Over time, the lesbian and gay movements were forced to work with the AIDS activist movement, as the two eventually became one and the same. But in recent years, the boundaries between the lesbian and gay movements and the AIDS activist movement have grown more rigid, as AIDS has receded from public and policy attention and other issues have become more prominent on the lesbian and gay movements' agenda. We now turn to a discussion of these issues—military integration and same-sex marriage—in Chapters 4 and 5.

4

Don't Ask, Don't Tell: Policy Perspectives on the Military Ban

Never in my wildest imagination had I thought I would end up challenging a military policy. I had spent a lifetime in uniform, believing in democracy, in freedom and justice for all. With four words my world was turned upside down and my belief system challenged. In response to questioning in a top secret investigation, I said, "I am a lesbian." Those words triggered the military to initiate discharge procedures against me based on military policy barring homosexuals from serving in the military.

—Colonel Margarethe Cammermeyer, quoted in
Gay Rights, Military Wrongs: Political Perspectives on Lesbians and Gays in the Military

The exclusion of gays and lesbians from the military has been a crucial issue for the gay movement for 65 years—in part because, during the postwar decades, it served as a model for anti-homosexual discrimination throughout the government and private sector.

—George Chauncey

THE CONTEMPORARY DEBATE OVER LESBIANS AND GAYS IN THE MILITARY has been forever transformed by President Barack Obama's decision in December 2010 to repeal the US Armed Forces' "Don't Ask, Don't Tell" policy, which prevented openly gay and bisexual people from serving in the military. Obama's decision was the culminating development in a number of policy changes affecting gay and bisexual service members over the years. Indeed, with the beginning of the war in Afghanistan in 2001, "discharges of openly gay service members have fallen by 40 percent" (Alvarez 2006, n.p.). Military expediency has led in recent years to the greater integration and assimilation activists have demanded. At the same time, however, some seventeen thousand US service members "have been, at the very least, discharged simply for being gay" (Lehmkuhl 2006, xii–xiii) since the implementation of DADT began in 1994. In some ways, the falling number of discharges was viewed as "progress" by those who embrace the assimilationist perspective. But for those who take a more radical liberationist perspective on US imperialism and military involvement across the globe, permitting lesbians, gays, and bisexuals to serve openly in the military means allowing them to support America's quest for global hegemony. This tension between the assimilationist and liberationist perspectives has been present since the debate over integration of the military exploded onto the public policy agenda in 1992–1993.

As we have already seen, a core component of recent social-movement theory is the belief that expanding political opportunities help to determine the overall strength of a social movement. The election of Bill Clinton in 1992 provides a context to evaluate the theoretical claim. After twelve years of conservative Republican dominance of national policymaking, the return of the Democrats to power was greeted with euphoria by many members of the lesbian and gay movements. Indeed, there was tremendous hope and excitement because for the first time a presidential candidate had courted the lesbian and gay vote, had been elected with the support of the community, and now would presumably have to govern with that reality in mind. But as we will see, the debate over the military ban and the subsequent passage of the DADT policy helped undermine that euphoria and introduced the lesbian and gay movements to the challenges faced by any movement that has so-called friends in power.

This chapter assesses the original circumstances under which the military-ban issue appeared on the policy agenda soon after Clinton was elected. Why did it emerge as an issue early in the first term of the Clinton presidency? What role did the lesbian and gay movements play in forcing the issue onto the agenda? And what role did the Christian Right play? We will also assess the circumstances that enabled Barack Obama to sign the repeal of the military's policy in December 2010. What role did the lesbian and gay movements play in forcing the issue onto the agenda in Obama's first and second terms in office? And what role did the Christian Right play in the military debate during the Obama presidency? In answering these questions, we will interrogate the role of the lesbian and gay movements in interacting with the Clinton administration, Congress, and the Christian Right during the 1993 debate over the military ban as well as during the Obama presidency beginning in 2009. In addition, it explores the implementation of the DADT compromise since the law was enacted, with an eye toward assessing the policy in light of the lesbian and gay movements' goals and political strategies. Finally, we assess the work that must continue to be done, even with the repeal of DADT, to allow openly lesbian, gay, and bisexual service members to serve openly and honestly in the United States military. As we address these issues, we examine the arguments for and against allowing openly lesbian and gay members to serve. But to fully understand the complexities of this issue, we first turn to an examination of the full historical context of the military ban.

Military Integration in Historical Context

To understand the history of homosexuality in the US military, we must first recognize that it "has been a struggle between two intransigent facts—the persistent presence of gays within the military and the equally persistent hostility toward them" (Shilts 1993, 3). It is also true that the place of lesbians and gays within the military has garnered policy attention by the military itself over the past seventy-five years. As historian Timothy Haggerty accurately points out, "the transition from prosecuting 'sodomists' to separating homosexuals that occurred during World War II, for example, was preceded by psychological and legal research that tried to rationalize the varied practices within the services before the war" (2003, 12).

World War I and World War II

During World War I, the punishment of homosexual soldiers was codified into law. The 1916 Articles of War classified assault with the intent to commit sodomy as a felony. This law did not criminalize sodomy itself, but revisions to the Articles of War three years later identified sodomy as a specific felony; the crime was the sexual act itself, whether it was consensual or involved assault. Throughout the 1920s and 1930s, many gay soldiers and sailors were imprisoned under this law (Shilts 1993, 15).

World War I also saw acceptance of the idea of "excluding people for having a homosexual orientation, as opposed to punishing only those who committed homosexual acts" (Shilts 1993, 15). A San Francisco psychiatrist, Dr. Albert Abrams, wrote in September 1918 (after San Francisco police discovered a number of soldiers during a raid on a gay club) that "while 'recruiting the elements which make up our invincible army, we cannot ignore what is obvious and which will militate against the combative prowess of our forces in this war. . . . From a military viewpoint, the homosexualist is not only dangerous, but an ineffective fighter. . . . It is imperative that homosexualists be recognized by the military authorities'" (253). As we will see later in this chapter, these arguments would be repeated over the years by those who wished to prohibit openly lesbian and gay people from serving in the US armed forces.

But the earliest attempts to regulate homosexuality in the military were inconsistent and sporadic. In 1919, "immoral behaviors" in the Newport, Rhode Island, naval facilities were the subject of the first attempt to purge an installation of homosexuals. A chief machinist's mate, Ervin Arnold launched his own personal investigation of gays in the navy there, gained approval of his plan from his superiors, "and then persuaded seven enlisted men to entrap suspected gays, largely at the local YMCA." Arnold soon expanded his investigation to the point that a number of "presumably" gay soldiers had been caught, were court-martialed for sodomy, and were sentenced to five-to six-year prison terms (Shilts 1993, 16). Civilians associated with the navy were also "outed" as part of Arnold's investigation.

During World War II, the move to transform homosexuality from a crime to an illness gained currency. Between 1941 and 1945, the US armed forces mobilized some sixteen million soldiers and sailors. The military establishment needed help devising guidelines for eliminating those who might not be fit to serve; it turned to the psychiatry profession, a relatively new field that was itself legitimated by its role in assisting the military issue its first regulations to military psychiatrists pertaining to new recruits. The regulations came with the following notation: "persons habitually or occasionally engaged in homosexual or other perverse sexual practices are unsuitable for military service." They furthermore introduced to the military establishment the notion that homosexuals were unfit to serve because they were mentally ill. Indeed, the belief that lesbians and gay men constituted a class of people who had to be excluded from the military became an important part of military policy (Berubé 1990, 33). Final regulations, which remained unchanged for some fifty years, were issued in 1943; they banned homosexuals from all branches of the military (Shilts 1993, 16–17).

The diverse policies of the different services were replaced by the Uniform Code of Military Justice (UCMJ) at the end of World War II. The Uniform Code provided for the following:

> Article 125 of the UCMJ prohibits sodomy, defined as anal or oral penetration, whether consensual or coerced and whether same-sex or opposite-sex, and does not exempt married couples. Under Article 125, the maximum penalty for sodomy with a consenting adult is five years at hard labor, forfeiture of pay and allowances, and dishonorable discharge. Article 134 of the UCMJ, also known as the "General Article," sanctions assault with the intent to commit sodomy, indecent assault, and indecent acts, and prohibits all conduct "to the prejudice of good order and discipline in the armed forces." The maximum penalty is the same for each of these offenses as for sodomy, except in the case of assault with intent, which has a maximum of ten rather than five years confinement. (D'Amico 1996, 6)

Research by several scholars has highlighted the importance of World War II in modern gay history. Historian Allan Berubé's *Coming Out Under Fire* is particularly important for pointing out that the wartime experience offered many young lesbians and gay men the opportunity to recognize that they were not alone. They also learned that certain cities allowed them to meet others of their kind and that they could have meaningful lesbian and gay friendships as well. As Berubé points out, "thousands of young lesbians and gay men, many from small towns and rural areas, met large numbers of other homosexuals for the first time on military bases, in nearby bars, or in hotels where service people congregated" (1990, 5). In these ways, the military's mobilization forced soldiers to confront homosexuality in their personal lives.

As the military expanded its antigay policies, it forced many officers and soldiers to come out against their will. Draftees were often forced out as well when they "declared themselves" and received undesirable discharges as a means to escape harassment (Berubé 1990, 7). During the World War II period, the military's "definition of homosexuality was extended to women engaged in same-sex behavior for the first time" (Haggerty 2003, 17). By the end of the war, as antihomosexual practices were vigilantly enforced, many gay men and lesbians were involuntarily discharged and returned to civilian life stigmatized, and in some cases lives were destroyed. Berubé offers the important argument that when veterans identified their struggles with the government in the broader context of justice and equal rights, they helped to provide ideas that later became cornerstones of the contemporary lesbian and gay movements.

The McCarthy Era and Beyond

During the anticommunist hysteria of the McCarthy era of the 1950s, concern for "national security" was identified as the central reason for keeping gays out of government service, including the military. By the early 1950s, the virulent anticommunist and antihomosexual views associated with McCarthyism pervaded the political and social milieus. Senator Joseph McCarthy and his colleagues claimed that "homosexuals and other sex perverts" threatened to undermine the nation's moral welfare (Benecke and Dodge 1996, 73). Throughout the 1950s and 1960s, individuals were barred from military service for acknowledging a homosexual orientation. For the pre-Stonewall lesbian and gay movements, challenging the military policy became an important goal. For example, the founder of the Washington, DC, Mattachine Society chapter, Franklin Kameny, had three goals as a political activist: "to end the Civil Service's ban on gays working for the government, to end discrimination against homosexuals seeking security clearances, and to end the exclusion of gays from the military" (Shilts 1993, 194).

As we saw in Chapter 2, the 1969 Stonewall Rebellion ushered in an array of challenges to discriminatory governmental policies. The military policy became a target of the movement, as reflected in the legal challenge made by air force technical sergeant Leonard Matlovich (Herek 1996, 6). On March 6, 1975, Matlovich hand delivered a letter to his superior, Captain Daniel Collins, the officer in charge of race-relations instruction at Langley Air Force Base in Hampton, Virginia. The letter, addressed to the secretary of the air force, began, "After some years of uncertainty, I have arrived at the conclusion that my sexual preferences are homosexual as opposed to heterosexual. I have also concluded that my sexual preferences will in no way interfere with my Air Force duties, as my preferences are now open. It is therefore requested that those provisions in AFM-39–12 relating to the discharge of homosexuals be waived in my case." It ended, "In sum, I consider myself to be a homosexual and fully qualified for military service. My almost twelve years of unblemished service supports the position" (Miller 1995, 411). Matlovich's letter signaled the beginning of the contemporary battle to overturn the US military's policy barring lesbians and gays. During the late 1970s, there were a number of challenges to the military ban, including one by Sergeant Perry Watkins, who was stripped of his army clearance and discharged for his homosexuality in 1984. He won a lengthy Supreme Court battle in 1990, as the court pointed out that the army, realizing he was gay, had re-enlisted him three times. With this decision, Watkins became the only openly gay man in history permitted to serve in the military by the Supreme Court. The other challenges were largely unsuccessful, but they highlighted the discretion afforded to military commanders responsible for implementing existing policy and applied different degrees of rigor and standards in the implementation process.

Matlovich's case had the highest profile in the media. He appeared on the cover of *Time* in uniform six months after his letter was delivered. The caption was "I Am Homosexual." On the inside were photos of him recovering from wounds in Da Nang, South Vietnam, and dancing in a gay bar. The prominent coverage that *Time* granted the Matlovich case encouraged Miriam Ben-Shalom to inform her commanding officer that she was a lesbian and inspired Ensign "Copy" Berg to fight his discharge from the navy (Miller 1995, 413).

In November 1975, Matlovich was discharged by the air force, and federal district court judge Gerhard Gesell refused to overturn the air force's decision. But there was legal momentum building in Matlovich's favor. The court of appeals ruled in December 1978 that the discharges of Matlovich and Berg were illegal. It did not order the reinstatement of either man. It did, however, force Judge Gesell to re-examine the Matlovich case. Gesell's September 1980 decision ordered Matlovich's reinstatement to the air force by December 5 of that year (Miller 1995, 413).

The air force responded by offering Matlovich a cash settlement in a last-ditch effort to avoid having to take him back in its ranks. Most observers thought that Matlovich would not accept such a settlement. And most realized as well that the air force would appeal Judge Gesell's decision to the United States Supreme Court. But in the end, within days of his reinstatement, Matlovich agreed to drop his case and accept the tax-free $160,000 offered by the air force (Miller 1995, 413–414). Matlovich's courageous battle and the prominent mainstream media coverage it received helped to dramatize the military's pernicious internal policies toward lesbians and gay men.

The military ban remained in place throughout the 1980s, despite occasional sympathetic lower-court decisions. Military regulations were toughened during the Reagan/Bush years. The military revised its policy concerning homosexuality in 1982. A General Accounting Office (GAO) report suggests that the revision was implemented for three central reasons: "(1) to establish uniform procedures concerning homosexuality across the service branches; (2) to clarify the specific actions for which a person could be separated; and (3) to define the extenuating circumstances under which persons found to have engaged in those actions might nevertheless be retained" (Herek 1996, 6). The 1982 policy mandated the following:

> Homosexuality is incompatible with military service. The presence in the military environment of persons who engage in homosexual conduct seriously impairs the accomplishment of the military mission. . . . The presence of such members adversely affects the ability of the Military Services to maintain discipline, good order, and morale; to foster mutual trust and confidence among service members; to ensure the integrity of the system of rank and command; to facilitate assignment and worldwide deployment of service members who frequently must live and work under close conditions affording minimal privacy; to recruit and retain members of the

> Military Services; to maintain the public acceptability of military service; and to prevent breaches of security. (7)

These are arguments that have been advanced by the military at various points over the years, and they were central components of the opposition to overturning the military ban.

That the 1980s were a particularly difficult decade for lesbians and gays in the military is reflected in discharge statistics. Between fiscal years 1980 and 1990, 16,919 men and women were discharged under the separate category of homosexuality. White women, in particular, were targeted. They "were discharged at a disproportionately high rate: 20.2 percent of those discharged for homosexuality were white women, although they constituted only 6.4 percent of personnel." The navy was disproportionately represented, accounting for 51 percent of all discharges related to homosexuality despite the fact that it constituted only 27 percent of the active force during this period. These figures do not even include those lesbians and gay men processed under other categories and involuntarily separated from the military (Herek 1996, 7).

Advocates for lesbian and gay civil rights embraced overturning the military ban as a priority in the 1980s. Legislation to overturn the ban was introduced by Senator Howard Metzenbaum (D-OH) and Representative Patricia Schroeder (D-CO) in 1992. At that point, there appeared to be mounting opposition to the military policy on the part of many national organizations, as well as colleges and universities that chose to ban military recruiters and ROTC programs from their campuses.

The Early Days of Don't Ask, Don't Tell: Debates and Policy

It was in this context that presidential candidate Bill Clinton announced that if he were elected president in 1992, one of his first acts would be to overturn the military ban through executive order. Then-candidate Clinton made this announcement in response to a question asked by a student at a Harvard University forum. Clinton then explained further: "I think people who are gay should be expected to work, and should be given the opportunity to serve the country." He continued to make this pledge as a presidential candidate and then very early in his presidency (Rimmerman 1996c, xix). Clinton's position did not provoke any challenge during the primaries because all of the Democratic contenders, including Jerry Brown, Tom Harkin, Bob Kerry, and Paul Tsongas, had joined him in taking this position on a questionnaire distributed by the Human Rights Campaign Fund (HRCF). And in May 1992, Clinton gave a "moving and unprecedented" speech to the Los Angeles lesbian and gay community, describing "a vision of America that included gay and lesbian Americans and in which discrimination, particularly the government's own bias-induced policy of keeping homosexuals from serving their country in uniform, would end" (McFeeley 2002, 239).

It was certainly not in Clinton's interest to focus attention on his promise as he tried to woo moderate voters. But why did then President Bush not make it an issue in the campaign? According to Tim McFeeley, who was executive director of HRCF (now HRC) at the time, "Why the Republicans, who had to be well aware of Clinton's stand on gays in the military, let it go is unclear, but the probable explanation was to distance Bush from the vitriol and extremism of the 1992 GOP National Convention in Houston, particularly Pat Buchanan's fuming and foaming in his August 13, 1992 address. . . . The assistance that Buchanan provided in the defeat of George Bush in 1992 cannot be overstated" (2002, 239–240). But the fact that the issue did not come up during the campaign meant that Clinton and his advisers were not ready for the vitriol unleashed by opponents of lifting the ban even before he took office. And the lesbian and gay movements were also unprepared and ill-equipped to provide the considerable organizing effort necessary to support the president's initial effort to overturn the military ban.

The military ban and Clinton's attempt to rescind it raise an array of important questions. Why did such furious and sustained opposition emerge to Clinton's original promise? What are the sources of this opposition? To what extent was Clinton's promise related to changing cultural factors regarding lesbians and gays in the larger society? Why did Congress toughen Clinton's compromise proposal? What are the broader implications of how this issue was resolved for the lesbian and gay movements? As we answer these questions, it makes sense to keep Nathaniel Frank's important perspective in mind: "what made homosexuality in the military a unique battleground in the 1990s was the looming train wreck of vocal gay rights advocates facing off against an even more vocal, and stunningly effective, coalition of religious conservatives convinced that their world—and the next one—hung in the balance" (2009, 30).

Military-Ban Debates and Clinton's Compromise

The first major news story in the period between Clinton's election and his inauguration was his announcement that he planned to adhere to his campaign promise and overturn the ban on lesbians and gays through an executive order. At the moment, Clinton had no idea that this promise would be an enduring controversy for the first six months of his presidency. After Clinton's inauguration, the controversy reached its zenith as the issue dominated radio call-in programs and newspaper headlines for a week. Congressional offices were flooded with postcards, telegrams, and phone calls from irate citizens who adamantly opposed the president's suggestion that the military ban be overturned. Some argued that the mobilization of the citizenry against overturning the military ban had been carefully orchestrated by the Christian Right. These religious conservatives gained considerable support when the Joint Chiefs of Staff, led by Chair Colin Powell, expressed strong opposition to Clinton's promise and when Sam Nunn, chair of the Senate Armed Services Committee, expressed public concern. Nunn held much-publicized hearings on the issue in the spring of 1993, hearings that those in favor of overturning the ban later characterized as biased in favor of the military. The hearings themselves produced several dramatic moments, most notably Colonel Fred Peck's outing of his own son, Scott Peck, who at the time was the US Army spokesperson in Somalia, when he testified in favor of the ban because of antigay prejudice in the ranks. He concluded that if his son were in the military hierarchy, he "would be very fearful his life would be in jeopardy from his own troops." Scott Peck later responded to his father by stating, "I have a little more faith in members of the military" (Rimmerman 1996c, 116).

The media's role in defining the context and setting the agenda for the debate was significant. For example, the television networks captured Colonel Peck's dramatic congressional testimony live, broadcast it into millions of homes, and gave it considerable coverage on the evening news. The brutal beating and murder of Seaman Allen Schindler after he had identified himself as a gay man and as he prepared for discharge was given coverage by the media as well. In addition, Sam Nunn and several of his colleagues in favor of the ban were given a tour of two navy ships so that they could get a better understanding of the close living quarters of military personnel. He identified for the accompanying C-SPAN camera the proximity of the bunks and shower stalls and asked groups of sailors how they felt about the idea of "open homosexuals" in the armed forces. The press reinforced the most negative stereotypes of lesbians and gays by covering this tour extensively. The role of the press, Sam Nunn's ability to dominate the debate with his hearings, and the mobilization of the Christian Right at the grassroots level all had the consequence of forcing the president on the defensive. Opponents of the ban never really recovered from this defensive posture.

Much attention was focused on Clinton's role in the debate, given that it was his attempt to overturn the ban that focused national attention on the issue. Just what role did Clinton play? When Clinton appeared on a live broadcast of *CBS This Morning* on May 27, 1993, a Virginia minister asked him about the issue of gays in the military. Clinton responded, "Most Americans believe that the gay lifestyle should not be promoted by the military or anybody else in this country. . . . We are trying to work this out so that our country does not appear to be endorsing a gay lifestyle. . . . I think most Americans will agree when it works out that people are treated properly if they behave properly without the government appearing to endorse a lifestyle" (Bawer 1993, 148–149). Clinton employed the worst form of language—*lifestyle, endorse, approve, promote*—from the antigay lexicon in his answer. Members of the lesbian and gay community responded quickly. David Mixner, Clinton's longtime friend and a leading openly gay member of the Democratic Party, claimed that he was physically sickened by Clinton's response. Of course, Mixner and others supporting overturning the ban had plenty of good reasons to be disturbed. Clinton had begun to backtrack in public on his promised executive order. One explanation for his actions is that he was trying to distance himself from lesbian and gay groups for political reasons. What better way to do this but to embrace elements of the language of the Christian Right groups that were so feverishly working to uphold the ban (Rimmerman 1996c, 116–117)?

But Clinton's comments signaled to lesbian and gay groups and their supporters that he would likely compromise on his original promise. There was little surprise, then, when Clinton introduced DADT in July 1993. His proposal contained the following elements:

1. The policy bars military recruiters from asking whether prospective enlistees are gay or lesbian.

2. Homosexual conduct is forbidden both on base and off.

3. What constitutes homosexual conduct?
   A. Same-sex intercourse
   B. Public acknowledgment of homosexuality
   C. Attempting a same-sex marriage
   D. Same-sex hand-holding or kissing

4. What constitutes permissible activity?
   A. Telling a spouse, attorney, or member of the clergy about your homosexuality
   B. Associating with openly gay and lesbian people
   C. Going to a gay or lesbian bar
   D. Marching in a gay pride march in civilian clothes

5. Military personnel found to have engaged in homosexual conduct can be discharged.

6. Military officials cannot launch probes merely to whether if an enlistee is gay or lesbian, but if they suspect, based on "articulatable facts," that a person has engaged in prohibited activity, they may investigate.

7. Capricious outing of suspected gays and lesbians by fellow personnel without evidence is forbidden, and any attempt to blackmail a suspected gay or lesbian member of the armed forces is punishable by a dishonorable discharge, a $2,000 fine, and a one-year jail term. (Bull 1993a, 24)

Clinton's proposal was modified by Sam Nunn, whose goal was to make it more punitive toward lesbians and gays in the military. Nunn's efforts were ultimately codified into law by Congress under the rubric of "Don't Ask, Don't Tell, Don't Pursue," thus making it more difficult for opponents of the ban to offer serious structural reforms in the future. Because the previous ban was enforced through an executive order, which could at least be changed through presidential missive, the codification meant that any future changes to Nunn's congressional policy would require congressional consent. Nunn's tough congressional language enabled the specifics of the Clinton plan to take effect while codifying the law into a broad statement of policy that prohibits accepting lesbians and gays in the military (see Appendix 2). In addition, the congressional version states that lesbians and gays have no constitutional right to serve in the armed forces (Rimmerman 1996c, 118). This final element of Nunn's plan is "exactly what President Clinton hoped to challenge in his original determination to overturn the ban through executive order" ("The Legislative Word on Gays" 1993, 2076).

Why did President Clinton support a compromise on this issue? How could he do so, given his clear promise as a presidential candidate and as the newly elected president of the United States? A number of explanations have been offered by individuals both inside and outside the administration. Clinton's approach to governance has always been rooted in building consensus. This was true when he was governor of Arkansas, and his two-term presidency demonstrates his embrace of consensus as a governing methodology rather than adherence to ideology or principle. In addition, Clinton was obviously motivated by political considerations. His chief advisers—Rahm Emanuel, David Gergen, Bruce Lindsey, Thomas "Mack" McLarty, and George Stephanopoulos—clearly wanted him to put this divisive "no-win" issue behind the new administration. Clinton and his advisers believed that it was important for him to embrace the center of the political spectrum as a proud "new kind of Democrat." It made sense, then, for purely political reasons to distance himself from an unpopular special interest—lesbians and gays. Clinton certainly did not want to associate himself with Democrats such as Michael Dukakis and Walter Mondale, both of whom had reputations as individuals who could be pushed around by liberal special interests. As one political analyst suggested, "When he made a change in the rules that prohibited homosexuals from serving in the armed forces as one of his first executive orders, Clinton appeared to be taking a stand on the very kind of social issue that had driven so many Democrats away from their party in the first place" (Radosh 1996, 220–221).

It is clear as well that Clinton realized that, without a major fight, he did not have the congressional votes needed to uphold his original desire to rescind the ban. This view was reinforced by Representative Barney Frank, when he publicly proposed a compromise plan, much to the consternation of many lesbian and gay activists (Rimmerman 1996c, 118).

Under Frank's proposal, which he named "Don't Ask, Don't Tell, Don't Investigate," Pentagon officials would have been forbidden to ask recruits about their sexual orientation. In addition, military personnel also would have been "forbidden to disclose their homosexuality while on duty but would be free to do so during off-duty hours." In providing a rationale for his proposal, Frank argued that it was an improved version of the Clinton-Nunn compromise proposal and said he was worried that Congress was about to codify an even more restrictive proposal into law (Bull 1993b, 25–27). In the end, then, Frank believed that it was better to get something for lesbians and gays in the military rather than nothing at all. President Clinton obviously shared this compromise spirit, and this rationale underlay his entire approach to resolving the broader issue.

By backing away from his original promise, Clinton could also appease and meet the demands of the Joint Chiefs of Staff and Chair Colin Powell. As commander in chief of the armed forces, President Clinton had the authority to order the joint chiefs to obey his directives. But in this case, Clinton chose not to do so. Ultimately, he was convinced that the joint chiefs' perspective deserved more attention in the final policy resolution of the issue than did the concerns of lesbian and gay activists. Clinton would not forget either that the 1992 presidential campaign devoted considerable attention to his activities during the Vietnam War. George Bush and the Republicans hammered away at Clinton's opposition to the war and his lack of foreign-policy experience. For Clinton, backing away from overturning the ban meant that he could win some much-needed support from the military, the group that seemed most threatened by his original campaign promise (Rimmerman 1996c, 119).

Finally, Clinton and his political advisers feared that they were squandering valuable political capital during his honeymoon period over such an emotionally charged issue. From Clinton's vantage point, his first budget plan, health care, and the ratification of the North American Free Trade Agreement were far more important policy initiatives. As a result, he did not even lobby members of Congress to overturn the ban because he did not want to squander their support.

How did Clinton defend his own compromise plan? He publicly identified it as an "honest compromise" and acknowledged that the plan's specifics were not necessarily identical to his own goals. In the face of intense congressional and military opposition to lifting the ban, Clinton believed that the policy was the closest he could come to fulfilling his campaign promise. One administration official said, "The President believes that it is a solid advance forward in terms of extending rights to gays and lesbians in the military" (Rimmerman 1996c, 119).

The Response of the Lesbian and Gay Movements to Clinton's Compromise

Lesbian and gay activists and their supporters did not share the president's optimism. Tom Stoddard, the coordinator of the Campaign for Military Service, a Washington, DC–based organization established during the debate to help rally support for overturning the ban, stated, "The President could have lifted up the conscience of the country. Instead, he acceded without a fight to the stereotypes of prejudices he himself had disparaged." Torie Osborn, at the time the executive director of the National Gay and Lesbian Task Force, argued that the plan is "simply a repackaging of discrimination." And Tim McFeeley, then executive director of the Human Rights Campaign Fund, called the Clinton proposal a "shattering disappointment" (Rimmerman 1996c, 119). McFeeley later argued that "the political loss sustained by Clinton and the gay community was the result of inexperience, bad timing, and a romantic but naïve conviction that the ideal of fairness could trump the politics of fear" (2002, 237). Author and columnist Bruce Bawer assailed the Nunn proposal and Clinton's support for it: "This compromise . . . would essentially write into law the institution of the closet: while heterosexuals would continue to enjoy their right to lead private lives and to discuss those lives freely, gays would be allowed to remain in the armed forces only so long as they didn't mention their homosexuality to anyone or have relationships on or off base" (1993, 117). But it was a *New Republic* editorial that perhaps best captured the fury of those who expected the president to follow through on his original campaign promise: "And the most demeaning assumption about the new provisions is that they single out the deepest moment of emotional intimacy—the private sexual act—as that which is most repugnant. Its assumption about the dignity and humanity of gay people, in and out of the military, in public and in private, is sickening" (62). In the end, however, Nathaniel Frank, an analyst of the military ban fight, is right to conclude that "'don't ask, don't tell' was the result of a bitter battle over the acceptability of homosexuality in the United States" (2009, xix).

How the Clinton Administration Might Have Avoided Compromise

To supporters of rescinding the ban, the Clinton administration made a number of very serious strategic mistakes, mistakes that could have been avoided. Some believe that the president should have introduced the executive order as he had promised and then allowed Congress to do what it wished, even if that meant passing legislation that challenged the executive order. By embracing such a strategy, the president would have been given credit for following through with a policy promise rooted in principle (Rimmerman 1996c, 120).

In addition, the administration clearly underestimated the opposition of Congress (most notably Sam Nunn), the Joint Chiefs of Staff, the military, and the Christian Right. The Clinton administration was surprised that Nunn would attempt to embarrass a new president of his own political party who generally supported "New Democratic principles." Indeed, Frank argues persuasively that "to Clinton the issue of gays in the military probably seemed like an easy win: AIDS could not be cured with a snap of the fingers, and the research that was needed cost money; private intolerance and discrimination could not be ended overnight; and same-sex marriage was not on the agenda in a serious way. But ending overt discrimination against gays in the 1990s seemed, by comparison, almost simple, and long overdue" (2009, 84).

The administration also failed to establish an honest and open line of communication with lesbian and gay groups. Several officials from an array of organizations charged that they were deliberately misled about Clinton's intentions from the outset. Apparently during the presidential transition and the first weeks of the Clinton presidency, lesbian and gay groups were told by influential presidential advisers not to lift a finger in organizing grassroots support, because the president would do everything necessary to overturn the ban. In a much-publicized April 1993 White House meeting, just before the March on Washington, President Clinton told lesbian and gay activists in attendance that he would persuade Colin Powell and the joint chiefs to support his plan.

Yet another serious problem was that, during the first several months of the Clinton presidency, no one at the White House was assigned the responsibility of overseeing legislative strategy for overturning the ban. This was the case until David Gergen joined the Clinton White House, at which point George Stephanopoulos was given the responsibility for coordinating the Clinton strategy.

The Clinton administration did little lobbying on Capitol Hill. It is possible that the ban might well have received more congressional support had the president used the powers of his office to enlist it. But Congress was thrown on the defensive in the face of the administration's emphasis on such an unpopular issue in the early months of the Clinton presidency. Leon Panetta, a former member of the House of Representatives (R-CA) who had been appointed by Clinton as the new director of the Office of Management and Budget, offers this analysis of why the Democratically controlled Congress hesitated to support the newly elected president: "once there's some blood in the water, the Hill begins to tighten up a little bit, in terms of 'What's coming next?' and 'Where are we headed?'" (Hamilton 2007, 51).

In retrospect, it is obvious that the timing of the issue did not work to the president's advantage. His plan to rescind the ban was not a way to begin his presidency. Panetta, for one, recognizes this as a serious problem: "anyone with an ounce of experience in Washington knew that you certainly don't want to take on the gays in the military issue as one of the first ones after going into office" (Hamilton 2007, 47). Some have argued that Clinton would have been much better off raising the issue after his first year in office. At that point, he would have established the credibility of his administration with concrete legislative accomplishments. This might have given him more clout in dealing with Congress.

Finally, it is clear to critics that President Clinton did not perform his important leadership role in educating the public about why it was necessary to rescind the ban. Many presidential scholars have identified the importance of the president's potential role as an educator. In the words of Leon Wieseltier, "It is not leadership to tell people what they want to hear. It is leadership to tell people what they do not want to hear, and to give them a reason to listen" (1993, 77).

Flaws in the Lesbian and Gay Movements' Political Strategies

In his thoughtful analysis of the military-ban debate, McFeeley identifies three reasons President Clinton lost control of the policy agenda with respect to the military ban. McFeeley points to then senate minority leader Bob Dole, "who saw this issue as one with which he could wound the president and start his own 1996 campaign for the White House" as his first reason. Senator Dole first presented the issue to Congress in the form of an amendment proposal to the Family and Medical Leave Act, "designated S. 1 because it was such a top priority for Democrats, in order to force a vote within the first two weeks of the new administration" (2002, 240–241). A second reason "was the inexperience and ineptitude" of the newly elected president's political team. To support his argument, McFeeley reminds us that "during the weeks leading up to the late-January confrontation with Congress over lifting the gay ban, and even after the controversy erupted, the Clinton staff was not coordinating strategies or sharing information with gay lobbying groups." As McFeeley accurately points out, it was not only the Clinton presidency that made strategic errors in the debate over lesbians and gays in the military. The lesbian and gay movements also made a number of tactical mistakes that undermined their attempt to garner greater public support for overturning the ban. The third major reason that Clinton lost control of the policy agenda "was the overconfidence and insufficient grassroots support in the gay community. Despite the incessant warnings of Barney Frank, Pat Schroeder, and others on Capitol Hill, little constituent pressure had been orchestrated with which to support the president's position" (2002, 241). The Campaign for Military Service was largely a Washington, DC, organizing effort; it failed to generate the kind of grassroots support needed in states whose congressional representatives were wavering on whether to rescind the ban. In addition, lesbian and gay rights advocates were never able to marshal the volume of calls and letters from constituents to win over legislators, who were being deluged with calls and mail organized largely by the Christian Right. Representative Barney Frank received considerable criticism from the lesbian and gay communities for identifying the problems associated with the lesbian and gay organizing efforts. Frank said, "We did a very bad job of mobilizing—getting people to write to members of the House and Senate. We spent a lot of our time and energy on things that are irrelevant to a short-term fight in Congress. People assumed that the March on Washington or demonstrations were a good thing. Those have no effect on members of Congress" (Osborne 1994, 53). Frank was particularly critical of the March on Washington's organizers' inability to generate a massive congressional lobbying effort.

At the outset of the debate, the mainstream lesbian and gay organizations also put far too much trust in Clinton. Delirious with excitement because a supposed friend had been elected to the White House, the movements largely ignored Clinton's less-than-stellar record on lesbian and gay issues while governor of Arkansas. Historian John D'Emilio captures the challenges facing the lesbian and gay movements well:

> The Clinton administration is going to offer our movement and our community an alternative to outsider status. Will we be ready to accept it? Will we be able to shape our roles as insiders? Will we be able to use the openness of the Clinton presidency to further an agenda for justice? Or will the allure of the system, the perks of power, swallow us up? Can we walk the corridors of power and still retain the animating vision of justice and decency that comes to us from having been cast as outsiders? (2002, 139)

There were some notable exceptions to the prevailing view that the Clinton presidency would lead to tangible public policy gains. Michael Petrelis, a member of the Washington, DC, chapters of ACT UP and Queer Nation, distributed "Impeach Clinton" buttons the weekend before the November 1992 presidential election. Unlike many of his counterparts in the mainstream lesbian and gay movements, Petrelis recognized that supposedly having Clinton on his side was simply not enough. From the outset, Petrelis and other more radical members of the movements distrusted Clinton's motives, sincerity, and seriousness of purpose in overturning the ban and addressing HIV/AIDS policy meaningfully. Gary Lehring makes the astute observation that the "enthusiasm for candidate Clinton seemed undeserved given his lackluster support of lesbian and gay issues prior to coming to Washington, and that enthusiasm translated into greater trust and a greater benefit of the doubt than Clinton deserved." He is understandably critical of the response of the lesbian and gay movements' leaders. He cites a letter by McFeeley that marked the first time the HRCF had ever endorsed a presidential candidate: "Bill Clinton and Bill Clinton alone, has clearly and unequivocally articulated positive stands on the issues. . . . In the past several months, Bill Clinton has met with lesbian and gay groups and AIDS activists. He has incorporated our agenda and our goals into his own." The letter further explained that Bill Clinton would "use 'whatever means necessary' to eradicate AIDS . . . advocate for the National Lesbian and Gay Civil Rights Law, and who 'with the stroke of a pen' would 'end the exclusion of gays and lesbians from the U.S. military and [would] end discrimination in federal employment based on sexual orientation'" (1996, 283). McFeeley's letter was just one of the many encomiums that candidate Clinton received from the mainstream lesbian and gay movements, praise and enthusiastic support that he did not deserve.

For those supporting overturning the ban, there were further complications. Some lesbians and gays simply could not garner excitement about the issue. This lack of excitement was due to several factors. Many people thought that the fight had been won by having Clinton as president, especially because he was the one who promised to rescind the ban. The movements had no real experience in dealing with a president who seemingly supported lesbian and gay concerns. In addition, the issue understandably did not seem nearly as important for a community that had been and continues to be ravaged by AIDS. Lehring correctly claims that "it is obvious that allowing lesbians and gays in the military would not have been the issue most people in the gay community would have had at the top of their list of wishes to be granted by a new administration in Washington. Greater funding and awareness for AIDS, or a federal civil rights law for lesbians, gays, and other sexual minorities, were issues that could have potentially generated more excitement at the grassroots level of the lesbian and gay movement" (1996, 282). Many lesbians and gays cut their political teeth in the antiwar movement of the 1960s and did not want to legitimate participation in the military. Others were frustrated by the narrow assimilationism of the call for overturning the ban and an inability to connect this organizing work to a larger political and social strategy. Historian Lisa Duggan captured this critique well ten years later when she linked the drive for same-sex marriage and military integration: "the push for gay marriage and military service has replaced the array of political, cultural, and economic issues that galvanized the national groups as they first emerged from a progressive social movement context several decades earlier" (2003, 45). We will return to this critique when we interrogate the response of the lesbian and gay movements to same-sex marriage in Chapter 5.

Implementation of the Don't Ask, Don't Tell Policy

As codified into law, DADT "was supposed to allow gays and lesbians to serve quietly, minimize troop loss, and protect the privacy of all service members so they would not be distracted from defending the nation" (Frank 2009, xix). In the end, "it was supposed to make sexuality a nonissue in the U.S. military." But as Nathaniel Frank points out, what occurred over time is the exact opposite of what was intended by the creators of the compromise proposal: "expulsions swelled, privacy was compromised for gays and straights alike, and the trust and cohesion of fighting units were torn apart by forced dishonesty, suspicion, and unnecessary troop losses" (2009, 167). The initial reports of policy implementation outlined themes that were present since the policy was first implemented in 1994. Eric Schmitt's *New York Times* account claimed that it "has not made life easier for many gay servicemen and women and in some ways has made it worse." The principal concern in the early stages of implementation is that although the policy may have been designed to enable lesbians and gays to "serve without fear of persecution if they kept their sexual orientation private," it has been carried out by commanders who have misused "the broad new authority granted under the policy to ferret out homosexuals." Schmitt also revealed that, "while a few gay servicemen and women said they felt the new policy had improved conditions, most of those who were interviewed said it had instead polarized attitudes toward homosexuals and had shifted the burden of proof to the servicemember if accused of engaging in homosexual acts" (1994, A1). These problems were to emerge over and over again in both press accounts and studies undertaken by the Servicemembers Legal Defense Network (SLDN), a Washington, DC–based organization founded by Michelle Benecke and C. Dixon Osburn that represents lesbian and gay service members. As the sole national legal aid and watchdog organization for those targeted by the military's new policy on homosexuals, SLDN was (and remains) the only means currently available to document abuses. SLDN published a "survival guide" for lesbian and gay service members who were negotiating the realities of DADT on a daily basis. The guide provided an illuminating overview of the kinds of precautions that lesbian, gay, and bisexual service members should practice under DADT: "extra caution during room inspections, during phone calls, in online profiles, when receiving letters or magazines, during security clearance interviews and visits to the doctors and psychologists, while filing insurance paperwork, and in any unexpected encounter with the law, civilian police, or during family or personal crises" (Frank 2009, 198).

One important policy question is "how well has the 'Don't Ask, Don't Tell' policy worked to create a 'zone of privacy' for military members since its enactment?" (D'Amico 2000, 253). The short answer is not well

FIGURE 4.1 Total Military Lesbian, Gay, and Bisexual Discharges Under "Don't Ask, Don't Tell"

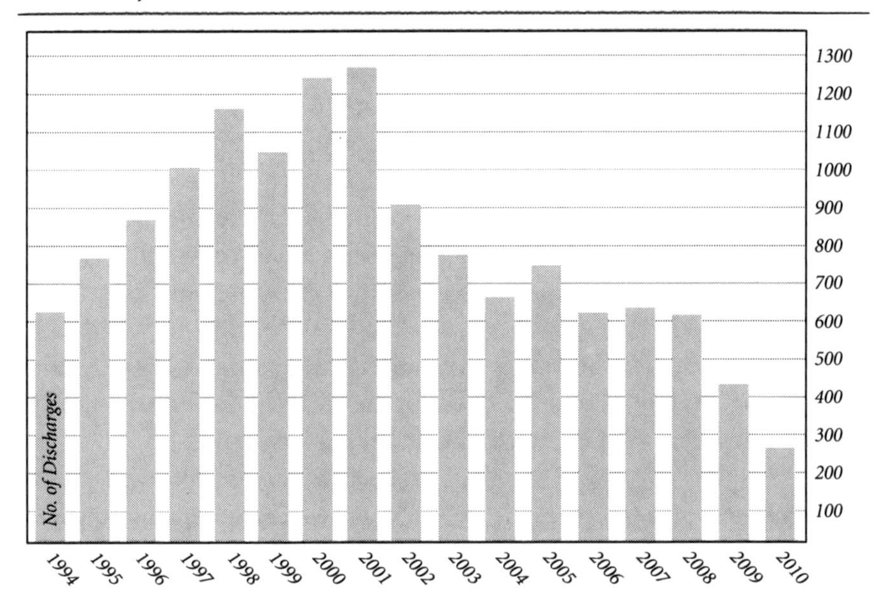

Source for 1994–2006: Servicemembers Legal Defense Network (http://www.sldn.org); and for 2007–2010: "Don't Ask, Don't Tell." *Wikipedia*. Accessed February 17, 2014, http://wikipedia.org.

at all. The number of discharges declined steadily since 1982 and reached a low point in 1994, but they began to rise again in 1995 before peaking at their highest point in ten years in 1998 (D'Amico 2000, 254). We also know that since 2001 and the beginning of the war in Afghanistan, "'Don't Ask, Don't Tell' discharges have declined by almost half" (Figure 4.1). The SLDN reports that lesbian and gay discharges have dropped during every major military mobilization, including World War II, the Korean War, Vietnam War, Persian Gulf War, and the war in Iraq. In addition, the SLDN reports that "women account for 30% of 'Don't Ask, Don't Tell' discharges, but comprise only 15% of the military" (http://www.sldn.org, n.p.).

One aspect of the recent implementation of the policy that has understandably received considerable attention in the media is the military's decision to discharge fifty-eight Arabic linguists because they are gay. These talented linguists have much to offer the military and the country at large, given American foreign-policy interests in the Middle East. The GAO has noted that "nearly 800 dismissed gay or lesbian service members had critical abilities, including 300 with important language skills." The financial cost of replacing these specialized service people is exorbitant. According to the Center for the Study of Sexual Minorities in the Military at the University of California–Santa Barbara, "Discharging and replacing them has cost the Pentagon nearly $369 million" ("Army Dismisses Gay Arabic Linguist" 2006, n.p.). Nathaniel Frank captures well the negative consequences: "These losses have torn a hole in the nation's defenses against Arab insurgents in the Middle East, as the thousands of fellow scholars who relied on these linguists were forced to drift through Iraq and elsewhere with one fewer conduit to the Arabic speaking world" (2009, 220).

What accounts for all of these developments? Sharon Debbage Alexander, former deputy director for policy at the SLDN and a former US Army lieutenant, offers these explanations for the current trends:

> I think that many people inside the Pentagon do realize the insanity of discharging anyone—linguist or otherwise—on the sole basis of their sexual orientation. But since the Congressional action in 1993, this is not a Pentagon policy or regulation that Pentagon leaders or the Commander in Chief could just change at their discretion. "Don't Ask, Don't Tell" is a federal statute—10 USC 654, and the Pentagon is bound to enforce it. While many commanders (smartly, in my view) look for ways to avoid enforcing "Don't Ask, Don't Tell" when doing so will hurt their units' abilities to perform their missions, most folks take the law at face value and try to comply with it. And I think that what's happening in practice is also very telling. More military leaders at the operational level are looking the other way when presented with evidence that one of their charges is lesbian, gay, or bisexual. (e-mail to author, June 8, 2007)

And why have we seen the significant drop in gay discharges by nearly half when compared to the soaring rates of the late 1990s? Alexander offers a perceptive answer in response to that important policy question:

> It's not because there are fewer gay people serving, nor is it because they're doing a better job staying in the closet—from our legal services case load, we actually see that many more service members are taking a risk and coming out to their colleagues, in most cases with little or no negative consequences. The generation of young officers and enlisted personnel fighting

> this war by and large doesn't have the same prejudices about gay people that even my generation of officers did. (e-mail to author, June 8, 2007)

For the DADT policy to be repealed, Congress needed to swing into legislative action. Representative Martin Meehan (D-MA) introduced the Military Readiness Enhancement Act in March 2005, which would repeal the military's ban on openly lesbian and gay service personnel. As of November 2006, the bill had 122 cosponsors, and Meehan and his supporters hoped to force legislative action on the proposed legislation (Rosenberg 2006, 8).

The Repeal of Don't Ask, Don't Tell

The election of Barack Obama in 2008 signaled a change in political opportunities for the lesbian and gay movements, especially when compared to the often hostile George W. Bush presidency. As a presidential candidate, Obama promised to repeal two policies that were of strong interest to his mainstream lesbian and gay supporters: the Defense of Marriage Act (DOMA) and DADT. But within six months of taking office, Obama was accused of dragging his feet by some, especially with respect to the military ban, because he could have used "his executive authority to order the military not to enforce the rule." Obama reiterated his opposition to DADT in June 2010 but also pointed out that he thought that the best strategic course was to work with lawmakers and the Pentagon to overturn it. Obama made this argument to a group of lesbians and gays in the East Room of the White House to commemorate the fortieth anniversary of the Stonewall Rebellion: "I know that many in this room don't believe progress has come fast enough, and I understand that. It's not easy for me to tell you to be patient any more than it was for others to counsel patience to African-Americans who were petitioning for equal rights a half-century ago. . . . As commander in chief, I do have a responsibility to see that this change is administered in a practical way that takes over the long term" (Stolberg 2009).

He followed through on his promise in 2010. The Obama administration announced that the repeal of DADT would be a top priority after his signature health-care reform effort was enacted in 2010. Unlike President Clinton, Obama received support from his chair of the Joint Chiefs of Staff, Admiral Mike Mullen, who testified before a Senate panel in

February 2010 that his "personal and professional belief [is] that allowing homosexuals to serve openly would be the right thing to do" (Radnofsky 2010, A5), and his secretary of defense, Robert Gates, though both asked "that Congress put off action for a year, during which time the Pentagon could study the impact of changing the policy" (Klarman 2013, 156–157). In addition, although Marine Corps commandant General James Amos opposed repealing the ban, he made it clear that "the Marine Corps will step out smartly to faithfully implement this new policy" after the ban was overturned (Burns 2010). Gates announced in March 2010 that, while the study was pending, the Pentagon would begin the process of easing enforcement. The Pentagon's change in policy meant that it would be "harder for the military to investigate troops who were outed against their will by third-parties and will put higher-ranking officers in charge of deciding whether to pursue such cases" (Radnofsky 2010, A5). Despite these positive developments, much to the understandable disappointment and anger of lesbian and gay activists, the Obama administration "continued to defend the constitutionality of 'don't ask, don't tell' in court" (Klarman 2013, 157).

What had changed since Bill Clinton signed the military ban into law in 1993? For one, public opinion polls revealed major shifts in support of overturning the ban. A 2009 Gallup poll, for example, "showed that 69 percent of Americans believed that gays should be permitted to serve openly in the military, up from 43 percent in 1993" (Klarman 2013, 157). This is a significant change in public opinion that was registered by other polling organizations as well. And as Michael Klarman points out accurately, "Even among three voting blocs that traditionally have been the least supportive of gay rights—conservatives, Republicans, and weekly church-goers—about six in ten now supported permitting gays to serve openly in the military."

In addition, many of those military experts who had previously supported the ban had either changed their positions or had passed away by 2010. And those countries that still barred gays from serving—China, Cuba, Iran, North Korea, and Pakistan—were countries to which the United States did not like to compare itself (Klarman 2013, 157).

Finally, in the summer of 2010, the Obama administration "found itself in the uncomfortable position of defending in court two statutes—'Don't Ask, Don't Tell' and DOMA—that it wanted repealed and which lower courts were starting to invalidate" (Klarman 2013, 157). Lesbian and gay movements' activists continued to pressure the White House at the grassroots, through blogs, and through insider political channels to overturn the ban. But it all took considerable organizing effort by many people over the years, and, as Michelangelo Signorile has pointed out persuasively, "only sustained pressure and continued media attention to the cause—which led to outright embarrassment for an administration and a Congress that failed to deliver all they had promised" inspired the repeal of the ban (2011, 26). Indeed, Signorile explains that the grassroots activist group GetEQUAL played an integral role in inspiring the Obama administration and Congress to finally repeal the ban by embracing unconventional politics. In March 2010, the arrests of GetEqual activists, including Robin McGehee, Lieutenant Dan Choi, and Autumn Sandeen, "for chaining themselves to the White House gates, among other protests, sent a message to the administration and Congress that patience was no virtue to those demanding an end to 'don't ask, don't tell'" (27). In addition, OutServe, "a secret Facebook group that became a larger organization, enabled a new level of community support and allowed gays in the military to realize just how populous they were" (Wilson 2011, 62), thus performing an integral organizing effort and building on the long and hard work of the SLDN.

The Case for the Military Ban

During the first several months of the Clinton administration, it became clear that the opposition to overturning the ban was rooted in a number of deep-seated concerns that reflect the larger society's long-standing hostility toward lesbians and gays. Bruce Bawer points out that an individual might be threatened by homosexuality because of several factors. First is utter incomprehension: the inability to understand how other human beings could have such feelings and could experience sexual attraction to a member of the same sex. The idea is so foreign as to be threatening, frightening, and repulsive. The sexual insecurity of men who are used to being in control of their relationships with women often results in fear of being the "object of affection" of other men. This fear is reflected in a Michigan airman's response to the idea of lifting the ban on lesbians and gays in the military: "I couldn't sleep at night. I'd be worried that some homosexual is going to sneak over and make a pass at me" (1993, 266).

These concerns underlie some of the more specific arguments offered by those opposed to overturning the ban. It is interesting to note that some of these same arguments were posited by those opposed to Harry Truman's executive order to integrate the military racially in 1948. As one historian's extensive analysis of the comparisons of the debates over race and sexuality in the armed forces shows, those in favor of the ban resisted any meaningful comparisons between race and sexual orientation, despite the clear parallels. For example, Colin Powell, as chair of the Joint Chiefs of Staff, wrote in a letter to Representative Patricia Schroeder, "I can assure you I need no reminders concerning the history of African Americans in the defense of their Nation and the tribulations they faced. I am a part of that history. Skin color is a benign, nonbehavioral characteristic. Sexual orientation is perhaps the most profound of human behavioral characteristics. Comparison of the two is a convenient but invalid argument" (Bianco 1996, 47).

Powell's open opposition to rescinding the military ban had a tremendous impact on the ultimate outcome of the debate. Others certainly shared Powell's views. One scholar wrote at the time that "to lump blacks with homosexuals is an affront to most African Americans" (Bianco 1996, 48). As David Ari Bianco suggests, however, few participants in the debate based their conclusions on thoughtful comparisons between the integration of African Americans in the late 1940s and the contemporary debate over lesbians and gays. He concludes that "the arguments used to keep African Americans segregated are so similar to those that barred lesbians and gays in the early 1990s that a gay newspaper, the *Washington Blade,* argued that the history of the military's exclusion of African Americans 'seems to be serving as a blueprint for the military on how to dissuade the government from allowing gays to serve openly in the ranks'" (49).

Just what are some of the arguments shared by proponents of the military ban on lesbians and gays and proponents of racial segregation in the late 1940s? Several are informed by the notion of inferiority. One such argument is the belief that gay men have such relentless sexual appetites that they simply cannot be controlled in a military setting. As Bianco points out, "the defenders of the military's ban on lesbians and gays frequently raised the specter of homosexual rapists and pedophiles endangering young soldiers and sailors." Likewise, during the racial integration debate of 1948, southern conservatives claimed that the higher rate of rape and other crimes attributed to African Americans would endanger the daily functions of the military (1996, 50).

Another line of argument used to defend the military ban on lesbians and gays was to highlight the higher prevalence of sexually transmitted diseases, specifically AIDS, associated with gay men. The Family Research Council, a conservative organization, made this argument in one of its publications:

> The AIDS risk is very real, since two-thirds of all current AIDS cases involved the transmission through homosexual activity, according to the Centers for Disease Control. Homosexuals also account for a disproportionate number of cases of sexually transmitted diseases, such as syphilis, gonorrhea, genital warts, hepatitis A, hepatitis B and also diseases associated with anal intercourse, such as the parasites collectively referred to as "gay bowel syndrome." According to the American Medical Association, homosexual youths are 23 times more likely to contract a sexually transmitted disease than are heterosexuals. (Bianco 1996, 51)

A similar argument was offered by Kevin Tededo, a cofounder of the conservative group Colorado for Family Values: "There is no question that the homosexual community, particularly males, are [*sic*] very diseased." During hearings on the military ban, one colonel testified, "At the very least homosexuals would have to be specially identified to ensure their blood not be used as a protection to other soldiers." Similar arguments were raised in the racial integration debate. As Bianco notes, "During World War II the Red Cross—with no scientific justification—maintained racially segregated blood banks at the demand of the armed forces." And former senator Richard Russell highlighted disease rates among African Americans in the quest to keep the military segregated (Bianco 1996, 51).

In addition, those opposed to Clinton's campaign promise contended that the presence of lesbians and gays in the armed forces would undermine the "good order, discipline, and morale of the fighting forces" (Shilts 1993, 17). Norman Schwarzkopf reinforced this point of view in a 1982 sworn deposition in which he "characterized homosexuality as being 'incompatible with military service'" on precisely these grounds (426). Conservative legal scholar Bruce Fein echoed Schwarzkopf's argument and raised the important connection between masculinity and the criteria for being a good soldier as a justification for opposing attempts to integrate lesbians and gays: "The lifeblood of a soldier is masculinity, bravery, and gallantry. The battlefield soldier is inspired to risk all by fighting with comrades whose attributes conform to his view of manhood. . . . And it is inarguable that the majority of a fighting force would be psychologically and emotionally deflated by the close presence of homosexuals who evoke effeminate or repugnant but not manly visions" (730).

Like Schwarzkopf and Fein, decorated Vietnam veteran David H. Hackworth worried that openly lesbian and gay soldiers would undermine the military's illusion of masculine invincibility: "To survive in a killing field, a warrior has to believe he's invincible, that he's wearing golden armor; that he can buck 1,000 to 1 odds and live. To think that way, he has to be macho. Fairly or unfairly, gays threaten that macho. When it goes, the warrior starts thinking, 'Maybe I won't make it.' And from that moment, the unit goes to hell." The perceived danger of lesbians and gays in the military is so threatening that Hackworth warned, "I cannot think of a better way to destroy the fighting spirit and gut U.S. combat effectiveness." Visions of masculinity were similarly deployed during the racial integration debate. Writing in 1948, *New York Times* military editor Hanson W. Baldwin wrote that "one of the surest ways to break down the morale of the army and to destroy its efficiency" is to support racial integration of the military (Bianco 1996, 53).

Supporters of the military ban on lesbians and gays argued, too, that integration would undermine the ability of the military "to recruit and retain members of the armed forces," and the United States would face "the specter of a depleted military force and weakened recruitment efforts if those who join or remain were forced to associate with people known to be lesbian or gay." Schwarzkopf said, "The impact on the army's public image would also endanger recruitment and retention, by causing potential servicemembers to hesitate to enlist, making parents of potential servicemembers reluctant to recommend or approve the enlistment of their sons and daughters in an organization in which they would be forced to live and work with known homosexuals, and causing members of the army to hesitate to reenlist." Schwarzkopf's views were supported by others in the military hierarchy. A four-star general reported to the *Washington Times*, "It would be a wrenching change. . . . We're not ready for it. Good people will leave the military in droves over this." Similarly, the threat of white desertion was invoked during the debate over racial integration in the late 1940s (Bianco 1996, 55).

The navy defined the rationale for its gay policies by making several arguments. An individual's daily performance of military duties could be hindered by emotional or sexual relationships with other individuals and would interfere with proper military hierarchical and command relationships. There was also the concern that homosexual individuals might force their sexual desires on others, resulting in sexual assaults. In the early 1980s, the Pentagon argued that lesbians and gays must be banned to "facilitate assignment and worldwide deployment of servicemembers who frequently must live and work under close conditions affording minimal privacy" (Mohr 1993, 92). Furthermore, an internal navy memorandum revealed that "an officer or senior enlisted person who exhibits homosexual tendencies will be unable to maintain the necessary respect and trust from the great majority of naval personnel who detest/abhor homosexuality. This lack of respect and trust would most certainly degrade the officer's ability to successfully perform his duties of supervision and command" (Shilts 1993, 281).

All of these arguments were "part of a larger effort to preserve and expand the Christian character of the military and the nation." Indeed Nathaniel Frank points out that "many of the most vocal and influential military leaders were evangelicals themselves, who came to the services with an unyielding belief in the sinful nature of homosexuality and who violently opposed its acceptance on religious grounds." The Family Leadership Council, under Gary Bauer's leadership, focused on the military ban issue "and disseminated position papers that cast gay rights as a threat to the family. The idea was to mobilize their constituency to fight reform while simultaneously convincing the rest of the country that, whatever they believed about God and morality, gays had no place in the nation's armed forces" (Frank 2009, 35).

All of the above arguments rely on bigoted and negative stereotypes of lesbians and gays. Indeed, when former head of the Joint Chiefs of Staff Peter Pace said in 2005 that "the U.S. military mission fundamentally rests on the trust among its members and the homosexual lifestyle does not comport with that," he was merely making public his bigotry, which he reinforced in March 2007 when he called homosexual acts "immoral" (Ephron 2007, 34). As Richard Mohr points out, "none of [the arguments] is based on the ability of gay soldiers to fulfill the duties of their stations" (1993, 93). But these are the arguments that served to define the broader context of the debate, arguments that both Clinton and proponents of overturning the ban have had difficulty engaging in ways that would shift the grounds of the discussion (Rimmerman 1996c, 114).

The Case Against the Military Ban

Those in favor of lifting the military ban have offered several arguments. Many suggested that the ban itself is rooted in discrimination and prejudice against lesbians and gays, and we should not countenance any discrimination against individuals or groups in our society. In addition, lesbians, gays, and bisexuals have already fought and died on behalf of this country in an array of wars over the years. As a result, they should be afforded the kind of respect and support that their outstanding service to their country has earned. In practice, this means that they should be treated with decency and dignity in their daily lives. By its very nature, the ban is rooted in the most ugly assumptions about the connections between sexuality and military performance—assumptions that are not confirmed by any evidence. Indeed, one early study provided evidence for overturning the ban. In the spring of 1992, the Pentagon commissioned a Rand Corporation study, which concluded that "the ban could be dropped without damaging the 'order, discipline, and individual behavior necessary to maintain cohesion, and performance.'" The report also stated that "many of the problems that opponents of lifting the ban anticipate are exaggerated through education and discipline" (Gallagher 1993, 28). Unfortunately, the Clinton administration chose to delay its release in a way that diminished its potential impact. News stories circulated that the report was ready long before August 1993, when it was finally shared with the public. Indeed, it was released to the press and public at a downtime in Washington, when everyone was on vacation (including the president), so little attention would be focused on it. The release was inspired by a joint congressional letter signed by those committed to overturning the ban, urging the Clinton administration to make the report's findings public (Rimmerman 1996c, 115).

Furthermore, the financial costs of enforcement are exorbitant. Ultimately, these costs are paid by taxpayers. Writing in 1993, Randy Shilts concluded that "the cost of investigations and the dollars spent replacing gay and lesbian personnel easily amount to hundreds of millions of dollars" (4). A June 1992 congressional study revealed that "the ban on homosexuals in the armed forces costs the Pentagon at least $27 million a year" (Bawer 1993, 58). These costs have been corroborated by an array of sources since 1992. A 2011 GAO report revealed that the "Pentagon spent at least $193 million from 2004 to 2009 to discharge 3,664 members of the military" under DADT. The GAO reported that the Army enforced the ban more strictly than any other military service, "sending 1, 774 soldiers back to civilian life. The Navy kicked out 913 sailors. The Air Force discharged 540 airmen. And the Marines separated 437 Marines. Additionally, the GAO found that 1, 442 of those discharged held critical jobs such as linguists and intelligence officers" (DiMascio 2011).

Opponents of the ban also point out that most democracies allow lesbians and gays to serve with dignity in their militaries. More than twenty countries allow gays to serve, including all NATO countries except for Portugal and the United States.[1] Canada's 1992 decision to revoke its military ban caused little or no controversy, and its experience could have been an excellent lesson for the United States. In 2000, Britain was forced to overturn its military ban by the European Court of Human Rights, but by 2005 the Royal Navy was calling on gay rights groups to help recruit gay soldiers, and gay partners have been afforded full benefits (Alvarez 2006, n.p.). Britain, too, could have been a role model for the United States. Unfortunately, we appear to have learned little from either nation's successful experiences in eliminating the military ban.

Many opponents of the ban have argued that, since the 1993 debate, the US military (and the United States more broadly) has become more open to lesbians and gays serving in the armed forces. For example, former retired army general and chair of the Joint Chiefs of Staff from 1993 to 1997, John Shalikashvili, argues that "the military has changed, and that gays and lesbians can be accepted by their peers." He bases this claim on a number of meetings with gay soldiers and marines, some of whom have had combat experience in Iraq. He also spoke to an "openly gay senior sailor who was serving effectively as a member of a nuclear submarine crew." Shalikashvili also points out that this greater openness is mirrored in public opinion, as evidenced by a late 2006 "Zogby poll of more than 500 service members returning from Afghanistan and Iraq, three quarters of whom said they were comfortable interacting with gay people" (2007, n.p.).

Finally, and perhaps most disturbingly, the ban reinforces the horrors of the closet for lesbians and gays in the military: "The chief problem of the social institution of the closet is not that it promotes hypocrisy, requires lies, sets snares, blames the victim when snared, and causes unhappiness—though it does have all these results. No, the chief problem with the closet is that it treats gays as less than human, less than animal, less even than vegetable—it treats gays as reeking scum, the breath of death" (Mohr 1993, 114). Through the ban, then, the closet is then sanctioned by the institutional forces of the US government in ways that prevent human beings from living open and fully developed lives.

The incalculable human costs of the military ban have taken a number of forms, as lives have been ruined and careers destroyed. Aaron Belkin has pointed out that "'Don't ask, don't tell' has taken a disastrous toll on gay troops. I know gay and lesbian service members who have been raped and not reported their assaults to commanders. Doing so could have generated rumors about their sexual orientation, and such rumors could have been used as evidence in discharge hearings" (2011, 16). Despairing women and men occasionally commit suicide in the face of the pressure associated with a purge and the accompanying rumors that often precede one. This is certainly not surprising, given that military policies have created an atmosphere wherein discrimination, harassment, and violence against lesbians and gays are tolerated and often encouraged. Shilts's analysis of the consequences of the ban provides particularly chilling accounts of how lesbians face significant discrimination and harassment in their daily lives. For this and other reasons, opponents of the military ban argued that it must be overturned.

Wayne Besen's overview of the consequences of overturning the ban is especially pertinent as we consider work that must continue in the years ahead as we implement the new policy and as service members who were discharged under DADT now try to re-enlist: "Repealing don't ask-don't tell was a monumental victory. Not only was this an impressive and meaningful legislative win, but the fight for repeal flooded the media with positive gay and lesbian role models, which significantly undermined the propaganda of anti-gay organizations. The images of brave gay service members will endure in our culture long after the celebrations stop. What's more, just as the desegregation of the U.S. military by President Truman was a tipping point in the civil rights struggle for African-Americans' equality, this event could well prove the beginning of the end of anti-gay discrimination and prejudice" (Besen 2011, 5).

Conclusion

This chapter has offered a comprehensive overview of DADT by placing it within its appropriate historical, political, and policy contexts. In doing so, we have explored the tensions between the assimilationist and liberationist perspectives on whether military integration should be a central goal of the lesbian and gay movements and, if so, how to pursue that goal. We have interrogated the interactions between the movements and the Clinton presidency around this issue with an eye to how the movements interacted with a president who as a candidate promised to overturn the ban but ran into enormous obstacles as he attempted to implement that promise. The mainstream movements went from being outsiders to insiders in the policy process, as they were granted access to power in ways that they had never experienced before. This increased access did not necessarily lead to concrete policy accomplishments, as the Clinton years suggest. But it did lead to increased conflicts among assimilationists and liberationists over political organizing strategies. These conflicts continued to materialize during the Obama presidency. And these same conflicts have increasingly manifested themselves in other contentious policy areas, most notably the politics of same-sex marriage, which we will now explore in Chapter 5.

5

Jilted at the Altar: The Debate over Same-Sex Marriage

Equality is a good start, but it is not sufficient. Equality for queers inevitably means equal rights on straight terms, since they are the ones who determine the existing legal framework. We conform—albeit equally—with their screwed-up system. That is not liberation. It is capitulation.

—Peter Tatchell

Certainly nobody expected that an arrest that night of two gay men for a minor criminal offense would reverberate in American constitutional law, challenging not only the traditional understanding of what makes a family but also the proper role of government in maintaining that understanding. Nobody foresaw the cultural storm that would gather from the events that transpired in a modest second-floor apartment. Nor could anyone have foreseen how a single arrest might expose the deep malignity in a law that was superficially directed at a certain conduct, but that in practice was used to brand an entire group of people as strangers to moral tradition.

—Dale Carpenter on the background to *Lawrence v. Texas*

We won and got everything we hoped for. If I had to survive Thea, what a glorious way to do it.

—Edith Windsor, the lead plaintiff in the Defense of Marriage Act case, *United States v. Windsor*

THE FIGHT OVER SAME-SEX MARRIAGE HAS BECOME A CENTRAL ISSUE in the ongoing cultural wars in the United States. Some analysts have argued that gay marriage has replaced abortion as *the* focal issue of cultural conflict. In recent years, we have seen considerable political and organizing activity on all sides of the same-sex-marriage debate. Conservative activists have marched in Washington and throughout the United States and have flooded the US Senate with letters, telegrams, and e-mails supporting a constitutional ban limiting marriage to heterosexual couples. Lesbian and gay rights activists have also marched, lobbied, and accessed the legal system to challenge state and local laws that prevent them from marrying. For political scientist Gary Mucciaroni, "same-sex marriage is the culmination of the long march toward gender and sexual equality rooted in the feminist movement" (2008, 24). The conflict over same-sex marriage has engulfed all branches and levels of government, has been the focus of many state referenda, and has come before the Supreme Court of the United States. The tremendous publicity that the issue has received has also forced presidential and congressional candidates to take positions on same-sex marriage. Candidates over time have chosen to use the subject as a wedge issue in their electoral strategies. But there are signs that this is now changing as "polls show that about fifty-five per cent of the American people now support same-sex marriage" (Toobin 2013a, 28). And among younger people support is even stronger. Indeed, a June 2013 Field poll indicated that "78 percent of voters under 39 favor making gay marriage legal" (Medina 2013). A November 2012 Gallup poll reported that "73 percent of people between 18 and 29 years old said they favored it, while only 39 percent of people older than 65 did" (Connelly 2012). At the same time, it is important to remember "that support for same-sex marriage in polls has not necessarily translated into support at the ballot booth," as the discussion of California's Proposition 8 later in this chapter will reveal, and as the adoption in at least twenty-nine states, including most recently North Carolina, constitutional bans on same-sex marriage reflects (Silver 2012).

The issue itself is complex. As we will see in this chapter, the debates over same-sex marriage extend back several decades. From the vantage point of many lesbian and gay activists, the right to marry is a logical extension of the assimilationist approach to political and social change. It is viewed as one of an array of issues that are all rights based: decriminalizing same-sex behavior, prohibiting discrimination in employment and housing, and serving openly in the military. All of these political and policy fights share a common goal: to extend the rights, benefits, and privileges that have been and are enjoyed by heterosexual citizens to lesbians, gays, bisexuals, and transgender individuals (Wilcox 2007, ix–x).

As we will see, however, there have been vocal critics of same-sex marriage both within and outside of the lesbian and gay movements. Why has this issue engendered such emotional responses? How has the fight for same-sex marriage affected the goals of the broader lesbian and gay movements? Why has there been disagreement among lesbian and gay activists regarding the desirability of placing marriage on the political organizing and policy agenda? What progress has been made in the fight for same-sex marriage? How has the Christian Right responded with its own organizing efforts? Should the power to legalize same-sex marriage rest with the federal government or the states? This chapter will address these questions and more. And as we do so, it is important to recognize, in the words of the distinguished historian George Chauncey, that "marriage equality was neither inevitable nor, until recently, even conceivable" (2013). But before we can do so, we must turn our attention to how and when the issue emerged on the policy agenda in the United States.

Same-Sex Marriage in Historical Context

The same-sex marriage debate exploded on the national scene in the early 1990s, despite the fact that lesbians and gay men had been challenging their exclusion from the rights of marriage since the early 1970s. Early legal challenges were pursued without the support of organized lesbian and gay interests, though somewhat surprisingly, "from the earliest days of gay liberation, some activists demanded the right to marry," even as others who identified with the gay liberationist agenda denounced marriage "as a discredited patriarchal institution." Indeed, many liberationists coming out of the 1969 Stonewall Rebellion "rejected everything they associated with heterosexuality, including sex roles, marriage, and the family" (Chauncey 2004, 89). But others claimed that they should have the right to do anything and everything that heterosexuals could do, including holding hands with a partner in public or getting married. Given the repressive context of the times, either of these activities was viewed by many as a radical challenge to straight society. In the end, though, support for marriage was a minority position within the larger lesbian and gay movements' agenda. As Chauncey points out, lesbian feminist activists were understandably hostile to pursuing marriage rights as a key component of the movements' agenda. To most lesbian feminists, "marriage was an inherently patriarchal institution, which played a central role in structuring the domination of women. As they sought to build a new women's culture shorn of patriarchal influence, many questioned monogamy and worked to construct new kinds of relationships and living patterns" (93).

National organizations that were established in the 1970s, including the Gay Rights National Lobby (which later became the Human Rights Campaign), the Lambda Legal Defense and Education Fund, the Lesbian Rights Project, and the National Gay Task Force, and a growing number of local organizations largely ignored the issue, "either because they were critical of marriage, saw it as a hopeless cause, or most commonly, simply had other priorities. Instead of focusing on the rights of same-sex *couples*, gay politics at the time focused on securing the rights of *individuals* against discrimination in employment and on building *community* institutions and a collective culture" (Chauncey 2004, 94).

Lone couples who filed legal challenges did so within this broad movement context and without the support of experienced legal advocates (Pinello 2006, 23). In May 1970, Jack Baker and J. Michael McConnell became the first gay couple to apply for a marriage license. Their application was denied by the Hennepin County, Minnesota, clerk, and in *Baker v. Nelson* (1971), the Minnesota Supreme Court ruled that "the men had no federal due process or equal protection rights to marry. The first marriage case involving a lesbian couple arose in Kentucky and met a similarly unsuccessful fate" in the 1973 decision *Jones v. Hallahan* (22).

Over the course of the next two decades there were "at least four more failed attempts to seek judicial recognition of same-sex marriage (*Singer v. Hara* 1974; *Adams v. Howerton* 1980; *DeSanto v. Barnsley* 1984; and *Dean v. District of Columbia* 1992)." These developments prompted Yale law professor William Eskridge to conclude that "legal agitation for gay marriage in the 1970s [and 1980s and 1990s] was a complete flop" (Pinello 2006, 22). But a number of important factors came to the fore by the early 1990s that allowed same-sex marriage to emerge as an issue for national debate: "The stage for the national marriage debate was set by the changing character of marriage, the changing circumstances of gay life, and the changing place of gay people in American society. . . . But it was the vision of a few key legal strategists and the decisions of a few state courts that took the issue to the next level" (Chauncey 2004, 123).

One of the most important developments in the lesbian and gay movements' organizing strategy was the emphasis on family issues by the early 1990s. These family issues included parenting by same-sex couples, partnership recognition, spousal benefits in the workplace, gay-supportive public school policies, and policies to support lesbian, gay, bisexual, and transgender youth. Several factors contributed to the changing historical circumstances, with consequences for the larger lesbian and gay movements and for the human beings that were the basis for the movements. One key development was the case of Sharon Kowalski:

> In 1983 Kowalski was involved in an automobile accident that left her ability to communicate seriously impaired. The courts awarded guardianship to Kowalski's father rather than to her partner, Karen Thompson, who for years was denied access to Kowalski. Across the United States, lesbian communities hosted forums, organized fundraisers, and worked to raise public awareness about the case. After an eight-year battle the courts eventually made Thompson the legal guardian, but in the meantime "Free Sharon Kowalski" became a rallying cry among lesbians concerned about the lack of legal recognition for their relationships. (D'Emilio 2007, 49)

The *Kowalski* case received considerable coverage in the gay press, heightening attention of the broader policy issues involved. Some gay pride marches opened with an empty wheelchair to dramatize the injustices associated with the case (Chauncey 2004, 113).

The AIDS crisis that emerged in the 1980s also inspired a call for full legal recognition of gay marriage by some movement activists. The reality of AIDS "suddenly forced tens of thousands of committed gay couples to deal with powerful institutions—hospitals, funeral homes, state agencies—that did not recognize their commitments. Even if AIDS patients were on their deathbeds, their life-partners were often excluded from visiting because they were not officially 'spouses' or next of kin" (Eisenbach 2006, 307). Indeed, "AIDS patients and their partners discovered that they weren't covered by each other's medical insurance, weren't entitled to enter the doctors' offices and hospital rooms of their loved ones, weren't authorized to claim remains or plan funerals or inherit estates. Grieving survivors were barred from collecting Social Security and pension benefits" (Von Drehle 2013, 22). What made matters even worse is that hospitals were under no obligation to inform partners or loved ones about the medical-care process. This situation was devastating; those personally enveloped in these untenable circumstances and their supporters in the larger lesbian and gay movements looked for meaningful policy change in the form of same-sex marriage.

Another important factor contributing to the emphasis on family issues and the attention to same-sex marriage was the lesbian and gay baby boom. More people were choosing to become parents, thus challenging traditional notions of "family." The process varied considerably, as babies were "conceived through the cooperation of gay men with the procreative desires of lesbian friends to the use of sperm banks, adoption agencies, surrogacy, and sex among friends" (D'Emilio 2007, 50). These developments all meant that children and families became a more visible face of the lesbian and gay movements, thus challenging traditional notions of heteronormativity while at the same time reinforcing the assimilationist approach to political, social, and cultural change. In the end, the *Kowalski* case, the AIDS crisis, and the lesbian and gay baby boom all helped to catapult same-sex marriage onto the movements' policy agenda by the late 1980s and early 1990s.

The 1990s witnessed legal developments that had profound consequences for the same-sex marriage debate, consequences that still reverberate today. Indeed, the campaign for same-sex marriage has depended on the courts for much of its success. The broad assimilationist legal-rights strategy adopted by the lesbian and gay movements in the 1980s and early 1990s received judicial legitimacy with the Supreme Court of Hawaii's decision in *Baehr v. Lewin*.

Baehr v. Lewin

In 1991, three couples who were all residents of Hawaii filed a declaratory judgment stating that the state's marriage law was unconstitutional because it "denied same-sex couples the same marriage rights as different-sex couples." They based their claims on the privacy and equal-protection clauses of the Hawaii Constitution. The Hawaii Supreme Court's 1993 decision rejected the privacy argument but responded more positively to the equal-protection argument. It found nothing in the state constitution that prevented lesbian and gay marriage, and it concluded that denying same-sex couples access to the benefits and rights associated with marriage is a form of sex discrimination (Dolkart 1998, 316–317). With this decision, the Hawaii Supreme Court "challenged volumes of existing legal doctrine" (O'Connor and Yanus 2007, 294). It appeared that same-sex marriage might be headed toward approval in Hawaii and the United States as a whole.

But the Supreme Court of Hawaii remanded the case to the state trial court, affording Hawaii the opportunity to present evidence at trial to justify the marriage statute. Prior to the trial, the Hawaii state legislature responded to the *Baehr* decision by passing a bill that "defined marriage in Hawaii as the union of a man and a woman. This bill also called for the establishment of a Commission on Sexual Orientation and the Law, which was to investigate and issue a report describing the legal and economic benefits of marriage and stating whether public policy reasons existed to extend these benefits to same-sex couples" (O'Connor and Yanus 2007, 300). The new trial was held during the summer of 1996, and because it found that "the state had failed to prove a compelling interest in denying same-sex couples the right to marry," the trial court ruled the state's marriage law unconstitutional. The decision itself "was stayed pending appeal" (Dolkart 1998, 316–317). The case returned to the Hawaii Supreme Court, which on December 9, 1999, issued a ruling of fewer than five hundred words stating, in essence, that the state of Hawaii can bar lesbian and gay couples from obtaining marriage licenses. It also ruled that a 1998 initiative passed by voters legitimated a previous statute that restricted licenses to one man and one woman. The court also, however, opened the door to the possibility that same-sex couples could still be eligible for "the same benefits of marriage—even without the license" (Keen 1999, 1).

Shortly after the 1993 *Baehr* decision, there was a well-organized conservative backlash, which served as an augury of things to come over the next fifteen years. For example, the Hawaii legislature passed a law forbidding same-sex marriage, thus codifying the heterosexual character of marriage. Later, after the trial judge's 1996 decision, the state legislature also proposed a constitutional amendment that "would permit the legislature to restrict marriage to opposite-sex couples." This amendment, which appeared on the ballot during the November 1998 elections, was accepted by Hawaii voters, thus dealing same-sex-marriage advocates a serious blow (Dolkart 1998, 317).

As part of this broader backlash, conservative groups created strategies designed to be implemented prior to the judicial resolution of the *Baehr* case: "they provided conservative legislators in every state with draft legislation that would direct their state's courts and other agencies to refuse to recognize a marriage between two persons of the same sex conducted in another state" (Chambers 2000, 294). Why did promoting this legislation prove to be such an effective strategy? It was because the legislation itself served as an important wedge issue by rallying conservatives and dividing liberal legislators from their lesbian and gay constituents. The conservative Right has used this strategy with great success in recent years. David L. Chambers offers a compelling explanation for its effectiveness in 1996 that remains relevant for understanding how the same-sex-marriage issue is played out today:

> Many Democratic state legislators across the country either themselves believed that marriage should be limited to one man and one woman, or at least believed that they could not vote against the far right's bill because of the views of most of their heterosexual constituents. So, just as the far right had hoped, many otherwise liberal legislators voted for the bills and infuriated gay and lesbian voters. Gay groups, local and national, were forced to devote huge amounts of effort in nearly every state to persuade legislators to reject the bills. (276)

From 1993 to 2003, forty-eight of the fifty states "introduced laws that limited legal recognition of marriage to opposite-sex couples." In Alaska (1998), Hawaii (1998), California (2000), Nebraska (2000), and Nevada (2000 and 2002), citizens used a direct democracy process to "codify same-sex marriage bans in statutory or constitutional law" (Lofton and Haider-Markel 2007, 314).

The 1996 Defense of Marriage Act

The conservative backlash also manifested itself in politics at the national level. During the 1996 campaign, conservative activists and politicians organized a rally condemning the practice three days prior to the Iowa caucuses. Three of the announced Republican presidential candidates attended, addressed the rally, and "signed a pledge to 'defend' heterosexual marriage against the threat posed by three lesbian and gay couples in Hawaii who had sued the state for the right to marry" (Cahill 2004, 81). This pledge, the Marriage Protection Resolution, was introduced by a coalition of eight conservative religious groups (Rimmerman 2002, 75). The *Los Angeles Times* observed in April 1996 that "homosexual marriage has abruptly emerged as an emotional flashpoint in the debate about America's social mores" (Cahill 2004, 81). It was no surprise, then, that Republican presidential nominee, Bob Dole, introduced the federal Defense of Marriage Act (DOMA) in the Senate, though it was surprising to some that President Clinton ultimately signed it into law on September 21, 1996. The Senate had voted 85–14 in September 1996 in favor of the act, which the House had passed by a vote of 342–67 that summer. Congressional hearings about the legislation had turned ugly, as members of Congress and witnesses warned that if men were allowed to marry other men, "they would soon be permitted to marry children and other animals" (Chambers 2000, 295). Others worried that same-sex marriage would lead to the collapse of Western civilization. The official Republican Party position was a conservative one: "Let the people of each state decide whether or not to allow homosexuals to marry in their state. If a state decides to permit such unions, so be it" (Whitman 2005, 97). Proposed by Republicans with the enthusiastic support of their Christian Right supporters, the legislation was timed perfectly to coincide with the 1996 election season. The law was designed to accomplish two goals: "(1) prevent states from being forced by the Full Faith and Credit Clause to recognize same-sex marriages validly celebrated in other states, and (2) define marriages for federal purposes as the union of one man and one woman" (Strasser 1997, 127). What the law meant in practice is that gay couples, even once they can actually legally be married, would be excluded "from all federal protections, responsibilities, and benefits that ordinarily accompany any other marriage in America" (Wolfson 2004, 42).

What prompted Clinton to sign DOMA into law? He was clearly worried that the same-sex-marriage issue could achieve heightened saliency as a potential wedge issue during the 1996 general election. Having endured the unpleasantness of the debate about gays in the military during the first six months of his presidency, he wanted to avoid a similar controversy about marriage. With this in mind, he signed it into law after midnight, eschewing the Rose Garden ceremony that often accompanies White House bill signings. Understandably, Clinton received strong criticism from some members of the lesbian and gay movements. But, whereas he had reversed his position regarding the military ban, he at least was consistent with regard to lesbian and gay marriage: he had announced his opposition in the 1992 campaign. But those who were most critical of the president argued that DOMA was both unnecessary and highly discriminatory and that Clinton was forced to sign the law to avoid attacks by the Christian Right during the 1996 presidential campaign. Indeed, the Dole campaign had run a radio ad that criticized Clinton for supporting an end to the military ban. The Clinton forces responded by releasing their own ad celebrating the president's signing of DOMA. This ad was run on Christian radio stations across the country, despite the fact that the president criticized the authors of the act for attempting to inject such a difficult issue into presidential politics during an election year.

Lesbian and gay rights groups protested the radio ad loudly. In response, the Clinton campaign pulled it after two days (Rimmerman 2002, 76). Ever the politician, Clinton recognized the potency of same-sex marriage as a potential wedge issue during the 1996 campaign. In stopping the ad, he helped remind other candidates of how they might balance their desire for electoral victory with the interests of their lesbian and gay supporters.

Could the lesbian and gay movements have done more to force the Clinton administration to support same-sex marriage? Note that it was not a crucial issue for many movement members at that time. Those who think it should be a key goal—individuals such as Jonathan Rauch, Andrew Sullivan, and Bruce Bawer—generally represent the movements' more moderate to conservative element. But, as we know from the military debate discussed in Chapter 4, the movements cannot control when specific issues will come to the fore. And, in many ways, the issue of same-sex marriage could not have come up at a worse time. The Republicans now controlled both houses of Congress, it was a presidential election year, and the movements simply did not have the time, skills, or resources to mount an effective organizing and educational campaign for an issue that appeared to be unpopular with the American public—certainly not a campaign equal to challenging the Christian Right's vast organizational resources. Indeed, the Republicans were searching for a wedge issue when they introduced DOMA on May 8, 1996. Rich Tafel, then executive director of the Log Cabin Republicans, supported several of these points when he said, "Marriage is so visceral, such a negative in the polls. My experience in debating this issue is that if I have an hour or two hours, I can win, but if I have five minutes, I can't. This is all being done in five minutes" (Gallagher 1996, 21). As a campaign issue, opposition to same-sex marriage served several purposes. It was an opportunity for some politicians to reach out to both the center and the Right, given the larger public's apparent lack of support for the issue. And it forced Clinton to tackle a difficult issue at a time when he did not want to relive the military fiasco of several years before. Clinton had no choice, then, but to alienate some members of his voting base.

How might Clinton have handled the situation differently? He could have forbidden his campaign team to broadcast a radio ad supporting DOMA on Christian radio. That they did so suggests how badly Clinton and his campaign advisers wanted to straddle both sides of the issue. He might also have vetoed DOMA while expressing his own opposition to same-sex marriage, arguing that such legislation was being used as a political weapon, without the kind of lengthy public education and discussion that the issue deserved. We should not be surprised that Clinton did not follow the latter strategy, given his previous record with regard to the military ban. For him to take a bold and creative position, one rooted in educational leadership, would have been out of step with his political character. Not surprisingly, Clinton endorsed overturning DOMA in March 2013 when it was politically safe for him to do so and when he understandably thought that his endorsement could help. In a March 2013 editorial in the *Washington Post,* Clinton wrote, "I join with the Obama administration, the petitioner Edith Windsor, and the many dedicated men and women who have engaged in this struggle for decades in urging the Supreme Court to overturn the Defense of Marriage Act" (2013).

Clinton's position would have been inconceivable as president of the United States in the fall of 1996. But fortunately for advocates of same-sex marriage, the issue moved out of the national arena and back to the states with the historic December 1999 decision by Vermont's chief justice, Jeffrey Amestoy, that Vermont's legislature must grant lesbian and gay couples the "common benefits and protections" that heterosexuals receive. Not surprisingly, a conservative backlash soon followed. Vermont legislators who supported the civil union legislation were targeted for defeat by Christian Right organizers, and some lost their re-election bids in 2000.

Conservative forces throughout the United States immediately moved to pre-empt recognition of same-sex marriages in their own states. The publicity surrounding the *Baehr* case appears to have done much more for opponents of lesbian and gay marriage than for its proponents. Further, the marriage issue vaulted to the forefront of the movements' agenda without a full and frank discussion of what this rights-based strategy would mean for the movements' organizing and educational efforts and for the direction of both short-term and long-term political and cultural change. Same-sex marriage would not manifest itself in the national political scene again until the June 16, 2003, US Supreme Court decision in *Lawrence v. Texas,* a ruling that political scientist H. N. Hirsch has called "a stunning federal Supreme Court decision" (2005, ix).

The Implications of Lawrence v. Texas *for the Same-Sex Marriage Debate*

Analyst Andrew Sullivan has argued persuasively that "the single most serious barrier to recognizing the right to marry was a 1986 Supreme Court decision, *Bowers v. Hardwick,* which upheld state laws criminalizing consensual sodomy" (2004, 106). Another analyst, Dale Carpenter, has argued that the court simply was not ready to overturn sodomy laws as early as 1986: "It was a little too soon. The Court and its members needed more time and experience with actual, known gay people before they could associate homosexuality with families and appreciate the importance of intimacy for gay couples and individuals" (2012, 210). This is why same-sex marriage proponents (and opponents) viewed *Lawrence v. Texas,* which overturned *Bowers,* as a landmark decision in advancing the interests of the lesbian and gay movements. With the *Lawrence* decision the Court struck down the sodomy laws of thirteen states that ban "private, consensual sexual intimacy" (Cahill 2004, 2), and it "extended the right to privacy—which includes the right to make decisions about one's intimate life—to lesbians and gay men." In essence, the court admitted that it had made a grave mistake when it ruled in *Bowers* that states could regulate sodomy. Writing for the six-to-three majority, Justice Anthony Kennedy celebrated "the liberty" of gay people to form relationships, "whether or not [they are] entitled to formal recognition in the law," and condemned the *Bowers* decision for "demeaning the lives of homosexual persons" (Chauncey 2004, 1). But Kennedy also cautioned that the decision does not apply to marriage per se by noting that the legal case opposing the Texas sodomy law "does not involve whether the government must give formal recognition to any relationship homosexual persons seek to enter." From Kennedy's vantage point, then, "*Lawrence v. Texas* was not about same-sex marriage" (Toobin, 2013a, 21). And Justice Sandra Day O'Connor argued in her concurrence that the "'traditional institution of marriage' was not an issue" (Cahill 2004, 3).

But Justice Antonin Scalia (joined by Chief Justice William Rehnquist) warned of the dangers to the institution of marriage that might result from the *Lawrence* decision: "today's opinion dismantles the structure of constitutional law that has permitted a distinction to be made between heterosexual and homosexual unions, insofar as formal recognition in marriage is concerned" (Cahill 2004, 3). Scalia's concerns, which included the fear that the court's decision would ultimately lead to the legalization of same-sex marriage, were seconded by conservative politicians and activists in ways that contributed to a shift in coverage by the mainstream news media.

Lesbian and gay movement activists also reacted in ways that provided support for Scalia's claim. For example, Lambda Legal Defense Fund attorney Ruth Harlow, who served as the lead attorney in *Lawrence,* argued, "The ruling makes it much harder for society to continue banning gay marriages." And Patricia Logue, cocounsel in *Lawrence* and also a Lambda attorney, claimed, "I think it's inevitable now. In what time frame, we don't know" (Cahill 2004, 3). Judicial scholar David Garrow perhaps put it best when he said, "There's no getting around the fact that this changes the political and legal landscape forever" (Bull 2003, 36).

The *Lawrence* decision elicited responses from national politicians as well. At a press conference in late July 2003, President Bush endorsed a federal definition of marriage as being between a man and a woman. He also faced increasing pressure to endorse an amendment to the US Constitution enshrining that definition. Some Republican Party leaders, including Senate Majority Leader Bill Frist (R-TN), went public with their concerns almost immediately. Frist endorsed sodomy laws on the June 29, 2003, episode of ABC's *This Week:* "'I have this fear' that the ruling could create an environment in which 'criminal activity within the home would in some way be condoned . . . whether it's prostitution or illegal commercial drug activity'" (Cahill 2004, 38). Frist then endorsed a constitutional amendment that would ban same-sex marriage. "I very much feel that marriage is a sacrament, and that sacrament should extend and can extend to that legal entity of a union between—what is traditionally in our Western values has been defined—as between a man and a woman" (Crea 2003, 1). And he had the continued and enthusiastic support of Senator Rick Santorum (R-PA), who claimed that "the greatest near-term consequence of the *Lawrence v. Texas* anti-sodomy ruling could be the legalization of homosexual marriage" (Cahill 2004, 3). Of course, Santorum's support was no surprise, given his April 2003 warning that if the Supreme Court legitimated the right to gay sex "within your home, then you have the right to bigamy, you have the right to polygamy, you have the right to incest, you have the right to adultery. You have the right to anything" (Hertzberg 2003, 33).

The constitutional amendment that Frist endorsed had been introduced in the House of Representatives by Marilyn Musgrave (R-CO) and five other sponsors on May 23, 2003. Drafted by the Alliance for Marriage, the amendment defines marriage as the union of a man and a woman. Musgrave and her cosponsors later introduced a slightly different version on March 22, 2004, that would not "bar same-sex civil unions allowed by state law." The goal of the revised amendment was to "broaden support for the initiative and blunt the appeal of alternatives that could leave the definition of marriage up to individual states." Some supporters of the gay marriage ban also had worried that the original amendment went too far and would frighten more moderate voters by nullifying the nation's domestic partner laws and Vermont's civil unions law as well as ban same-sex marriage. The revised amendment therefore stated, "Marriage in the United States shall consist only of the union of a man and a woman. Neither this Constitution, nor the constitution of any state, shall be construed to require that marriage or the legal incidents thereof be conferred upon any union other than the union of a man and woman" (Hulse 2004, n.p.). Musgrave justified the introduction of her original amendment (Senator Wayne Allard, a Colorado Republican, introduced a companion measure in the Senate) by asking, "If we are going to be redefining marriage, who should decide: unelected judges, or the people and their elected representatives?" (Perine and Dlouhy 2004, 84). It was no surprise that Musgrave, serving her first term in Congress at the time, would lead the charge against same-sex marriage, given that she had organized a successful drive to abolish it as a Colorado state representative prior to her arrival in the

House of Representatives. In this way, she linked her state-level experience with her new career on the national stage.

For Musgrave's constitutional amendment to be codified into law, it would need a two-thirds supermajority in the House and the Senate. If Musgrave and her supporters in both chambers could garner that much support for it, it would then go to the states, where thirty-eight of the fifty state legislatures (three-fourths of the states) would have to vote to ratify it before it could become law. Assuming that all of these challenging constitutional hurdles were overcome, Musgrave's amendment would replace the 1996 DOMA and protect the ban on same-sex marriages from all legal challenges (Perine and Dlouhy 2004, 85).

How did President Bush react to the possibility of such an amendment? In late June 2003 Bush's spokesperson, Ari Fleischer, claimed that the president had never discussed the idea of a constitutional amendment with Frist. Instead, Fleischer said that "the president is proud to support the Defense of Marriage Act. We have a law on the books right now that was signed by President Clinton, that passed with massive, overwhelming bipartisan majorities in 1996. And the president supports that legislation and that's where he stands now" (Crea 2003, 14).

But the president's position evolved as he and his advisers perceived political opportunities in making same-sex marriage an electoral issue. Bush served notice that he recognized the power of same-sex marriage as a wedge issue when he proclaimed October 12–18, 2003, "Marriage Protection Week." In doing so, Bush signaled his support "for the proposed Federal Marriage Amendment, which would amend the U.S. Constitution to ban same-sex marriage and government recognition of civil unions or domestic partnerships" ("Declaration of Intolerance" 2003, 15). In introducing his proclamation, Bush underscored the importance of traditional marriage for children:

> Research has shown that, on average, children raised in households headed by married parents fare better than children who grow up in other family structures. Through education and counseling programs, faith-based, community, and government organizations promote healthy marriages and a better quality of life for children. By supporting responsible child-rearing and strong families, my Administration is seeking to ensure that every child can grow up in a safe and loving home. (Office of the Press Secretary 2003, n.p.)

His statement also highlights the importance of his faith-based approach to social policy and its connections to traditional family structures.

The Log Cabin Republicans' response was swift and severe. Executive director Patrick Guerriero recognized the political rationale for Bush's approach to same-sex marriage almost a full year before the 2004 elections: "Early polls indicate that opposition to same-sex marriage could become a wedge issue." Guerriero also recognized that Bush's approach would lead to a "civil war in the Republican party. We are very disappointed to see Bush catering to the extraordinary hypocrisy of the antimarriage groups, which call themselves pro-family and then go around encouraging discrimination against gay and lesbian families" ("Declaration of Intolerance" 2003, 15). He later argued that "using the Constitution as a campaign tool and using gay families as a political wedge sets a new low for shameful campaigning" (Guerriero 2004, n.p.). And Mark Mead, the political director of the organization, warned that "a federal marriage amendment has the potential to ignite a culture war. As conservative Republicans, we know what can happen when you ignite a cultural war" (Perine and Dlouhy 2004, 84).

The Austin Twelve, the group of handpicked gay Republicans who had met with George W. Bush in Texas during the 2000 presidential campaign, also reacted with consternation to the president's handling of the marriage issue. Once viewed as the base of Bush's support among gays, the group became increasingly critical of Bush's support of the federal marriage amendment. Rebecca Maestri, the only lesbian in the original group and president of the northern Virginia Log Cabin Republicans chapter, said that "the Bush campaign people were principally concerned with getting elected [in 2000]. I do feel we were Bushwhacked." David Catania, a DC council member and an outspoken critic of the president's position regarding same-sex marriage, announced his support for John Kerry in the 2004 election. John Hutch, another member of the Austin Twelve and president of a direct-marketing firm, claimed that "there's nothing that Bush can possibly do right now to regain the support of gays and lesbians. He would have to publicly go on television, repudiate his position on the amendment and acknowledge that he was wrong to get involved in the process. And he would probably have to go further than that. I just don't see it happening" (Crea 2004, n.p.). The responses of the Log Cabin Republicans and some Austin Twelve members are reminders of how presidents often disappoint their most fervent supporters. To be sure, as we have already seen, Bill Clinton's lesbian and gay supporters reacted similarly to his betrayal with regard to the military and same-sex-marriage bans after he had campaigned fervently for their votes in the 1992 and 1996 campaigns.

The Massachusetts Supreme Court's 2003 Decision

With the Massachusetts Supreme Judicial Court ruling in *Goodridge v. Department of Public Health* (November 17, 2003), the same-sex marriage issue was catapulted further onto the national stage. Politicians in both parties were forced to respond to the court's ruling that "the ban on marriage licenses to gay couples violated the Commonwealth's guarantee of equal protection of the laws." The court ruled in 2004 that "no separate-but-equal institution of 'civil unions' would suffice to meet constitutional requirements" (Sullivan 2004, xvii). Richard Land, president of the Southern Baptist Ethics and Religious Commission, offered an opening salvo in the debate that followed the court's initial decision, and his view represents the Christian Right's perspective well: "the Federal Marriage Amendment is the only way to adequately deal with this judicial assault on the sanctity of marriage being defined as God intended it, the union of one man and one woman" (Foust 2003, n.p.).

It was only a matter of time before Bush announced his support for the Musgrave amendment. He did so on February 24, 2004, after highlighting the issue in his State of the Union address. Bush declared that "the union of a man and woman is the most enduring human institution" (Sokolove 2004, 1). Why did Bush announce his endorsement at this time? It is clear that he was not eager to take such a step, but the possibility of using marriage as a winning wedge issue during his re-election campaign proved to be too attractive. Once the Massachusetts Supreme Judicial Court legalized same-sex marriage in that state and San Francisco mayor Gavin Newsom began the process of granting marriage licenses to lesbian and gay couples. On February 10, 2004, Newsom mandated that the San Francisco county clerk must "provide marriage licenses on a nondiscriminatory basis, without regard to gender or sexual orientation." In doing so, he called "the ability of lesbian and gay couples to marry a 'fundamental right.'" He argued that his commitment to upholding the "California state constitution required him to overrule a state law prohibiting same sex marriage because it violates the constitutional principle of legal equality." But on August 12, 2004, the California Supreme Court ruled that the mayor's decision was unconstitutional because it "had violated the principle of 'separation of powers'" (Snyder 2006, 1–2). Bush and his advisers perceived that his endorsement of the amendment was part of a winning electoral strategy. In addition, John Micklethwait and Adrian Wooldridge have argued that "with social conservatives up in arms, Bush had little alternative to backing the amendment" (2004, 149). Of course, his position should come as no surprise, given his administration's overall record on lesbian and gay rights during Bush's first term.

Nor did it come as a surprise when Bush endorsed a constitutional ban on same-sex marriage on the eve of a Senate vote on the amendment in early June 2006, well into his second term in office. The bill's Senate sponsor, Wayne Allard, introduced the measure with the support of the White House and the Christian Right. They perceived that it could help rally the conservative base in the November 2006 midterm elections, when Democrats stood to make large gains in light of the setbacks associated with the war in Iraq and rising energy prices. It is especially noteworthy that Bush highlighted his support for the amendment with a news conference in the White House Rose Garden on Monday, June 5, the day before the vote. In the end, the Republicans suffered a stinging defeat in the Senate, the 49–48 vote falling well short of the 60 votes needed to have an up-or-down vote on the amendment itself.

Bush's attempt to distance himself from the Log Cabin Republicans and the Republican Unity Coalition revealed how far he would go to avoid antagonizing his Christian Right supporters, whose votes he had desperately needed to win the 2000 election and whose votes he perceived he would need to win in 2004 and keep congressional Republicans in power in 2006. The president was also undoubtedly aware that the Christian Right had caused his father considerable difficulty during his one-term presidency when they perceived him as compromising too much on conservative principles. George W. Bush clearly did not want to repeat his father's political mistakes. Slightly more than 70 percent of self-identified lesbian and gay voters (more than 2.8 million Americans) cast their ballots for Al Gore in the 2000 election, while Bush received the votes of more than 11 million religious conservatives (Rimmerman 2002, 163). Bush owed his conservative base his loyalty, given their strong support for him in such a close election and their role in his victory over John Kerry in 2004. Journalist Chris Bull captured well the challenges confronting Bush following his 2000 election "victory": "Gay rights is a no-win situation for Bush. If he aligns with the antigay right wing, the media will accuse him of bigotry. If he doesn't, he'll get attacked by conservatives" (2001, 26). Bush and some congressional Republicans also recognized that support for a constitutional amendment could turn off potential swing voters who might view the Republican Party as too intolerant. In addition, Republican strategists were well aware that President Bush secured 25 percent of the lesbian and gay vote in the 2000 election, support that both he and Republican congressional members needed in future elections. During a December 2003 interview on ABC, Bush was asked whether he supported a constitutional amendment that would abolish same-sex marriage. His response reveals his attempt to balance competing interests: "If necessary, I will support a constitutional amendment which would honor marriage between a man and a woman, codify that . . . the position of this administration is that, you know, whatever legal arrangements people want to make, they're allowed to make, so long as it's embraced by the state" (Perine and Dlouhy 2004, 85). But, despite these various political concerns, soon after the *Lawrence* decision was handed down, Bush and his advisers recognized the utility of using same-sex marriage as a divisive political issue.

The Massachusetts Supreme Judicial Court decision provided more support for conservatives, who believed that the Republican Party should use same-sex marriage as a wedge issue. Indeed, a little more than a month before the November 2004 elections, social conservatives in Congress recognized the potential of using the same-sex marriage issue to mobilize their political base. House leaders brought the revised Musgrave amendment to the floor on September 30, 2004, bypassing the Judiciary Committee and its chair, F. James Sensenbrenner (R-WI). Sensenbrenner opposed same-sex marriage but had also voiced serious concerns about amending the US Constitution, thus revealing an important split among social conservatives. In justifying the procedural maneuver, House Majority Leader Tom DeLay (R-TX) claimed that "this debate will spill over into the elections, I think, and rightly so." And Marilyn Musgrave used the latest procedural debate as an opportunity to bash the court system, which, she claimed, had stymied the will of the people: "the trajectory of the courts' decisions is unmistakable" (Perine 2004, 2322). Both DeLay and Musgrave helped President Bush's cause by highlighting the saliency of the same-sex-marriage issue in a volatile election year and making the case against the practice with a stridency that the president could not emulate. He was hampered by Vice President Dick Cheney's announcement in August 2004 that he did not support the president's determination to amend the US Constitution, presumably out of consideration for his lesbian daughter, Mary.

Bush's attempts to appease the Christian Right help explain his discomfort with addressing lesbian and gay civil rights issues during his first term. Since assuming the presidency, Bush had done little to support issues that were of broad interest to the lesbian and gay movements. If anything, he was openly hostile, as reflected in some of his appointments, such as that of John Ashcroft (R-MO) as attorney general during his first term. As a member of the United States Senate, Ashcroft had consistently voted in support of the Christian Right's positions on lesbian and gay issues. Bush's appointment of former Colorado attorney general Gale Norton also did little to comfort the movements, as Norton was a vigorous defender of Colorado's Amendment 2, which would have eliminated all lesbian and gay rights laws in the state. Indeed, by the end of his first term, Bush had no real policy achievements that lesbians and gays could justifiably celebrate. Therefore, his support for a constitutional amendment was merely an extension of his overall approach to gay rights issues since assuming office. His support also represented a point of departure from his first presidential campaign in 2000, when he indicated that he "did not believe in punitive action against gays" and refused to support a constitutional amendment against same-sex marriage (Wald and Glover 2007, 123).

The United States v. Windsor *and* Hollingsworth v. Perry *2013 Supreme Court Decisions*

On June 26, 2013, the United States Supreme Court issued two landmark decisions that brought some legal and policy clarity to the debate over same-sex marriage. Justice Anthony Kennedy issued an opinion in the *Windsor* case that vindicated the rights of lesbian and gay Americans as he and the court had done previously in *Romer v. Evans* (1996) and *Lawrence v. Texas* (2003). In writing for the 5–4 majority that struck down DOMA, Kennedy claimed that "'DOMA instructs all federal officials, and indeed all persons with whom same-sex couples interact, including their own children, that their marriage is less worthy than the marriages of others. The principal purpose and the necessary effect of this law are to demean those persons who are in a lawful same-sex marriage'" (Toobin 2013a, 27). In making this decision, the Court ruled that married-same sex couples are entitled to federal benefits, which is a major policy advance. As commentator Adam Liptak pointed out, "the decision on federal benefits will immediately extend many benefits to couples in the states where same-sex marriage is legal, and it will give the Obama administration the ability to broaden other benefits through executive actions" (Liptak 2013). More specifically, "the ruling makes clear that gay couples living in states that recognize their unions will immediately gain access to more than 1,000 federal benefits, like Social Security and family leave rights. Less certain is how couples in the remaining 37 states will fare" (Bernard 2013). Indeed, "Kennedy's decision was carefully limited to the question of Congress's authority to restrict marriage to opposite-sex couples; he insisted that he was not deciding the much larger question of whether states can restrict marriage along those lines" (Cole 2013, 28). And by declining to decide on the case from California, *Hollingsworth v. Perry*, the court essentially permitted same-sex marriages there. Writing for the 5–4 majority, Chief Justice John Roberts announced that the court would not intervene in the controversy over California's Proposition 8, which lower courts had invalidated previously. But what the court did not say in both of these rulings is perhaps just as important as what it did say: "the rulings leave in place laws banning same-sex marriage around the nation, and the court declined to say whether there was a constitutional right to same-sex marriage" (Liptak 2013). In the end, the court essentially said that it is not yet ready "to cut off the unfolding state-by-state legislative debate on gay marriage." Harvard Law professor Richard Fallon reflected on the implications of both court decisions for the future of same-sex marriage: "the five-justice coalition favoring gay rights was willing to go only so far at this point." And the court's decisions in June 2013 obviously have consequences for the future of same-sex marriage, as Fallon points out: "although a majority thought it was important to resolve the DOMA issue, a majority did not believe it was not similarly desirable to resolve the larger equal protection issue" that is posed by laws on the books against marriage ("Analysis" 2013). Legal commentator David Cole offered this trenchant assessment of the two Court decisions:

> Together, these decisions are a consummate act of judicial statesmanship. They extend federal benefits to all same-sex married couples in states that recognize gay marriage, expand the number of states recognizing gay marriage to thirteen, yet leave open for the time being the ultimate issue of state

> power to limit marriage to the union of a man and woman. The Court took a significant step toward recognition of the equality rights of gays and lesbians. But by not imposing same-sex marriage on the three quarters of the states whose laws still forbid it, the Court has allowed the issue to develop further through the political process—where its trajectory is all but inevitable. (2013, 28)

Andrew Rosenthal pointed out that "the rulings leave a lot unsettled." Why do they do so? Because the "surviving part of DOMA frees states from having to recognize marriages legally performed in other states—which seems clearly unconstitutional . . . but was not part of this case. So, if you're a same-sex couple married in New York and you're driving west through the Lincoln Tunnel, when you see that yellow line marking the border of New Jersey, you're no longer married. How ridiculous" (2013).

Some voices on the political right offered a much more negative interpretation of the Court's marriage decisions. For example, Representative Michelle Bachman (R-MN) offered this statement to the press: "Marriage was created by the hand of God. No man, not even a Supreme Court, can undo what a holy God has instituted." Longtime Christian Right activist Ralph Reed promised that "we will now seek the passage of federal legislation to remedy this situation as much as possible given the parameters of the decision" (Chait 2013). Tony Perkins, president of the Family Research Council, predicted in light of the Court's rulings that it will be "difficult for pro-gay marriage forces to institute same-sex marriage in the 38 states that have not yet." Perkins claimed that "there are very few states that I think are easy pickings for them. I think they have reached a wall here. So the idea that this is inevitable was shown today that it is not. They are not going to be able to impose same sex marriage on the nation" (Goodstein 2013).

But in the end Chauncey is certainly right about the broader implications of the court's decision to strike down DOMA: "lesbian and gay couples will no longer suffer the indignity of having the government treat their marriages as inferior" (2013). And political analyst Nate Silver pointed out in the aftermath of the court's decisions that "by August 1 [2013], same-sex marriage will be legal in California, Delaware, Maine, Maryland, Minnesota, Rhode Island and Washington—all states where it was not legal one year earlier. There are about 59 million people living in these seven states, which means that the availability of same-sex marriage in the United States as a percentage of population will have more than doubled within the year." Silver's analysis points to the dramatic change in the same-sex marriage legal landscape in just over one year: "as of early last year [2012], same-sex marriage was legal only in Connecticut, Iowa, Massachusetts, New Hampshire, New York, Vermont and the District of Columbia, which have 35 million people among them" (Silver, 2013). All of this suggests that the march toward legalized same-sex marriage in the United States has gathered significant momentum in recent years and the court's decisions in the *Windsor* and Proposition 8 cases have helped to build that momentum.

The background to the *Windsor* case is fascinating and important as we try to understand the trajectory of the lesbian and gay movements over time. Edith Schlain Windsor is an eighty-four-year-old lesbian who married her long-term partner, Thea Clara Spyer, in Canada in 2007. Spyer died in 2009 and Windsor inherited her property. DOMA "did not allow the Internal Revenue Service to treat Ms. Windsor as a surviving spouse, and she faced a tax bill of about $360,000 that a spouse in an opposite-sex marriage would not have had to pay." Windsor sued and the US Court of Appeals for the Second Circuit in New York, "struck down the 1996 law" in 2012 (Liptak 2013). The Justice Department defended the law in court until 2011, "as it typically does all acts of Congress." Attorney General Eric H. Holder Jr. announced in 2011 "that he and President Obama had concluded that the law was unconstitutional and unworthy of defense in court, but that the administration would continue to enforce the law." House Republicans intervened to defend the law after the Justice Department stepped aside. The "administration's position prevailed in the lower courts," but "the Justice Department filed an appeal to the Supreme Court, saying that the final decision should come from the Supreme Court," thus setting the stage for the Court's 5–4 decision in *United States v. Windsor.*

One of the most compelling background stories to the Proposition 8 case, *Hollingsworth v. Perry,* is that Theodore Olson and David Boies, two prominent lawyers on opposite sides of the case that decided the 2000 presidential election, *Bush v. Gore,* filed the challenge to Proposition 8 that culminated in the Court's decision. "The dismissal of the Proposition 8 challenge leaves intact" a 2010 ruling by now retired San Francisco trial judge, Vaughan Walker. "Following a much publicized three-week trial, he found that same-sex marriage caused no harm whatsoever to the state or society but substantial harm to same-sex couples by depriving them of their rights to equal protection and due process" ("Same-Sex Marriage Rulings," 2013). In doing so, Walker had overturned California's proposition 8, which had "outlawed same-sex marriage in spite of the fact that thousands of same-sex couples already had married during a brief period when their marriages were considered legal in the state" (Andriote 2011, 397). Proposition 8, which passed by a 52–48 percent majority, had "added a new section 7.5 to Article I of the California state constitution with the following words: 'Only marriage between a man and woman is valid or recognized in California'" (Feldblum 2009, 34). For advocates of same-sex marriage, the results of the Proposition 8 referendum were particularly disconcerting, as many of the same California voters who turned out to vote for Barack Obama in 2008 voted to overrule a state Supreme Court ruling that had legalized same-sex marriage. Exit polls in the aftermath of the 2008 election revealed that seven in ten African Americans and "fifty-three percent of Latinos . . . backed Proposition 8, overcoming the bare majority of white Californians who voted to let the court ruling stand" (Vick and Surdin, 2008). Evan Wolfson argued that the basic issue raised by the Proposition 8 case was that it challenged "California's stripping away the freedom to marry from one group of couples—those of the same sex—and ask[ed] whether it is acceptable for a majority to vote away freedoms (like the freedom to marry) from a minority" (2012).

And what role has President Obama played in same-sex marriage policy debates? As a 2008 presidential candidate, Obama supported gay rights and opposed DOMA, though he pointed out often that "he was not personally in favor of gay marriage." At the same time, however, he suggested "that his view on gay marriage was 'evolving.'" But, much to the disappointment of supporters of same-sex marriage, Obama's Department of Justice defended DOMA's constitutionality. Justice Department officials defended this position by arguing "that the executive branch historically defends laws passed by Congress as presumptively constitutional" (Schwartz 2012, 213). For many supporters of same-sex marriage, this position was unacceptable. Indeed, some members of the lesbian and gay movements who were already furious about the loss on Proposition 8 in California turned their anger on President Obama through the blogosphere, led by blogger John Aravosis. In response, "the Obama administration hurried up its new executive order extending partnership benefits to the same-sex couples employed by the federal government, in a transparent effort to calm the waters" (Hirshman 2012, 319). Critics pointed out that Obama's extension of benefits was far too limited: it applied only to federal employees and did not include health and retirement benefits, because that was prohibited under the DOMA. Frustration continued to mount among some in the lesbian and gay movements, especially given Obama's promises in the 2008 presidential campaign and the reality that he received "70 percent of the vote from those who identified themselves as gay, lesbian or bisexual according to CNN exit polls." President Obama had already irritated his supporters within the lesbian and gay movements when he chose the Reverend Rick Warren to deliver the invocation at his January 2009 inauguration, because Warren supported California's Proposition 8 and "likened homosexuality to bestiality and incest" in an interview with Belief.net (Keck 2009).

Some have defended Obama's approach by pointing to the formidable obstacles that Bill Clinton faced as he tried to overturn the ban on lesbians and gays in the military, not to mention the amount of time that then president Clinton had to devote to the issue in his first six months in office. For example, Michael Klarman reminds us that when Obama assumed office he faced a number of serious challenges that warranted immediate legislative attention, including "an economic stimulus package, health care reform, and environmental legislation. . . . Furthermore, many newly elected Democrats in Congress represented fairly conservative districts, which would not have supported gay marriage." What did the Obama administration do soon after taking office to appease the lesbian and gay movements instead of fighting to overturn the military ban and supporting same-sex marriage? He invited lesbian and gay couples to visit the White House in honor of the annual Easter Egg Roll. In addition to issuing an executive order that extended "limited benefits to same-sex partners of federal employees," the administration also "lifted visa restrictions on people with HIV, reversed Bush administration policy on allowing same-sex couples to identify themselves as married in the census, approved regulations protecting gays and lesbians from discrimination in the sale and rental of housing and declared June to be Gay Pride Month in commemoration of Stonewall's fortieth anniversary" (Klarman 2013, 140).

But in February 2011 the Obama administration finally responded to the demands of the lesbian and gay movements, when the Justice Department announced "that it would no longer defend DOMA as constitutional." And in May 2012 Vice President Biden said on NBC's *Meet the Press* that "'I am absolutely comfortable with the fact that men and women marrying one another are entitled to the same exact rights, all the civil rights, all the civil liberties'" (Knowlton 2012). Biden's apparently unscripted comments appeared to catch the White House by surprise, so much so that the vice president apologized to the president in the Oval Office several days later (Wallsten and Wilson, 2012). It is also worth noting, however, that it is possible that the Obama White House was sending top surrogates out to test the waters and to send a message to the lesbian and gay movements about Obama's ultimate support for their cause. For example, in 2011, Secretary of State Hillary Rodham Clinton announced in Geneva, Switzerland, that "'gay rights are human rights, and human rights are gay rights,'" a position that Obama later endorsed with enthusiasm. And when Shaun Donovan, Housing and Urban Development secretary, reported in an interview that he supported same-sex marriage, "a senior administration official said that Mr. Donovan enjoyed 'the trust and respect of the president.'" Finally, Obama's own evolution culminated in his statement on May 9, 2012, in an ABC interview with Robin Roberts that "'I think same-sex couples should be able to get married'" (Knowlton 2012). Long a proponent of civil unions, Obama cited encouragement by gay friends as well as conversations with his wife and daughters as inspiring him to embrace same-sex marriage. In addition, he cited his Christianity as a source for his endorsement: "Not only Christ sacrificing himself on our behalf, but it's also the golden rule—you know, treat others the way you would want to be treated. And I think that's what we try to impart to our kids, and that's what motivates me as president" (Calmes and Baker, 2012). Another explanation is his "affirmation of gay couples as parents" and his "contact not only with gay couples but also with their children." In the course of the Roberts interview, President Obama spoke of his own White House staff members "who are incredibly committed, in monogamous relationships, same-sex relationships, who are raising kids together." In addition, he spoke in eloquent terms of "how caring they are, how much love they have in their hearts—how they're taking care of their kids" (Yoshino 2012). A second explanation is that President Obama and his political advisers finally recognized that changing public opinion in favor of same-sex marriage meant that he could publicly embrace the issue without retribution at the ballot box in November 2012. And what has Obama's support meant for same-sex marriage and it supporters? As one lesbian activist said, "It was a sea change. Not in the law, but politically and culturally, the earth moved" (Bernstein 2012, 10).

The Implications of the Marriage Debate for the Lesbian and Gay Movements

As we have already seen, the campaign for same-sex marriage has been rooted in litigation, and it has now garnered the support of most major national lesbian and gay organizations, including the Lambda Legal Defense and Education Fund, the National Gay and Lesbian Task Force, and the Human Rights Campaign. Its status as one of the leading issues of the late 1990s and early twenty-first century is evidenced by the contention of Lambda's Evan Wolfson that, in the wake of the Hawaii Supreme Court's *Baehr* decision, there should be no "intra-community debate over whether to seek marriage. The ship has sailed" (Warner 1999, 83). For strategic reasons, Wolfson believes that the lesbian and gay movements should present a united front in support of same-sex marriage if homophobic Christian Right initiatives are to be defeated.

The results of the 2004 election—which saw the re-election of George W. Bush, the election of a more conservative Congress, the passage of eleven state ballot initiatives banning same-sex marriage, and election-day polls indicating that 22 percent of voters focused more on "moral values" than on other factors (Keen 2004, 20)—did not bode well for those supporting same-sex marriage and lesbian, gay, bisexual, and transgender issues more broadly. In the wake of the election, movement leaders held discussions about future strategy and whether more moderate goals and strategies should be pursued in light of the grim election results. The Human Rights Campaign, the country's largest lesbian and gay advocacy group, accepted the resignation of Cheryl Jacques as its executive director, appointed the first nongay cochair to its board, and publicly announced a more moderate political and electoral strategy, one that would focus less on "legalizing same-sex marriages and more on strengthening personal relationships" (Broder 2004, A1).

But the reality is that same-sex marriage is now a part of the national political debate about lesbian, gay, bisexual, and transgender rights for the foreseeable future. Indeed, scholar Michael Klarman believes that "not all of *Bowers*'s consequences for the gay rights movement were adverse. The Court's decision made gay rights issues highly salient" (2013, 38), even though "the gay rights community was devastated by *Bowers*" to the point that Tom Stoddard of Lambda Legal Defense and Education Fund cited the *Bowers* decision as "the gay community's *Dred Scott*" (37).

We are seeing the consequences of the *Bowers* decision in the amount of attention being devoted to same-sex marriage. And the movements have recognized over time that they must fashion a political and educational organizing strategy that recognizes and accepts this reality. It is a reality that has played to the strength of the Christian Right's grassroots organizing efforts over time, because same-sex marriage is the kind of hot-button social issue that can mobilize voters to support conservative candidates and conservative ballot initiatives, as the 2004 and 2006 election results indicate. "The efforts to build a diverse coalition—in terms of race and religion—underscore the political sophistication of the religious activists who oppose gay marriage. . . . And for the battle over gay marriage, the coalition of opponents has been broad indeed" (Campbell and Robinson 2007, 146). Since the legalization of same-sex marriage in Massachusetts in 2003, thirty-one states have adopted a constitutional amendment that preserves traditional marriage, while as of February 2014 California, Connecticut, Delaware, the District of Columbia, Illinois, Iowa, Maine, Maryland, Massachusetts, Minnesota, New Jersey, New Hampshire, New Mexico, New York, Rhode Island, Vermont, and Washington allow same-sex marriage. In the 2006 midterm elections, only Arizona rejected a constitutional amendment that would have defined "marriage as a one-man, one-woman institution. The measure also would have forbid civil unions and domestic partnerships" (Crary 2006, n.p.).

Although the Arizona results and the Massachusetts legislature's June 2007 overwhelming 151–45 vote that defeated an effort to place same-sex marriage before voters in a statewide referendum were reason for celebration, the overall view from the states is sobering (Figure 5.1) ("World at a Glance" 2007, 7). John D'Emilio offers this dismal assessment of where things stand for those who support same-sex marriage: "Simply put, the marriage campaign has been a disaster. It is far better to assess the damage and learn from it, better to figure out if a course correction can be made, than to proceed down the current road blissfully in denial, claiming that night is day, stop means go, and defeats are victories" (2007, 45). D'Emilio believes that reliance on a judicial strategy has been a "catastrophe" because it has helped to foster "new legislation and state constitutional provisions" that have undermined the entire same-sex-marriage campaign (61).

FIGURE 5.1 The State of the States

States Allowing Same-Sex Marriage	Massachusetts
States Allowing Civil Unions	New Jersey Vermont
States with Laws Banning Discrimination Based on Sexual Orientation and Gender Identity	California Colorado Connecticut Delaware District of Columbia Hawaii Illinois Iowa Maine Massachusetts Minnesota Nevada New Jersey New Mexico Oregon Rhode Island Vermont Washington
States that Prohibit Discrimination Based on Sexual Orientation Only	Maryland New Hampshire New York Wisconsin

Source: www.hrc.org.

The Case for Same-Sex Marriage

Those who argue for same-sex marriage often invoke a practical argument. For example, the late gay political activist Thomas B. Stoddard pointed out that "the legal status of marriage rewards the two individuals who travel to the altar (or its secular equivalent) with substantial economic and practical advantages." What are these advantages? By filing a joint tax return, married couples can reduce their tax liabilities. In addition, "they are entitled to special government benefits, such as those given surviving spouses and dependents through the Social Security program." Even when there is no will, they can inherit from one another. Furthermore, "they are immune from subpoenas" that require testimony against the other spouse. Any foreigner who marries an American citizen gains "a right to residency in the United States" (1989, 754).

And there are advantages that accrue to married couples through custom as well. Health insurance is a major issue for everyone in a country that provides health care as a privilege or benefit rather than as a right. Many employers offer health care to their employees and to their spouses, but few employers "include a partner who is not married to an employee, whether of the same sex or not" (Stoddard 1989, 754). Stoddard offered this astute summary of the legal realities facing same-sex couples:

> In short, the law generally presumes in favor of every marital relationship, and acts to preserve and foster it, and to enhance the rights of the individuals who enter into it. It is usually possible, with enough money and the right advice, to replicate some of the benefits conferred by the legal status of marriage through the use of documents like wills and power of attorney forms, but that protection will inevitably, under current circumstances, be incomplete. (755)

But the reality is that this avenue for redress is unavailable to those without the resources to hire quality legal advisers.

A second set of arguments emanate from the privileged place that marriage occupies in our entire social structure. Marriage transcends what is sanctioned by law because it is at the core of what Americans mean by family. Marriage in every state but Massachusetts is conceptualized to suggest that "two men or two women are incapable of achieving such an exalted domestic state." Lesbian and gay relationships are viewed, then, as "somehow less significant, less valuable" (Stoddard 1989, 756). Furthermore, the US government "cannot legitimately pass laws discriminating against lesbian and gay citizens—denying them the civil right to marry or treating their relationships differently than those of heterosexuals" (Snyder 2006, 11). As a result, gays and lesbians must fight for full equality.

Same-sex-marriage advocate Claire Snyder offers an argument steeped in democratic theory: "The fundamental principles of American democracy not only allow, but also require the legalization of same-sex marriage" (2006, 2). How can people identify themselves as supporters of democracy but discriminate against a minority group?

> Lesbian and gay Americans are citizens, just like heterosexuals, and must be treated equally before the law. While many people may view the traditional heterosexual family as the most desirable family form, there is no evidence

> that it does a better job of producing democratic citizens. And even if there were, lesbian and gay citizens would still have the right to form families and raise children, just like anyone else. (11)

The underlying argument here is that for democracy to be alive and vibrant, to even exist, it requires equality among all citizens, including lesbians, gays, bisexuals, and transgender individuals. Marriage "has come to be regarded as a fundamental civil right and a powerful symbol of full equality and citizenship" (Chauncey 2004, 165). As a result, the opportunity to marry must be extended to all citizens.

A fourth set of arguments derives from the nature of "marriage as a symbol of personal commitment and as a means of gaining recognition for that commitment from others." The reasoning here is that domestic partnerships and civil unions are far too limiting, even though they had once appeared to be a huge advance (Figure 5.2). Why did some rush to get married as soon as they were legally permitted to do so? One woman said: "First and foremost, I love this woman and she loves me." Marriage is "the best sign of a commitment that you can make" (Chauncey 2004, 142).

The profound psychological benefits of marriage are offered as key justifications by other proponents. Andrew Sullivan, for one, has argued passionately that the right to marry is "the mark of ultimate human respect." If we deny human beings the right to marry, then we cause "the deepest psychological and political wound imaginable." With this in mind, Sullivan believes that allowing lesbians and gays to marry would afford "the highest form of social approval imaginable" and provide "the deepest means for the liberation of homosexuals" (P. Robinson 2005, 63). And he connects his advocacy for same-sex marriage to the larger lesbian and gay movements' political program: "If nothing else were done at all, and gay marriage were legalized, ninety percent of the political work necessary to achieve gay and lesbian equality would have been achieved. It is ultimately the only reform that truly matters" (62).

The positive impact of same-sex marriage on "the self perception and psychological well-being" of lesbian and gay children is also an argument made by some proponents (P. Robinson 2005, 62). Sullivan thinks that with the legalization of same-sex marriage, children would have important role models as they contemplate relationships as adults. But the key is for society to place its imprimatur of acceptance on same-sex relationships, an acceptance that would infuse the larger culture.

FIGURE 5.2 **Ways to Recognize Same-Sex Relationships: A Comparison**

Marriage	Domestic Partnership	Civil Union
Federal Law Federal protections conferred by 1,049 federal laws and policies, such as Social Security, federal taxation, family and medical leave, and immigration policy.	*Federal Law* No federal protections.	*Federal Law* No federal rights, responsibilities, or protections.
Region Available Available in all states, unless couple is the same sex.	*Region Available* Available in a range of states and cities, as well as in the context of some private and public employment. Provisions vary widely.	*Region Available* Available only to same-sex couples.
Benefits Provided The broadest array of federal and state benefits, including Social Security benefits, the right to inherit from a partner without a will, the right to take family leave under federal law, the right to file federal taxes jointly, the right to sponsor a partner for immigration, and many others.	*Benefits Provided* Benefits range from health care alone, provided by some public and private employers, to a broader array of state benefits, such as in California.	*Benefits Provided* Provides a separate form of equality at the level of state policy, except for eligibility for health insurance through private employers.

Source: Adapted from Cahill 2003, p. 7.

Sullivan makes another important argument in his fervent case for marriage. He claims that same-sex marriage will lead to a reduction of promiscuity in the lesbian and especially gay male community. This promiscuity undermines stable and healthy relationships and contributes significantly to the AIDS epidemic.

Finally, some argue that same-sex marriage would not only be good for lesbians and gays, but it would also be positive for American society as a whole—good for lesbians and gays, for heterosexuals, and for the broader institution of marriage. Jonathan Rauch is the foremost advocate of this position, and he justifies his argument in this way:

> Far from opening the door to all sorts of scary redefinitions of marriage, from polygamy to incest to who knows what, same-sex marriage is the surest way to shut that door. Far from decoupling marriage from its core mission, same-sex marriage clarifies and strengthens that mission. Far from hastening the social decline of marriage, same-sex marriage shores up the key values and commitments on which couples and families and society depend. Far from dividing America and weakening communities, same-sex marriage, if properly implemented, can make the country both better unified and truer to its ideals. (2004, 5–6)

To Rauch, then, the fight for same-sex marriage is a stabilizing rather than destabilizing force because it would normalize all marriages. But this argument and the other arguments outlined above are vehemently rejected by those who are opposed to same-sex marriage.

The Case Against Same-Sex Marriage

The arguments against same-sex marriage can be divided into two broad categories: those most often offered by the Christian Right and its supporters and those articulated by members of the lesbian and gay movements who argue that same-sex marriage is too accommodating and assimilationist and as a result should not be a central focus of the movements' policy and political agenda. Why did same-sex marriage provoke such virulent responses by the Christian Right? The most outspoken opponents to same-sex marriage are those who have been fighting against greater equality for lesbians, gays, bisexuals, and transgender individuals for many years. They are the people who have steadfastly "opposed gay rights ordinances, the right of gay couples to adopt children, and the appearance of gay characters in the media" (Chauncey 2004, 145).

A consistent argument offered by the Christian Right in its opposition to same-sex marriage is that children raised by lesbian or gay parents will be injured or abused in some way. Focus on the Family, a leading

Christian Right organization, states that "same-sex parenting situations make it impossible for a child to live with both biological parents, thus increasing their risk of abuse" (Cahill 2007, 161). It was no surprise, then, that in response to the Massachusetts *Goodridge* decision, Focus on the Family bought a full-page advertisement in the January 23, 2004, *Boston Globe* that stated, "Same-sex marriage advocates and the Massachusetts Supreme Court are asking our state and nation to enter a massive, untested social experiment with coming generations of children. We must ask one simple question: Is the same-sex 'family' good for children?" (162). This line of argument is not surprising, given the Christian Right's fixation over time on the negative consequences of homosexuality for children in the classroom, children in families, and children in society at large. They have consistently argued that "American democracy requires the traditional heterosexual family (two *heterosexual, married* parents) in order to function properly" (Snyder 2006, 10; emphasis in the original). In making this argument, the Christian Right ignores a "large body of social science research that confirms that children raised by gay or lesbian parents are not disadvantaged relative to their peers." For example, an array of child advocacy organizations, including the American Psychological Association, the American Academy of Pediatrics, and the National Association of Social Workers, all "recognize that gay and lesbian parents are just as good as heterosexual parents and that children thrive in gay-and lesbian-headed families" (Cahill 2007, 162).

The Christian Right and its supporters have defended traditional marriage ferociously—the issue has "special symbolic significance for the opponents of gay rights." They worry about any challenge to the institution of marriage and see same-sex marriage as "the ultimate sign of gay equality and the final blow to their traditional idea of marriage, which had been buffeted by thirty years of change" (Chauncey 2004, 145). And they are well aware that American acceptance of lesbians and gays has grown over time.

Antigay groups have also embraced the argument that "homosexuality is a choice" and that people can choose heterosexuality if they wish to do so and try hard enough. This has long been an argument of the Christian Right, which has supported reparative therapy, the process whereby people can be "cured" of their same-sex desires through therapy and support, which serves as the basis for the "ex-gay movement." This movement was founded in 1973 when the Love in Action ministry was created. A coalition of Christian Right groups paid for full-page advertisements in major US newspapers in 1998. These advertisements claimed that lesbians and gays could be "cured" through religious conversion (Cahill 2007, 171). Such assumptions have informed the Christian Right's campaign against same-sex marriage. For example, the Massachusetts Coalition for Marriage has justified its opposition to sexual-orientation nondiscrimination laws by stating on its website that "we do not believe that a person's sexual behavior is comparable to other protected categories such as race or sex—characteristics that are inborn, involuntary, immutable, innocuous and/or in the Constitution." The Christian Right has also used the "homosexuality as choice" claim to fight against programs that would create safe spaces in schools for kids who are grappling with sexual-orientation issues and against nondiscrimination laws. In doing so, they believe that rewarding "bad choices by granting 'special protections' or 'special rights' based on sexual behavior" is poor public policy (172).

The claim that "gay rights are special rights" goes back to Anita Bryant's Save Our Children campaign in the 1970s. It has been a fundamental tenet in the Christian Right's organizing efforts against same-sex marriage and other policy areas, including discussion of homosexuality in schools, sexual-orientation nondiscrimination laws, and domestic-partner recognition. Over time, the Christian Right has portrayed gay rights as "special rights" that would threaten "the civil rights of 'legitimate minorities,' that is, African Americans and other people of color" (Cahill 2007, 172). President Bush has used this language as well, most notably during the second presidential debate in October 2000. In response to the question of whether "gays and lesbians should have the same rights as other Americans," Bush said, "Yes. I don't think they ought to have special rights. But I think they ought to have the same rights." Bush was asked to clarify his use of the term *special rights*, and he said, "Well, it'd be if they're given special protective status" (173). These claims pivot on faulty rationale because, legally, there are no "special rights" in the United States.

The Christian Right has also argued that if sodomy laws are struck down and same-sex marriage is permitted, we would see many instances of bestiality, incest, pedophilia, and polygamy, all of which the Christian Right has long associated with homosexuality. Indeed, groups opposed to same-sex marriage often argue that "those seeking to legalize marriage for same-sex couples are also seeking the legalization of marriages among three or more people" (Cahill 2007, 176). Of course, no group advocating for same-sex marriage has argued for recognizing marriages between more than two people.

The second broad set of arguments against same-sex marriage emanates from activists within the lesbian and gay movements. For example, the most vocal critics of same-sex marriage within the movements argue from a feminist perspective that all marriage reinforces patriarchy and for that reason alone should be rejected. Paula Ettlebrick has articulated this position well: "Steeped in a patriarchal system that looks to ownership, property, and dominance of men over women as its basis, the institution of marriage long has been the focus of radical feminist revulsion. Marriage defines certain relationships as more valid than all others" (1997, 757). She develops her important critique even more fully in ways that cut to the heart of the dilemma underlying this book. For Ettlebrick and other critics of the assimilationist approach, "marriage will not liberate us as lesbians and gay men. In fact, it will constrain us, make us more invisible, force our assimilation into the mainstream, and undermine the goals of gay liberation" (758). Furthermore, she claims that the push for marriage undermines all other possible relationships that people might have with one another.

By looking to sameness and de-emphasizing our differences, the movements relinquish a position of power to transform marriage from an institution that emphasizes property and state regulation of relationships to an institution that recognizes one of many types of valid and respected relationships. Until the constitution is interpreted to respect and encourage differences, pursuing the legalization of same-sex marriage would be leading the movements into a trap; they would be demanding access to the very institution that, in its current form, would undermine the movements to recognize many different kinds of relationships. They would be perpetuating the elevation of married relationships and of "couples" in general, and further eclipsing other relationships of choice (Ettlebrick 1997, 759).

Michael Warner extends Ettlebrick's analysis by offering a scathing critique of marriage based on two arguments: first, it reinforces the worst elements of heteronormativity by "normalizing" the lesbian and gay movements; and second, by embracing same-sex marriage, the lesbian and gay movements are endorsing the real economic privileges associated with marriage as an institution in the United States, such as health-care coverage, inheritance rights, Social Security survivors' benefits, and tax breaks. Warner joins others in criticizing those national organizations that have "accepted the mainstreaming project and, in particular, the elevation of the marriage issue as the movement's leading goal" (1999, 46).

Like Warner, other critics worry about the primacy of marriage on the movements' political organizing and policy agenda. D'Emilio, for example, raises this important question as a possible response to the movements' focus on marriage in recent years: "What about *urgent* issues like AIDS prevention, homophobic violence, and the safety of queer youth, issues that legitimately might be termed matters of life and death?" (2007, 41). And Gary Mucciaroni joins those critics associated with BeyondMarriage.org by arguing that "the movement should stop making same-sex marriage a high priority and instead work to end the privileged position of marriage in legal entitlements and push for new legal arrangements that recognize and protect the majority of Americans who live in committed nonmarital relationships by separating government benefits and legal recognition from marital status. Many of the feelings of inferiority and disrespect that gay and lesbian couples experience arise from practical problems in daily life—like being denied control over medical decisions or having to pay inheritance taxes—and would be remedied with gaining civil unions or comprehensive packages of partner benefits" (2008, 268). Dean Spade's illuminating analysis of those who are transgender and the law points to the class and structural privilege of the same-sex marriage movement. Spade warns that the same-sex marriage movement is far too limiting, especially as a framing device: "the framing of marriage as the most essential legal need of queer people, and as the method through which queer people can obtain key benefits in many realms, ignores how race, class, ability, indigeneity, and immigration status determine access to those benefits and reduces the gay rights agenda to a project of restoring race, class, ability and immigration status privilege to the most privileged gays and lesbians" (2011, 62). Chapter 6 will explore these tensions over same-sex marriage when we discuss the movements' future organizing strategies and attempt to navigate possible common ground between those who call for a liberationist approach to political, social, and policy change and those who believe that the assimilationist perspective is more realistic and pragmatic.

Conclusion

This chapter began with several key questions: How has the fight for same-sex marriage affected the goals of the broader lesbian and gay movements? How has the Christian Right responded with its own organizing efforts? And what progress has been made in the fight for same-sex marriage? In answering these questions, we have placed the battle over same-sex marriage in its proper historical context. We have seen the role that the courts have played in advancing the cause of same-sex marriage over time, most notably in the *Baehr v. Lewin, Lawrence v. Texas, Goodridge v. Department of Public Health, United States v. Windsor,* and *Hollingsworth v. Perry* decisions. But we have also seen how all of these decisions have galvanized the Christian Right and other opponents of same-sex marriage.

Where do things stand now? One group of analysts believes that the term *marriage* is a major obstacle for many Americans: "They are torn between a desire to treat gay men and lesbians with equality and respect, on one hand, and core beliefs that marriage is a sacred institution designed by God, on the other. This suggests that it would be more profitable for gay and lesbian rights activists to focus first on building additional support for civil unions" (Wilcox et al. 2007, 239). The public supports civil unions in many states. But virtually all surveys reveal still-significant opposition to same-sex marriage, though that opposition is declining yearly, with young Americans leading the way. Indeed these public opinion developments have led Klarman to conclude accurately: "Once public opinion has shifted overwhelmingly in favor and many more states have enacted gay marriage, the Court will constitutionalize the emerging consensus and suppress resisting outliers. That is simply how constitutional law works in the United States" (2013, 207). And like other observers, Klarman recognizes that, "as more gays and lesbians have come out of the closet, the social environment has become more gay-friendly" (197). These developments have created a broader social context that is more conducive to support for same-sex marriage and adoption. In addition, Klarman offers the astute point that a major accomplishment of "gay marriage litigation from the perspective of the gay rights movement has been to 'open up the middle' by making domestic partnerships and civil unions seem more moderate by comparison" (211).

But we have also seen in this chapter that the Christian Right will use a full arsenal of resources and political tactics to undermine the promarriage forces at the grassroots level. And this undoubtedly will have an impact on American politics, as many politicians, certainly at the national level, will find the issue of same-sex marriage a difficult one to navigate. More and more Democrats are finding the political courage to openly support same-sex marriage, and even some Republicans, such as Senator Rob Portman (R-OH) are doing the same, though many other Republicans are largely hopeless on this issue (and other policy issues that we have discussed in this book).

But the other reality is that the issue does not enjoy the kind of fervent support among the larger lesbian and gay movements that is necessary to mount a sustained strategy for fighting the forces against same-sex marriage. Much of the conflict within the movements derives from the larger tension underlying this book regarding assimilationist and liberationist approaches to political and policy change. This tension grows out of the messy nature of social movements themselves, as we have seen. In this book's final chapter, we will explore possible ways that we might ameliorate this tension as we consider the movements' futures.

6

The Movements' Futures

Every successful social movement eventually moves from the unthinkable to the impossible to the inevitable.

—Laura Liswood, founder of Women World Leaders

Injustice anywhere is a threat to justice everywhere.

—Martin Luther King Jr.

Difference unites us. While each of these experiences can isolate those who are affected, together they compose an aggregate of millions whose struggles connect them profoundly. The exceptional is ubiquitous; to be entirely typical is the rare and only state.

—Andrew Solomon, *Far from the Tree: Parents, Children, and the Search for Identity*

ON THE NIGHT OF OCTOBER 6, 1998, A TWENTY-ONE-YEAR-OLD GAY University of Wyoming senior stopped in downtown Laramie for a drink at the Fireside Bar. One day later, he was found by a mountain biker "lashed to a fence on the outskirts of town, beaten, pistol-whipped, unconscious, and barely breathing" (Loffreda 2000, ix). The young man never regained consciousness and died five days later, on October 12. His name was Matthew Shepard. His murder, funeral, and the subsequent trials of his killers—Russell Henderson and Aaron McKinney, also from Laramie, also in their early twenties—received international attention.

Why did his murder happen? One explanation offered in the aftermath is that Matthew made a pass at his killers in a space that had become known as a "hospitable" place for lesbians and gays to gather, to share a drink, and to find the kind of community and solace that bars have often provided in the face of a hostile world. But another more important explanation is that we live in a country that fails to teach its children the importance of respecting and understanding racial, gender, and sexual-orientation differences. As one of my colleagues said to me in the wake of the murder, "This underscores the crucial importance of education." Had Henderson and McKinney been given the opportunity to confront their anxieties regarding their own sexualities and their views of those who fall outside the "heterosexual norm" in an educational setting many years before, perhaps the murder would not have happened. And had we had national hate-crimes legislation on the books at the time that applied to sexual orientation, perhaps the crime might not have occurred, but at least we would have had a clear policy regarding how to punish the perpetrators. But as we have seen in this book, we also live in a country where people who are lesbian, gay, bisexual, and transgender are reviled and targeted by many. For example, soon after Matthew Shepard's death, Fred Phelps, a defrocked minister from Kansas and creator of the Internet site GodHatesFags.com, "faxed reporters images of the signs he and his followers intended to carry at the funeral: 'Fag Matt in Hell,' 'God Hates Fags,' 'No Tears for Queers'" (Loffreda 2000, 18). The media's coverage of Phelps's attacks publicized his hatred and vitriol, thus giving them more attention than they deserved. Not to be outdone, in the wake of the September 11 attacks, the late Reverend Jerry Falwell, founder of the Moral Majority, said on the Reverend Pat Robertson's *700 Club*, "I really believe that the pagans and the abortionists, and the feminists, and the gays and the lesbians who are actually trying to make that an alternative lifestyle, the ACLU, People for the American Way, all of them who have tried to secularize America, I point the finger in their face and say 'you helped this happen'" (Duggan 2003, 43). His remarks were publicized and denounced by many, though once again the media saw fit to highlight them at a particularly difficult time for the country and the world. The revulsion expressed by Phelps and Falwell is reflected in the public debates that we have had about sex education, HIV/AIDS, military integration, and same-sex marriage (to name just a few of the most contentious issues) and in our laws. We are a country that forbids openly lesbian and gay people to get married, to serve in the military, to teach in our schools in many places, and, in most states, to adopt children as well.[1] It is no surprise, then, that the laws that we have crafted as a nation reflect a country that is and has been retrograde in its ability to have open, honest, mature, and dignified discussions of many of the issues underlying this book.

In light of these realities, what political organizing strategy is the most viable for addressing the policy issues discussed here? To what extent can we imagine a strategy that combines the best of what the assimilationist and liberationist perspectives have to offer? How much progress have we made in advancing the various issues of importance to the larger lesbian and gay movements? And why is educational curricular reform needed to help prevent the kind of vicious hate crimes that have been and are perpetrated against lesbians, gays, bisexuals, and transgender people? Before we can answer these questions, we must first review the strengths and weaknesses of the assimilationist and liberationist strategies in light of the analysis presented throughout this book. In doing so, we recognize that it is important for the members of any social movement to reflect critically upon strategies, tactics, accomplishments, and failures.

The Assimilationist and Liberationist Strategies Revisited

As we have already seen, much of the work of contemporary national and lesbian and gay organizations has relied on an insider assimilationist strategy that strives for access to those in power and is rooted in an interest-group and legislative-lobbying approach to change. The strategy is largely based on civil rights, legal reform, legitimation, political access, and visibility. It is an approach that works within the political and economic framework associated with classical liberal ideology. And it highlights the importance of allowing lesbians, gays, and bisexuals (but rarely those who are transgender) access to power and a seat at the table. This strategy often emphasizes national policymaking as opposed to organizing at the grassroots level, though in recent years the mainstream lesbian and gay movements have increasingly recognized the importance of organizing and educating at the local level.

The assimilationist approach recognizes that the American political system and the policy process growing out of that system are characterized by slow, gradual, incremental change. One way of thinking of political, policy, and cultural change is in terms of cycles of change. Incremental change means "creeping along" the path to reform, whereas more radical change means "leaping" toward more radical goals. The period of "creeping" is often associated with "strategic incoherence" on the part of social movements (D'Emilio 2000, 50). Assimilationists are typically more patient with creeping toward long-term movement goals, whereas liberationists are more likely to try to mount more radical and ambitious structural challenges to the system at large. The lesbian and gay movements have witnessed both, with three key moments of "leaping change" punctuating their history. The first leap forward occurred in the 1950s with the founding of the Mattachine Society and the Daughters of Bilitis, organizations that engaged in acts of courage and resistance, especially given the context of the times. By the time of the 1969 Stonewall Riot, the second great leaping moment, the rights-based strategy these groups called for seemed too assimilationist in the face of greater liberationist calls for change. The third major leap forward was framed "by the 1987 March on Washington and the debate over the military exclusion policy in 1993. Like gay liberation of the Stonewall era, activists in these years frequently used militant direct action tactics. But unlike the two earlier periods of leaping ahead, this one witnessed movement and community organizations sinking secure roots in every region of the country" (43).

We are now clearly in a period of creeping political, social, and policy change. Lesbians, gay men, bisexuals, and transgender individuals continue to be "outnumbered and despised." Political scientist Kenneth Sherrill has argued that "their quest for political power is disadvantaged by barriers to the formation of political community as well as by lack of access to significant power resources. The relative political powerlessness of gay people stands in contradistinction to their depiction by advocates of 'traditional values' as a powerful movement advancing a 'gay agenda' in American politics." Indeed, "the attention paid to the occasional electoral victories of openly lesbian and gay candidates distorts the reality that fewer than one tenth of 1% of all elected officials in the United States are openly lesbian, gay, or bisexual" (1996, 469). These numbers have not improved significantly since 1996. How can we expect creeping (or leaping) political and policy change when the larger political process is most often associated with the values and assumptions underlying heteronormativity? It is no surprise, then, that the lack of formal political power within the American policy process has yielded disappointing policy outcomes at all levels of government.

The quest for equal rights is at the core of the contemporary lesbian and gay rights movements' strategy. As we have seen throughout this book, this rights-based approach has dominated mainstream-movement thinking from the early years of the homophile movement to today's debates over the military-service ban and same-sex marriage. Over time, this rights-based strategy has pivoted on the state's relationship to lesbians and gay men. Lesbians and gay men have fought for the right to live their personal lives as fully and freely as possible from negative state intervention. At the same time, they have asked the state to intervene more positively to protect their ability to meet basic daily needs.

How have these issues manifested themselves politically? The movements have organized to abolish laws that restrict the right of individuals to engage in private, consensual sexual relations. In addition, they have fought against discrimination in employment, housing, and public accommodation and for equal legal protection. This claim of equal legal rights has led to the further demands that lesbians and gays should be entitled to have their intimate relationships recognized as marriages and to serve openly in the US military. These demands, if transformed by the State into rights, would enable lesbians and gays to enjoy the same privileges that are currently the province of heterosexuals. Finally, in light of the AIDS crisis, the movements have demanded that the State provide lesbians and gays with "distributive justice" in their right to pursue their sexual health, free from stigma and discrimination. These are the central elements of the rights-based assimilationist strategy, which have largely been unquestioned and unchallenged by the contemporary lesbian and gay movements.

How has this approach worked in the policy arenas that we have discussed? Same-sex marriage is the issue that has dwarfed nearly all others on the lesbian and gay movements' policy agenda in recent years. For a positive interpretation of the progress made in the fight for same-sex marriage and how that progress connects to larger movements' accomplishments, political scientist David Rayside claims:

> The United States is an unusual case, in part because of the extraordinary range of legal and political outcomes across states and localities. It is also unusual in several characteristics that impede the march to equity. But it is not as exceptional as is widely believed. A great majority of Americans now believe in extending recognition to lesbian and gay couples, if only a minority favor marriage. Most large corporations extend their family benefits coverage to the same-sex partners of employees. A steadily growing number of U.S. states and municipalities extend some form of recognition to such partners of their own employees. Openly lesbian and gay characters make regular appearances on American television dramas, even if their portrayals have limitations. In everyday life, sexual diversity is as visible in American society as in any. And across a wide range of regions and localities in the United States, countless lesbians, gays, bisexuals, and the transgendered are asserting their right to be visible. (2007, 361)

However, Rayside's positive assessment must be viewed in light of the Christian Right's success at mobilizing to fight same-sex marriage at the state and national levels in recent years. John D'Emilio is certainly right to remind us that the legal-rights strategy pursued by the lesbian and gay movements on this issue has largely been a failure thus far. Indeed, "the battle to win marriage equality through the courts has done something that no other campaign or issue in our movement has done: it has created a vast body of *new* antigay law" (2006, 10). Given this failure, should same-sex marriage occupy such an exalted position on the movements' organizing agenda? That is the question that should generate considerable discussion among the movements' activists.

The struggle to allow lesbians and gays to serve openly in the military finally reached fruition when President Obama overturned the ban in December 2010 with the support of Congress and the outstanding organizing efforts of the Servicemembers Legal Defense Network and other lesbian and gay rights organizations over the years. The campaign faced stiff opposition in light of the "Don't Ask, Don't Tell" policy passed by Congress and signed into law by a so-called friend, Bill Clinton. Integration of the military has also been an important hallmark of the assimilationist rights-based strategy. And as we know, much work still needs to be done so that people who serve in the United States military can serve openly and honestly free from discrimination and sexual harassment.

In the area of HIV/AIDS policy, we have seen attention shift in recent years. During the Bush years, a more conservative Congress and a president whose "compassionate conservatism" extended only as far as the global AIDS crisis put adequate funding for the Ryan White CARE Act in dispute. As a result, the many policy challenges growing out of the domestic HIV/AIDS crisis receded from the spotlight. These challenges included funding for community-based and local AIDS initiatives, recruiting committed and qualified people to the AIDS service-delivery communities at the local level given the paucity of resources available to pay them proper wages, and a sense that the AIDS crisis is not as immediate, since the advent of protease inhibitors has allowed people to live longer, "healthier," and more productive lives with HIV. But the Obama administration has done much better in focusing attention on the domestic HIV/AIDS crisis, as reflected in significant policy reforms at the federal level, most notably his December 2009 spending bill that eliminated federal funding for abstinence-only programs for the first time in nearly thirty years. At the same time, however, HIV/AIDS has not received the kind of urgent attention from the LGBT movements' national organizations that we have a right to expect, given the ongoing HIV/AIDS health-care policy and service-delivery challenges faced at all levels of government and in communities throughout the United States. And as we have seen, the primacy of same-sex marriage on the movements' policy agenda has displaced the urgency of fighting for a thoughtful and well-funded HIV/AIDS policy at the national level that would provide adequate resources to communities, health-care professionals, and community organizations battling the AIDS crisis on a daily basis.

But if the rights-based assimilationist strategy has provided us merely with the "virtual equality" that Urvashi Vaid and other liberationists deride, do the movements stand to gain more by embracing a more fully developed liberationist strategy and policy agenda? And what would such a strategy and agenda look like in practice? Scholar and activist Liz Highleyman offers an insightful overview of the challenges facing those who embrace a liberationist approach:

> Queer radicals today face a dilemma. Should we try to steer the mainstream GLBT movement in a more progressive direction or work with other progressive activists in groups that are not queer-focused? Can—and should—a movement focused on gay and lesbian identity expand to encompass a full range of progressive causes? And how can a movement organized around sexual identity embrace the intersecting identities of gay men and lesbians (and bisexuals? and transgendered people?) who are also women, people of color, disabled, youth, or working class? (2002, 110)

These theoretical and practical considerations challenge the larger lesbian and gay movements in compelling ways, and, as we have seen, they have been the source of considerable disagreement and tension among the movements over time. These are questions that the Gay Liberation Front was forced to confront coming out of Stonewall in the early 1970s. Activist-scholar Michael Bronski provides an excellent rationale for embracing a broader coalition-based, progressive organizing strategy:

> We need to reassess what kind of a movement we want it to be. Will it be a movement that continues arguing, with diminishing success, for the rights of its own people—and even at that, only for those who want to formalize a relationship? Or will we argue for a broader vision of justice and fairness that includes all Americans? If the movement does not choose the latter course, we risk becoming not just irrelevant, but a political stumbling block to progressive social change in general. (2006, 18)

Bronski's vision will require the movements to develop a broad coalition-building strategy, which is no easy task, especially given the disagreements among lesbians, gays, bisexuals, and transgender individuals over what the movements' central issues should be and how they should be addressed. It is to that coalition-building strategy that we now turn.

Coalition Politics

If our goal is to move beyond a narrow rights-based assimilationist strategy, one that is often focused on identity politics, we have two options. The first is what Vaid calls "the coalition-around-an-issue strategy," which involves working with people who share interests in the same issues. The second option is much more ambitious because it requires people to create a "common movement." The coalition-around-an-issue strategy could lead to the recognition of common ground, which is the precursor to a common movement, whereby individuals come together to talk about issues of interest and strategies for working toward common goals that have been identified through participatory democratic processes. Vaid poses three important questions organizers should ask at the outset of any campaign or political project: "How does this issue affect different populations within the gay and lesbian community? Can we build coalitions within the non-gay community around this issue? How can we educate the different segments of our community on the direct way this project or campaign affects them?" (1995, 303).

Beyond these questions, the movements need to identify the kinds of issues that will foster the building of short- and long-term alliances rooted in a radical democratic politics. Coalitions have surely been the catalyst behind virtually all of the movements' legislative victories, including the Americans with Disabilities Act, the Hate Crimes Statistics Act, the Ryan White CARE Act, the progay local laws that have been passed and the antigay referenda that have been defeated throughout the United States (Vaid 1997, 7). Indeed, perhaps the best recent example of the positive policy results of coalition building is when President Obama signed the Matthew Shepard and James Byrd, Jr., Hate Crimes Prevention Act into law on October 28, 2009. Antigay "violence rose to the national agenda with the murder of Matthew Shepard" on October 6, 1998 (Vaid 2012, 188). And racial violence had received considerable attention earlier that year when James Byrd, an African American man, was tied to the back of a pick-up truck and dragged to his death by three white men (two had ties to white supremacy organizations) in Jasper, Texas. The Byrd and

Shepard families (and their many supporters) came together to lobby national government officials over the course of a decade on behalf of federal hate crimes legislation. Their organizing work fell on deaf ears in the George W. Bush White House but received a positive and enthusiastic reception once Barack Obama assumed the presidency.

The importance of coalition building certainly has not been lost on those who are concerned with policy making at the national level. Tom Sheridan, a former high-ranking official at the AIDS Action Council, explains, "Coalition politics is effective because it's the hardest to get people to do. The Hill really respects its speaker because they figure that if you can get up here with a coalition that big and that diverse and have everyone agreeing on something, you must have hit something" (Andriote 1999, 230). A central goal of radical democratic politics is to build permanent coalitions around political strategies and concrete public policies that cut across race, class, and gender divides, coalitions that will be ready to respond to the Christian Right's distortions in all political arenas. Vaid believes that this important class-based organizing work will require a consolidation of "the presently fractured infrastructure of progressive queer institutions. We need a new federation that unites groups working for racial, economic, sexual and gender justice under a meaningful, common rubric." Vaid believes that such a "seriously organized and funded federation would enable the groups to actually have a greater influence on the national movement agenda" (2012, 98–99). The goal is to organize around issues that provide "a comprehensive system of social and economic protections for all families and household groupings" (Bronski 2006, 19). But Vaid also recognizes the challenges to this important goal: "as social movements that have come before the LGBT struggle have clearly shown, formal equality—and even progress towards greater cultural recognition of one's humanity—can be achieved while leaving larger structural manifestations of inequality and deeper cultural prejudice intact" (2012, 8). What issues might inspire individuals to work together to build a common movement?

Comprehensive Medical Care

"Comprehensive medical care will never happen in the United States. As a result, we need to be much more pragmatic about how we approach health care" (personal interview, February 5, 1997). That is the view of one member of the national movement's elite class. The pragmatism to which this person refers characterized the Clinton White House's health-care reform efforts in the administration's first term. When Bill Clinton took office in January 1993, some thirty-nine million Americans lacked adequate medical insurance. As I write this in the late summer of 2013, that number has ballooned to forty-six million, with many more Americans close to the edge of financial disaster because of escalating health care costs. It is in the interest of the lesbian and gay movements to support major health-care policy reform that moves toward comprehensive medical care in light of HIV/AIDS and the exorbitant costs of the medicines that people depend on to survive.

The Affordable Care Act, President Obama's signature domestic policy initiative, is certainly a step in the right direction. Indeed one commentator has accurately pointed out that "most of the changes happening under ACA benefit the general population, but because of the many disparities that lesbian, gay, bisexual, and transgender (LGBT) people and their families face—in employment, societal misunderstanding or discrimination, and health—the changes will greatly benefit LGBT lives." Here are some of the concrete benefits associated with the ACA: the state insurance exchanges that prevent discrimination against LGBT people and their families; insurance coverage for young people under twenty-six; insurance for people who have pre-existing conditions; federal assistance for individuals and families who qualify as low income; increased medical care coverage by community health-care centers; insuring that insurance premiums are targeted to health care and not to bonuses and salaries; and dissemination of "information on domestic partner insurance benefits." All of these reforms represent significant progress even as they stop far short of comprehensive medical care. And as Brad Jacklin correctly argues, "the Affordable Care Act does much to increase the rates at which LGBT people and their families, indeed all Americans, are covered for the basics of health care to the catastrophes. There's more work to be done, especially for transgender people, who still find their needs excluded from most insurance plans" (2012). We also need to finance further research and support for women's health issues, including breast, cervical, and ovarian cancers. And that work should include an organizing strategy that embraces comprehensive medical care.

How might we pay for comprehensive health care? Coalitions of citizens' groups can challenge the federal government to reduce spending for costly and unneeded weapons systems and to cut military spending on reckless military incursions of the kind that we witnessed in Iraq. These moneys could then be used to develop a comprehensive national health insurance program over time. This will not be easy, given the realities of the well-entrenched military-industrial complex. Such a plan would likely also require a substantial, progressive tax increase that would place the financial burden on those who can best afford it, no easy task given the power the wealthy exercise in the American policy process.

Comprehensive Government Responses to HIV/AIDS

As we saw in Chapter 3, AIDS has had devastating consequences on many communities in the United States, not to mention countries throughout the world. With this in mind, we need support for a new AIDS movement that recognizes AIDS as a global problem and also takes into account the specific needs of lesbians, gay men, African Americans, poor people, and others who are marginalized in American society.

This new AIDS movement envisions a society that refuses to stigmatize sex but instead provides accessible information about safer sex practices. We need a new AIDS movement that organizes on behalf of legalizing and financing the distribution of clean needles in inner cities throughout the United States. If these public policy goals are to be achieved, they will need the support of coalitions of diverse individuals committed to humane AIDS policies. But they will also need the support of the mainstream lesbian and gay movements, which appear to have lost interest in AIDS in recent years, as same-sex marriage has dominated their agenda. ACT UP / Philadelphia provides us with a model of how community-based organizing can link funding for programs in the United States with funding for programs on a global scale. The following appeared on the organization's website, as an announcement for a political rally to take place on November 29, 2006, that featured the following policy demands:

- $2.6 billion for the Ryan White CARE Act, the life-line for people living with AIDS in the U.S. The Care Act has been largely flat-funded since President Bush came into office, even as the number of HIV infections has continued to climb.

- $8 billion to train, retain and sustain enough healthcare workers in Africa to achieve universal access. Without significant new investments in the health workforce in Africa, current investments

> such as the President's Emergency Plan for AIDS Relief will not succeed. (http://www.critpath.org/actup, n.p.)

ACT UP / Philadelphia has been on the cutting edge of linking community-based organizing with global concerns. In recent years, it has protested the Obama administration's flatlining of funding for global AIDS initiatives. Its work is an excellent model for organizations at all levels associated with the American policy process.

In addition, the movements need to support those community institutions that were created in the midst of the epidemic's major infection wave in the 1980s. The movements need to continue to distribute information about HIV/AIDS prevention; organize to challenge discrimination; pressure federal, state, and local governments around AIDS-related issues; and provide the changing social services and support systems that become necessary as people who are HIV positive live longer. As they build coalitions with others (outside the lesbian and gay movements) around HIV/AIDS, they must work to ensure that more people have access to the information and drugs associated with these medical advances. This is challenging but crucial work, especially because some younger gays coming of age perceive AIDS as not nearly the threat that it was during the 1980s and 1990s, given the development of drugs that have allowed some to live "normal" lives.

Support for Lesbian, Gay, Bisexual, and Transgender Youth Issues

One of the most serious issues facing the lesbian and gay movements is the problem of teen suicide. One Canadian study "claims to provide the most compelling proof to date of a link between homosexuality and youth suicide, concluding that gay and bisexual males are nearly 14 times more at risk than their heterosexual contemporaries of making a serious attempt on their own lives" (King 1996, 41). A more recent study of Oregon youth found that "gay, lesbian and bisexual teens are five times more likely than their heterosexual counterparts to commit suicide but a supportive environment in their schools and communities can make a difference, new research suggests. Suicide is the leading cause of death among young adults from ages 15–24, and lesbian, gay, and bisexual teens are more likely to attempt suicide." In support of the study's conclusions, the lead researcher, Columbia University's Mark Hatzenbuehler, concluded that "the results of this study are pretty compelling. When communities support their gay young people, and schools adopt anti-bullying and anti-discrimination policies that specifically protect lesbian, gay, and bisexual youth, the risk of attempted suicide by all young people drops, especially for lgb youth" (Welsh 2011). The suicide of Rutgers University freshman Tyler Clementi, who jumped off the George Washington Bridge in New York City in September 2010, garnered tremendous publicity in light of the fact that his Rutgers freshman roommate, Dharun Ravi, posted a video on the internet of him having sex with another man. This tragic case raises many questions about cyberbullying, homophobia, and outing, and the resources that educational institutions (including high schools and junior high schools) have in place that might prevent such tragedies. The suicide of 14-year-old Jamie Rodemeyer in western New York in September 2011 is another tragic case of a boy who was consistently tormented by his classmates because he was gay. His case is particularly noteworthy because "it is a classic case of bullying: he was aggressively and repeatedly victimized" (Boyd and Marwick, 2011). And in February 2008, a 15-year-old out gay student, Lawrence King, was fatally shot by a classmate in Oxnard, California, after King had been repeatedly harassed in school. This case received considerable national publicity and is the subject of a documentary film, *Valentine Road*, released in October 2013. These sad stories are a reminder of the internal pressures that young people face as they struggle with sexual identity concerns and wrestle with all of the challenges of coming out of the closet. UCLA researcher Ilan H. Meyer explains it well: "there's a stress that's involved with concealing" (Schwartz 2012, 56). And Robert Kim has concluded, based on his research, that "bullying of [LGBT students and those perceived as LGBT] stems largely from discomfort with students who do not conform to traditional gender roles in their appearance or behavior, i.e., who are gender-nonconforming" (Biegel 2010, 117–118). Sociologist C. J. Pascoe thinks that we need to focus our research and attention on masculinity and in the schools: "What does not seem to be happening at the level of legislation, in online environments, or in academic research, is a discussion of the role of masculinity (apart from football perhaps) in homophobic harassment and heteronormative behavior. . . . Researchers and those who care about and work with youth need to begin to ask about the role of masculinity in all of these tragedies. This is what the conversation needs to be about, not some generic discussion about bullying or homophobia" (Pascoe 2012, xiv). And as Jason

Cianciotto and Sean Cahill point out accurately, as LGBT youth come out at a much earlier age, school administrators and policymakers face a number of interrelated public policy challenges relating to "school safety, curricular, and other education policy issues at the intersection of sexual orientation, gender identity, and public education. Self-identification at an earlier age can expose LGBT youth to rejection, harassment, and violence at home and at school, creating a greater need for appropriate advice, comprehensive and age-appropriate sex education, and referrals to available resources from supportive adults" (2012, 3).

Fortunately, there are organizations that provide support for those contemplating suicide around sexual identity concerns, organizations whose work is invaluable in the absence of a supportive environment for youth at home and in schools. The Trevor Project, which "is the leading national organization providing crisis intervention and suicide prevention services to lesbian, gay, bisexual, transgender and questioning youth" (www.thetrevorproject.org), has deservedly received considerable national attention. Another project aimed at supporting young people struggling with sexual identity concerns is Dan Savage's YouTube campaign, ItGetsBetter.org. The campaign features an array of lesbian, gay, bisexual, and transgender adults discussing their experiences with harassment when they were enduring their challenging teenage years. A subsequent book associated with the project, *It Gets Better: Coming Out, Overcoming Bullying, and Creating a Life Worth Living,* offers a collection of essays and testimonials targeted for teens and written by celebrities, everyday people, and political leaders. The book features an introductory essay by President Obama and offers essays by the transgender author and academic Jennifer Finney Boylan; the first out bishop in the Episcopal Church, Gene Robinson; lesbian activist and movements' analyst Urvashi Vaid; novelist Michael Cunningham; former US secretary of state Hillary Rodham Clinton; fashion designer Tim Gunn; lesbian author and graphic designer Alison Bechdel; and Senator Al Franken (D-MN), among others. Savage's campaign has understandably received considerable positive publicity, but it has also garnered criticism, primarily that the message itself is too passive. Kids need to know, so the critics understandably argue, that things do not just "get better," on their own and that it takes considerable organizing and educational work for structural conditions to improve for young people who are wrestling with sexual and gender identity concerns. Critics understandably worry that the message of the campaign is a passive call for accepting the status quo. But Savage's campaign has helped to inspire conversations about how to better support young people (and others) struggling with sexual identity and gender identity challenges in their daily lives. The resulting publicity has made a vital contribution to the broader conversations about suicide prevention that simply must be had.

While there may be disagreements about how to best support students who are coming out and who do not conform to what society deems to be "normal," there is little disagreement over this unfortunate reality: lesbian, gay, bisexual, and transgender youth are often subjected to considerable harassment in school. A significant number report having been physically assaulted as well.[2] One organization that is doing pioneering work in this area reports that "eight out of ten students are still harassed at school" (glsen.org). There is a connection between the harassment faced by lesbian and gay youth in their schools and suicide. Once again, these issues need a committed coalition of groups to come together to protect and promote the well-being of all our youth, but especially that of lesbian, gay, bisexual, and transgender youth, who, although they are particularly at risk, are often ignored in social policy. An organization that has done invaluable outreach work in this area is the Gay, Lesbian, and Straight Education Network (GLSEN), which was established in 1990. GLSEN's goal is to make America's schools safe for all youth: "We believe that a quality k-12 education is a fundamental right of every American. To that end, we work with elected officials and other policy makers at the local, state, and federal levels to ensure that the best and most inclusive safe schools policies are considered, passed, and implemented" (glsen.org). They have focused on four major fronts: (1) a fight for new laws that would extend equal protection to all students regardless of sexual orientation; (2) efforts to change the attitudes of all those who influence daily life in schools—"from public policy leaders in Washington, DC to state superintendents to local school board members"; (3) providing materials that can help train teachers about lesbian, gay, bisexual, and transgender issues in ways that help stop harassment and violence; and (4) organizing for change by strengthening grassroots activism (*GLSEN Fundraising and Information Newsletter* 2000, 3). GLSEN's national organization is located in New York City; it has eighty-five chapters nationwide. It plays a vital role in establishing a registry of Gay-Straight Alliances (www.gsanetwork.org) throughout the United States, "student clubs that, as of 2008, have been established in 4,000 schools around the country. The first such alliance was proposed by a straight student who wanted to curb bullying and harassment of fellow students who were gay" (Brody, 2011).

A number of other organizations already represent the interests of lesbian, gay, bisexual, and transgender youth. At the national level, there is the National Youth Advocacy Coalition (NYAC), which was formally established in 1994. It attempts to educate members of Congress and other decision makers on youth-related issues. NYAC also pushes other organizations to "develop the capacity to represent the concerns of gay, lesbian, bisexual, and transgendered people." All too often the national organizations discussed in this book largely ignore youth. Since its creation in 1994, NYAC has worked on a number of youth-related issues: supporting student groups in high school and even on some college campuses, supporting students who have been harassed in schools, fighting against federal funding cuts in programs that benefit youth, working on suicide issues in the context of mental health services, addressing youth substance abuse, supporting youth-related HIV education and treatment programs, and addressing youth homelessness (personal interview with NYAC staff member, March 4, 1997).

All of these important issues deserve a much higher profile in the contemporary lesbian and gay movements. Stuart Biegel, who is an expert on the interrelated issues of harassment and bullying of young people in the schools, believes that "not only has bullying by fellow students in a school setting consistently been found to have a negative impact on everyone's ability to learn, but recent research has also shown that bullying is more common and more potentially damaging to children than was previously thought" (Biegel 2010, 118). He warns that "studies continue to show that LGBTs feel disproportionately unsafe in school and that the mistreatment they face interferes with their ability to succeed. Gay and gender-nonconforming students often stop attending classes regularly and many drop out, run away from home, or attempt suicide" (xvii). Though hundreds of local and regional organizations provide social and educational services to lesbian and gay youth at the grassroots level, many lack the resources to provide services to the extent they are needed. In addition, in many small towns and rural communities throughout the United States, these crucial resources are nonexistent. This set of issues poses a unique opportunity for the lesbian and gay movements to build coalitions with others around providing basic services and support for all of our youth. It also opens the door to discussions about what can be done in the schools, where young people spend so much time in the formative years of their lives.

Education for Understanding of and Respect for Difference

Given that schools have long been regarded as having important responsibilities for the moral development of youth, it is no surprise that the Christian Right has organized in communities throughout the United States to prevent the discussion of sexual orientation in school curricula. These efforts have been generally effective, thus reinforcing the antilesbian and antigay climate in virtually all American educational institutions. Lesbian, gay, bisexual, and transgender students are the targets of daily verbal harassment, and some are physically abused as well. Educational institutions reinforce the larger society's heterosexism by tolerating antigay jokes and harassment and by promoting heterosexual coupling (Button, Rienzo, and Wald 1997, 139). As we have already seen, suicide and the threat of suicide are serious problems for adolescents who are struggling with how society treats their homosexuality.

In the 1990s, schools became an arena for the politics of lesbian and gay rights, as activists targeted school boards in an effort to persuade them to adopt curricula that promote nonjudgmental discussions of homosexuality and safe-sex education within the context of AIDS. Educator Karen Harbeck believes that when homosexuality and education come together for public discussion, they provoke "one of the most publicly volatile and personally threatening debates in our national history" (Button, Rienzo, and Wald 1997, 148). In 1992 New York City emerged as a battleground between the Christian Right and the lesbian and gay grassroots movements when Joseph Fernandez, then chancellor of the city's school system, attempted to implement his Children of the Rainbow multicultural curriculum. This curriculum was the "first-grade portion of the multicultural Rainbow Curriculum, which dealt with, among other issues, gay and lesbian families" (Bronski 1998, 133). Sexual orientation occupied a minor, but important, part of the entire plan; the curriculum was rooted in the assumption that the potential for homosexuality exists in students. Children of the Rainbow articulated this assumption in the following way: "Teachers of first graders have an opportunity to give children a healthy sense of identity at an early age. Classes should include references to lesbians and gays in curricular areas and should avoid exclusionary practices by presuming a person's sexual orientation, reinforcing stereotypes, or speaking of lesbians and gays as 'they' or 'other.'" Two related books chosen for classroom use were *Heather Has Two Mommies* and *Daddy's Roommate.* Children of the Rainbow and the broader multicultural Rainbow Curriculum received the support of former mayor David Dinkins in addition to Chancellor Fernandez.

The Christian Right responded to this curricular initiative with disdain and aggressive political organizing. New York's Roman Catholic archdiocese and a coalition of right-wing community groups organized against the curriculum while it was still being developed and considered for adoption. The conservative Family Defense Council distributed a flyer that said, "We will not accept two people of the same sex engaged in sex practices as 'family.' . . . In the fourth grade the Chancellor would demonstrate to pupils how to use condoms. . . . He would teach our kids that sodomy is acceptable but virginity is something weird" (Bronski 1998, 133). Ultimately, Fernandez lost his job as a result of the controversy generated by the Rainbow Curriculum, giving the Christian and antigay Right a major victory.

The highly visible curriculum battle in New York City is just one of many battles that have occurred in communities across the country with respect to teaching about issues relating to homosexuality and difference. The Christian Right is well ahead of the movements in challenging education-for-difference efforts in communities throughout the United States. They often attack local antibullying campaigns and "charge that liberals and gay rights groups are using the antibullying banner to pursue a hidden 'homosexual agenda,' implicitly endorsing, for example, same-sex marriage" (Eckholm 2010). Local school boards in some communities have been stacked with candidates supported by the Christian Right, making them morally and culturally conservative. This is the reality that the movements must face if they hope to reach out and build coalitions with others who have been the targets of hate and discrimination. The importance of education cannot be overestimated. In institutions where difficult issues are supposed to be examined with understanding and respect for difference, lesbian and gay teachers often remain closeted for fear of harassment, ridicule, and, even more seriously, loss of their jobs. Stuart Biegel identifies the challenges that the lesbian and gay movements face in this crucial area well:

> There's been so much focus on LGBT youth and rightly so, but not as much focus on educators. In many parts of the country, sizable numbers of parents and particularly sizeable numbers of folks in conservative religious communities are not comfortable with the idea of a gay or lesbian or transgendered person teaching their kids. Even though in the public sector educators do have the right to be out, there is great pressure on them to remain closeted and keep their identities to themselves. Instead of seeing LGBT educators as a valuable resource who can help LGBT youth, too many school districts are trying to keep them under wraps, so to speak. (Rogers 2010)

To the extent that the Christian and antigay Right continues to create a context for these sorts of attitudes, it challenges the fundamental tenets of the lesbian and gay liberation movements that are at the core of this book. Although winning the passage of assimilationist civil rights, antidiscrimination, or hate-crime laws may provide some tangible benefits for lesbians and gays, these measures will not challenge prejudices and fears that are deeply rooted. Properly trained and committed educators at all levels of education are in the best position to do so.

Hate Crimes

As we have already seen, the brutal murders of Matthew Shepard and James Byrd prompted a national debate over the merits of federal hate-crimes legislation that affords federal agencies jurisdiction over bias incidents. Shepard's and Byrd's deaths and the murder of Billy Jack Gaither, who in February 1999 was beaten to death and whose body was burned in Sylacauga, Alabama, galvanized the lesbian and gay movements and their straight allies around the Hate Crimes Prevention Act, signed into law by President Obama on October 28, 2009, but the reality is that hundreds of lesbians, gays, bisexuals, and transgender people (as well as people suspected of falling into these categories) have been the targets of bias-related crimes over the years, often with little response from the police, government officials, schoolteachers, principals, and community leaders.

The movements can build a number of natural coalitions around hate-related violence, such as with advocates for battered women and civil rights groups. If these groups fail to work together and instead organize themselves according to their separate identities, there will be no long-lasting coalition to address the sources of hate crimes. Hate-crimes legislation at the federal, state, and local levels is an important symbolic gesture, but most forms of the legislation address the issue *after* a crime has been committed. What is desperately needed is a long-term coalition to explore how the sources of hate crimes can be targeted before they occur. Many of these conversations are already occurring in communities throughout the United States, but the problem also needs the formal involvement of educators. Their research-based insights into the roots of bias crimes can help communities devise appropriate interventions, and they can also push for curricular innovations in schools that emphasize respect for and understanding of diversity.

Support for Transpeople

The lesbian and gay movements have struggled over time with integrating the day-to-day challenges facing transpeople into broader movement goals. Scholar Stuart Biegel has accurately pointed out that "the right to be out for transgender persons can prove to be quite different—both in its conception and in its application—from the right to be out on the basis of sexual orientation" (2010, 176). Andrew Solomon reminds us that "gay and trans are separate categories" and that "trans children are not manifesting sexuality; they are manifesting gender" (2012, 600). How are these differences manifested within the transgender community?

> Many gender nonconforming people, for example, may want to be out only as male or female. This is who they are, and this is how they want to be seen. Transgender, for at least some of these folks, is not necessarily the equivalent of an identity at all but may be the description of a process that they went through and have now completed. For others, transgender may be seen as primarily or perhaps even critically as the equivalent of a medical condition. Still others, of course, view transgender as central to their very persona, and it is highly important for these persons to be able to identify openly." (Biegel 2010, 176)

Another problem is that "many middle-class gay people don't truly know what transgender means, and when they do, some feel that transpeople are splitting the movement" (Beam 2007, 106), thus undermining the more mainstream, assimilationist goals of the lesbian and gay movements. Indeed, a further problem is that the "successes" of the lesbian and gay movements as described throughout this book and celebrated among mainstream lesbian and gay rights organizations—overturning the military ban, progress on same-sex marriage and adoption, for example—do not resonate as positively in the trans activist community. The trans community is understandably much more concerned with "economic marginalization, vulnerability to imprisonment, and other forms of state violence" (Spade 2011, 68). Transpeople face bias on a day-to-day basis, bias that can sometimes erupt into physical violence. A September 2010 survey of 6,450 transgender people released by the National Center for Transgender Equality and the National Gay and Lesbian Task Force "found that 97% of respondents experienced on-the-job harassment, ranging from colleagues repeatedly using the incorrect pronoun as a means of mocking to outright physical assaults" (Harmon 2009/2010, 50). In addition, a "web of inconsistent administrative rules governing gender—that produce 'significant vulnerability' must also be addressed by the larger lesbian and gay movements. These 'legal and administrative systems of domination' include prisons, welfare programs, foster care, drug treatment centers, homeless shelters, [and] job training centers that employ rigid gender binaries" (Spade 2011, 12). The good news is that there has been more mainstream media attention devoted to trans issues over the last twenty years or so. In addition, a new "critical trans politics" is emerging from membership-based organizations, including Southerners on New Ground, the Audre Lorde Project, Fabulous Educated Radicals for Community Empowerment, the Sylvia Rivera Law Project, and Communities United Against Violence (Spade 2011, 188). The challenge for the larger lesbian and gay movements is to build this new critical trans politics into the movements' strategies that have become much more aligned with assimilationist goals.

The Employment Non-Discrimination Act

The vast majority of lesbians and gay men can be fired for their sexual orientation, despite the fact that more than ten states and many cities now outlaw such job discrimination. There is a need for federal legislation, such as the proposed Employment Non-Discrimination Act (ENDA), that would ban discrimination in employment based on sexual orientation and gender identity. Support and publicity for this legislation serve an important symbolic purpose as well, because they highlight the reality of employment discrimination. Despite the fact that the legislation was defeated by the US Senate in 1996 by the narrowest of margins, ENDA will probably not pass in the short term unless a decidedly more liberal Congress is elected with a Democrat in the White House. President George W. Bush consistently opposed ENDA because he believed, erroneously, that it would constitute "special treatment." While President Obama supports ENDA, he has received considerable criticism from some within the lesbian and gay movements for refusing "to issue an executive order barring discrimination by federal contractors based on sexual orientation or gender identity, while ENDA remains stuck in Congress." GetEQUAL, an organization devoted to achieving "full legal and social equality" for lesbians, gays, bisexuals, those who are transgender, and those who identify as queer, organized a protest interruption of a June 2013 speech by Michelle Obama, in protest of the president's failure to be more aggressive in fighting for legal equality for all in the workplace. In addition, Get Equal activists were arrested in June 2013 during a protest in the Washington, DC, office of Speaker John Boehner (R-OH) (Terkel 2013).

ENDA has been introduced in every congressional term except one since 1994, but it still has not passed the Congress. The version introduced in 2007 was the first to include gender identity in proposed ENDA protections, which was controversial within the gay and lesbian movements. Democrats controlled both houses of Congress at that time, so transgender activists and their supporters believed that it was a propitious time to expand ENDA protections. "But when a preliminary vote in the House of Representatives reportedly failed to muster adequate support, Massachusetts representative Barney Frank split ENDA into two separate bills, one with gender identity protections, one without. The former died in committee; the latter passed the House, only to die in the Senate." Many movements' organizations criticized Frank's strategic move as undermining basic human rights for transpeople. Human Rights Campaign, which supported the bill without protection for transpeople in an effort to gather the necessary political support for lesbians and gays, was targeted by transgender activists and their allies, who protested their fund-raising dinners being held throughout the United States. All of this raised the important human rights and strategic question: "Are transgender individuals really part of the 'gay community'?" (Harmon 2009/2010, 51). In recent years, the proposed ENDA legislation has continued to include gender identity.

Employment rights are a set of issues where lesbians and gays can build an effective coalition with other civil rights groups, while recognizing that how the issue is framed will determine the American public's support.

Gregory B. Lewis and Marc A. Rogers have studied both demographic and attitudinal sources of support for lesbian and gay employment rights. They conclude:

> Americans support the concept of equal rights more than they favor laws to enforce them, especially when they are asked to expand legal coverage rather than just to support existing laws. If the debate over gay employment protections can be framed as simply preventing employment discrimination, gay rights supporters should garner majority support, but opponents have frequently been able to reframe the issue around morality or to focus attention on the occupations where public distrust is greatest, especially elementary school teachers. Defusing fears of gay teachers will be a key issue in winning employment protections for gay and lesbian people in all occupations. (1999, 130)

These findings suggest that passage of ENDA will require a broad-based coalition of civil rights activists to come together to educate the public about the importance of this legislation and to rally support around a basic civil rights issue. In the meantime, the lesbian and gay movements will need to work with coalitions of civil rights supporters at the state and local levels to combat job discrimination based on sexual orientation.

Barriers to Building Coalitions

Perhaps the most important barrier to building coalitions is that a narrow assimilationist rights-based organizing strategy is the political, cultural, and economic ethos of American society, as enshrined in the Bill of Rights and the Constitution, which uphold the importance of protecting *individual* rights. We are socialized to think in terms of protecting the individual's right to life, liberty, and happiness—often defined in ways that emphasize the acquisition of private wealth. An identity politics that embraces narrow civil rights goals, such as same-sex marriage or overturning the ban on lesbians and gays in the military, reinforces the primacy of the individual. And, in fact, there are practical advantages to a narrowly circumscribed identity-based organizing strategy, as writer and activist Suzanne Pharr suggests. These include "'clarity of focus in tactics and strategies, self-examination and education apart from the dominant culture' and the 'development of solidarity and group bonding. Creating organizations based on identity allows us to have visibility and collective power, to advance concerns that otherwise would never be recognized because of our marginalization within the dominant society'" (Vaid 1995, 286). Pharr's analysis goes a long way toward explaining why narrow identity politics will continue to dominate the mainstream lesbian and gay movements' strategic thinking, despite the setbacks of the Clinton and Bush eras and even disappointment with the Obama presidency. And Vaid reminds us that a narrowly focused identity politics that emphasizes traditional notions of families may "reproduce the isolation and abandonment many LGBT people experienced from their families of origin. Not everyone is in a couple or will be or wants to be; not everyone has children or wants to have them. Identities are at once individual and multiple, but interest group politics requires them to be homogenous" (2012, 19).

The other major barrier is one that we have seen repeatedly throughout this book, that is, the fact that the lesbian and gay movements are highly fragmented across identities and subject to conflicting and multiple cross-pressures. Given this reality, how can they build a coherent agenda that reflects agreement on a political and cultural strategy? And if the movements cannot agree on a coherent agenda, how can we expect them to build the coalitions needed to address the issues we have discussed? As Sherrill points out, "To the degree that there is any agenda in the United States, it is for equality and freedom from discrimination and violence. A more sophisticated agenda would require a level of collective identity among gay people not found anywhere in the world" (1996, 473).

And what does all of this mean for the central dilemma of this book—the tensions between the assimilationist and liberationist approaches to political and social change that has characterized the lesbian and gay movements over the years? One clear answer is that the movements should pursue a dual organizing strategy that builds on the best of the assimilationist perspective but that also always considers the possibilities for more radical, liberationist, structural, social, and policy change. We have seen in our discussion of the three major policy areas of this book—HIV/AIDS, the military ban, and same-sex marriage—that the assimilationist strategy has much to offer the movements, but in and of itself, it is far too limiting. We have also seen in this book that any social movement needs a variety of political organizing strategies that can be applied at different times in response to the Christian Right and at all levels of the political system. This chapter began with a quotation from Laura Liswood, the founder of Women World Leaders: "every successful social movement eventually moves from the unthinkable to the impossible to the inevitable" (Wilcox et al. 2007, 241). There are moments in any social movement's history when it seems as if very little progress can be achieved toward larger goals. The 1990s and the early twenty-first century have provided plenty of evidence that the larger lesbian and gay movements, working with others, have much work to do to make continued progress, so that the unthinkable and impossible can be turned into the inevitable. And to ensure that this happens, we rely on the courage and resistance of ordinary people who come together out of shared necessity and commitment across sexual-orientation, gender, race, and class divides. This is not easy work, but it is the necessary and messy work of social movements. And it is work that awaits, inspires, and challenges us all.

Conclusion

This chapter began with this key question: What political organizing strategy is the most viable for addressing the policy issues discussed in this book? The answer is that we need to build on the best of what the assimilationist and liberationist strategies have to offer. The assimilationist strategy, in and of itself, is far too limiting. And in the words of the late civil rights activist Bayard Rustin, those who embrace radical, outsider, unconventional, liberationist politics must eventually recognize the importance of moving "from protest to politics" (D'Emilio 2002, 5). All social movements recognize over time the importance of building coalitions with others across issues of common interest that will help bridge sexual-orientation, gender, race, and class divides. We have discussed the barriers to doing so throughout this book, but these barriers are not insurmountable. Indeed, much of the hope for the future resides in the attitudes and values of young people today, many of whom have indicated to pollsters and in classrooms across the country that those who are lesbian, gay, bisexual, and transgender deserve to live in a world free from prejudice, discrimination, and harassment, and they deserve, at a bare minimum, the rights afforded to those in the heterosexual majority. What we must ultimately do is reconceptualize what it is to be an American, challenge what Audre Lorde has called the American norm: someone who is "white, thin, male, young, heterosexual, christian, and financially secure." It is important to do so because "this mythical American norm" is socially constructed and is the locus of considerable power and privilege in American society (1984, 116). No single political strategy can begin to accomplish this goal; multiple strategies for political, social, cultural, and economic transformation are at the core of this radical democratic conception of politics. As we approach our task, we are challenging what it means to be a citizen in the United States and a citizen of the world. This book has been written with these goals in mind.

Appendix 1: AIDS Timeline

1981

- Doctors in New York and California begin to notice immune system disorders in otherwise healthy gay men.
- On June 5, the CDC reports the first case of the illness that will come to be called AIDS.
- Number of known AIDS deaths in the United States during 1981: 234.

1982

- The CDC links the new disease to blood. The name gay-related immune deficiency (GRID) is replaced with acquired immunodeficiency syndrome (AIDS). The disease is linked to four risk factors: male homosexuality, intravenous drug use, Haitian origin, and hemophilia A.
- Gay Men's Health Crisis, the first community AIDS service provider in the United States, established in New York City.
- First AIDS case reported in Africa.

1983

- The CDC warns blood banks of the risk of infection through transfusion; the first AIDS discrimination trial is held in the United States.
- People living with AIDS, as they want to be called instead of "AIDS sufferers" or "AIDS victims," take over plenary stage at US conference on AIDS in Denver, Colorado, and issue statement on the rights of PWAs referred to as the Denver Principles.
- National Association of People with AIDS formed.

1984

- Virus isolated by Luc Montagnier of the Pasteur Institute and Robert Gallo of the National Cancer Institute determined to be cause of AIDS; later named the human immunodeficiency virus (HIV).

- The secretary of health and human services announces that "a vaccine will be ready for testing within two years."
- San Francisco officials order gay bathhouses shut down; major public controversies over bathhouses rage in New York and other cities.

1985

- First International AIDS Conference held in Atlanta.
- Rock Hudson, fifty-nine, dies of AIDS complications.
- Ryan White, fourteen, is barred from attending public school in Indiana because he is HIV positive.
- First HIV test licensed by the US Food and Drug Administration.

1986

- President Ronald Reagan uses the acronym *AIDS* in public for the first time.
- The Reagan administration proposes rejecting immigrants who test positive for HIV.
- Surgeon General C. Everett Koop calls for AIDS education of children of all ages and for widespread use of condoms.
- Ricky Ray, a nine-year-old hemophiliac with HIV, is barred from Florida school, and his family's home is burned by arsonists in the following year. Ray died in 1991.
- Fifth anniversary of AIDS. Cumulative known AIDS deaths: 16,301.

1987

- ACT UP—the AIDS Coalition to Unleash Power—founded after a speech by Larry Kramer at the Lesbian and Gay Community Services Center in New York.
- AZT is approved to fight AIDS itself.
- The United States adds HIV as a "dangerous contagious disease" to its immigration exclusion list.
- Pianist and performer Liberace dies of AIDS.
- AIDS memorial quilt founded.

1988

- First World AIDS Day held on December 1.
- ACT UP members demonstrate at FDA offices in Washington, DC, over slow process for drug approval.

- Surgeon General Koop and CDC distribute the pamphlet *Understanding AIDS* to each of the 107 million homes in the United States.
- Congress authorizes an $800 million AIDS research initiative; the legislation contains a provision from Senator Jesse Helms (R-NC) requiring that testing confidentiality be eliminated.

1989

- The CDC issues guidelines for preventing *Pneumocystis carinii* pneumonia, a major cause of death for people with AIDS.
- Choreographer Alvin Ailey dies of AIDS.
- Artist Robert Mapplethorpe dies of AIDS.

1990

- Ryan White dies from AIDS at age eighteen. The Ryan White Comprehensive AIDS Resources Emergency (CARE) Act of 1990 is approved by Congress, providing federal funds for community services.
- President George H. W. Bush signs the Americans with Disabilities Act, which in part prohibits discrimination against people with HIV.
- Artist Keith Haring dies of AIDS.
- Fashion designer Halston dies of AIDS.
- *Longtime Companion* is released and becomes one of the first American feature films to address AIDS.

1991

- NBA superstar Magic Johnson announces that he has tested positive for HIV and will retire from professional basketball.
- Red ribbon introduced as the international symbol of AIDS awareness at the Tony Awards by Broadway Cares / Equity Fights AIDS and by Visual AIDS.
- Freddie Mercury, lead singer of the rock band Queen, dies of AIDS.
- Housing Opportunities for People with AIDS Act of 1991 enacted by US Congress to provide housing assistance to people living with AIDS through grants to states and local communities.
- Protests over the cost of AZT, which are up to $7,000 a year for one person, lead manufacturer Burroughs Wellcome to reduce the price by 20 percent in September. A major research study is released providing evidence that AZT can slow progression to AIDS in asymptomatic HIV-positive people.

1992

- The International Olympic Committee rules that athletes with HIV can compete. First clinical trial of multiple drug therapy is held.
- AIDS becomes number-one cause of death for US men ages twenty-five to forty-two.
- The White House permits the FDA to place experimental anti-HIV drugs on the fast track for approval.
- HIV-positive speakers Mary Fisher and Bob Hattoy address the Republican and Democratic National Conventions, respectively.
- Tennis star Arthur Ashe announces he has AIDS.
- *Brady Bunch* star Robert Reed dies of AIDS.

1993

- Arthur Ashe dies of AIDS.
- President Clinton establishes White House Office on National AIDS Policy, commonly known as the office of the "AIDS czar."
- *Angels in America,* a play about AIDS by Tony Kushner, wins the Tony Award and Pulitzer Prize.
- Ballet dancer Rudolf Nureyev dies of AIDS.

1994

- AIDS becomes leading cause of death for all Americans ages twenty-five to forty-four; remains so through 1995.
- A new study indicates that AZT can cut mother-to-child transmission of HIV by two-thirds.
- Elizabeth Glaser, cofounder of the Pediatric AIDS Foundation, dies of AIDS.
- Pedro Zamora, an HIV-positive gay man, appears in the cast of MTV's popular show *The Real World.* Zamora dies later that year at twenty-two.
- Randy Shilts, author of *And the Band Played On,* dies of AIDS at age forty-two.

1995

- First protease inhibitor, saquinavir, approved in record time by the FDA, ushering in new era of highly active antiretroviral therapy.
- First guidelines for the prevention of opportunistic infections in persons infected with HIV issued by the CDC.
- By executive order, President Clinton establishes the Presidential Advisory Council on HIV/AIDS.

- First National HIV Testing Day created by the National Association of People with AIDS.
- Olympic gold medal diver Greg Louganis announces that he is living with HIV.
- Rap star Easy E (Eric Wright) dies of AIDS.

1996

- At Eleventh AIDS Conference in Vancouver, new protease inhibitors and combination therapies bring renewed optimism.
- The FDA approves viral-load test, a new test that measures the level of HIV in the body.
- The number of new AIDS cases diagnosed in the United States declines for first time in the history of the epidemic, though experience varies by sex, race, and ethnicity.
- HIV is no longer leading cause of death for all Americans ages twenty-five to forty-four; remains leading cause of death of African Americans in this age group.

1997

- AIDS-related deaths in the United States decline by more than 40 percent compared to the prior year, largely due to highly active antiretroviral therapy.
- New York City health officials report that the number of city residents dying of the disease declined 30 percent from 1995 to 1996; this is the first documented drop in AIDS deaths in New York City.
- President Clinton announces goal of finding an effective vaccine in ten years.

1998

- Minority AIDS Initiative created in United States after African American leaders declare a state of emergency and Congressional Black Caucus Foundation calls on the Department of Health and Human Services to do the same.
- The US Department of Health and Human Services issues the first national guidelines for the use of antiretroviral therapy in adults.
- First large-scale human trials (Phase III) for an HIV vaccine begin.
- The US Supreme Court rules in *Bragdon v. Abbot* that the Americans with Disabilities Act covers those in earlier stages of HIV disease, not just AIDS.

1999

- Study finds that numbers of new HIV infections are rising among gay men.

- New York City health officials announce that a study reveals that 12 percent of young gay men in the city have been infected with HIV. African American and mixed-race men have the highest infection rates.

2000

- At the Thirteenth AIDS Conference in Durban, South Africa, five thousand doctors and scientists sign the Durban Declaration, stating that HIV causes AIDS, in response to South African president Thabo Mbeki's statements to the contrary.
- The CDC reports that, among men who have sex with men in the United States, African American and Latino HIV cases exceed those among whites for the year 1998. This is the first time that this has occurred.

2001

- The UN General Assembly convenes first-ever special session on AIDS.
- First National Black HIV/AIDS Awareness Day in the United States.
- A study focusing on six large US cities finds that 30 percent of young black gay men are HIV positive.
- The World Trade Organization, meeting in Doha, Qatar, announces the Doha Agreement to allow developing countries to buy or manufacture generic medications to meet public health crises.

2002

- HIV is leading cause of death worldwide among those ages fifteen to fifty-nine.
- UNAIDS reports that women constitute about half of all adults living with HIV and AIDS worldwide.
- The World Health Organization introduces a plan to insure that antiretroviral drugs are more accessible to people living in poor nations.
- FDA approval of OraQuick Rapid HIV-1 Antibody Test, the first rapid test to use finger prick.
- Cumulative AIDS deaths in United States through 2002: 501,669.

2003

- President Bush announces the President's Emergency Plan for AIDS Relief during the State of the Union Address, a five-year, $15 billion initiative to address HIV/AIDS, tuberculosis, and malaria, primarily in hard-hit countries.
- First National Latino AIDS Awareness Day in the United States.

- On World AIDS Day the WHO announces its 3 by 5 Plan to ensure that three million people who live in resource-poor countries are on antiretroviral drugs by 2005.

2004

- Leaders of the Group of Eight nations call for creation of the Global HIV Vaccine Enterprise, a consortium to accelerate research efforts to find an HIV vaccine.
- OraQuick Rapid HIV-1 Antibody Test approved by the FDA for use with oral fluid.

2005

- First National Asian and Pacific Islander HIV/AIDS Awareness Day in the United States.
- In a historic and unprecedented joint news conference, the WHO, UNAIDS, the US government, and the Global Fund to Fight AIDS, Tuberculosis, and Malaria announce results of joint efforts to increase the availability of antiretroviral drugs in developing countries.

2006

- Twenty-fifth anniversary of the outbreak of AIDS.
- The FDA approves Atripla, which is the first single-tablet, once-a-day regimen. It combines efavirenz, emtrictabine, and tenofovir and represents a joint initiative from Bristol-Myers Squibb and Gilead Sciences.

2007

- The WHO endorses male circumcision as part of a comprehensive AIDS prevention strategy. This policy decision is based on studies released in December 2006.

2008

- UNAIDS's annual report explains that AIDS deaths worldwide dropped from 2.2 million in 2005 to 2 million in 2007. It also reports that at the end of 2007 there were 33 million people living with HIV globally.

2009

- Pope Benedict XVI reiterates virulent opposition to condom use from the Roman Catholic Church. He claims that condom use may actually contribute to the spread of HIV.

2010

- President Barack Obama signs into law the historic $940 billion Patient Protection and Affordable Care Act on March 23, 2010.

2011

- A study led by researchers at the University of Washington, which involved 3,800 couples in six African countries, found that an injectable hormonal contraceptive used on a widespread scale by women in Africa appears to double the risk that they will become infected with HIV.

2012

- The CDC implements Take Charge, Take the Test, an inaugural campaign designed to increase HIV awareness and testing among African American women. The campaign was launched in ten cities where African American women have especially suffered the ravages of HIV: Atlanta, Chicago, Detroit, Fort Lauderdale, Houston, Memphis, Newark, New Orleans, Hyattsville, and St. Louis.

2013

- A study in the journal *PLOS Pathogens* reported that the virus that causes AIDS can be controlled through early antiretroviral treatment, thus preventing further therapy. The study tracked fourteen patients with HIV and found that those who had received antiretroviral treatment within the first ten weeks of infection were deemed to be "functionally cured" because their viral loads had decreased so significantly.
- PrePex, a new nonsurgical circumcision tool, is introduced by the FDA and approved by the WHO. HIV/AIDS prevention experts believe that it could lead to revolutionary strategies for preventing HIV/AIDS in sub-Saharan Africa.

Sources: Lee 2006b, "Thirty Years' War" 2011, Adams 2013, and Landau, 2013.

Appendix 2: The Don't Ask, Don't Tell Law

107 STAT 1671, PUBLIC LAW 103-160—November 30, 1993

SUBTITLE G—OTHER MATTERS

SEC. 571. POLICY CONCERNING HOMOSEXUALITY IN THE ARMED FORCES.

(a) CODIFICATION.—(1) Chapter 37 of title 10, United States Code, is amended by adding at the end the following new section:

"Sec. 654. Policy concerning homosexuality in the armed forces

"(a) FINDINGS.—Congress makes the following findings:

"(1) Section 8 of article I of the Constitution of the United States commits exclusively to the Congress the powers to raise and support armies, provide and maintain a navy, and make rules for the government and regulation of the land and naval forces.

"(2) There is no constitutional right to serve in the armed forces.

"(3) Pursuant to the powers conferred by section 8 of article I of the Constitution of the United States, it lies within the discretion of the Congress to establish qualifications for and conditions of service in the armed forces.

"(4) The primary purpose of the armed forces is to prepare for and to prevail in combat should the need arise.

"(5) The conduct of military operations requires members of the armed forces to make extraordinary sacrifices, including the ultimate sacrifice, in order to provide for the common defense.

"(6) Success in combat requires military units that are characterized by high morale, good order and discipline, and unit cohesion.

"(7) One of the most critical elements in combat capability is unit cohesion, that is, the bonds of trust among individual service members that make the combat effectiveness of a military unit greater than the sum of the combat effectiveness of the individual unit members.

"(8) Military life is fundamentally different from civilian life in that

"(A) the extraordinary responsibilities of the armed forces, the unique conditions of military service, and the critical role of unit cohesion, require that the military community, while subject to civilian control, exist as a specialized society; and

"(B) the military society is characterized by its own laws, rules, customs, and traditions, including numerous restrictions on personal behavior, that would be acceptable in civilian society.

"(9) The standards of conduct for members of the armed forces regulate a member's life for 24 hours each day beginning at the moment the member enters military status and not ending until that person is discharged or separated from the armed forces.

"(10) Those standards of conduct, including the Uniform Code of Military Justice, apply to a member of the armed forces at all times that the member has a military status, whether the member is on base or off base, and whether the member is on duty or off duty.

"(11) The pervasive application of the standards of conduct is necessary because members of the armed forces must be ready at all times for worldwide deployment to a combat environment.

"(12) The worldwide deployment of United States military forces, the international responsibilities of the United States, and the potential for involvement of the armed forces in actual combat routinely make it necessary for members of the armed forces involuntarily to accept living conditions and working conditions that are often Spartan, primitive, and characterized by forced intimacy with little or no privacy.

"(13) The prohibition against homosexual conduct is a longstanding element of military law that continues to be necessary in the unique circumstances of military service.

"(14) The armed forces must maintain personnel policies that exclude persons whose presence in the armed forces would create an unacceptable risk to the armed forces' high standards of morale, good order and discipline, and unit cohesion that are the essence of military capability.

"(15) The presence in the armed forces of persons who demonstrate a propensity or intent to engage in homosexual acts would create an unacceptable risk to the high standards of morale, good order and discipline, and unit cohesion that are the essence of military capability.

"(b) POLICY.—A member of the armed forces shall be separated from the armed forces under regulations prescribed by the Secretary of Defense if one or more of the following findings is made and approved in accordance with procedures set forth in such regulations:

"(1) That the member has engaged in, attempted to engage in, or solicited another to engage in a homosexual act or acts unless there are further findings, made and approved in accordance with procedures set forth in such regulations, that the member has demonstrated that—

"(A) such conduct is a departure from the member's usual and customary behavior;

"(B) such conduct, under all the circumstances, is unlikely to recur;

"(C) such conduct was not accomplished by use of force, coercion, or intimidation;

"(D) under the particular circumstances of the case, the member's continued presence in the armed forces is consistent with the interests of the armed forces in proper discipline, good order, and morale; and

"(E) the member does not have a propensity or intent to engage in homosexual acts.

"(2) That the member has stated that he or she is a homosexual or bisexual, or words to that effect, unless there is a further finding, made and approved in accordance with procedures set forth in the regulations, that the member has demonstrated that he or she is not a person who engages in, attempts to engage in, has a propensity to engage in, or intends to engage in homosexual acts.

"(3) That the member has married or attempted to marry a person known to be of the same biological sex.

"(c) ENTRY STANDARDS AND DOCUMENTS.—(1) The Secretary of Defense shall ensure that the standards for enlistment and appointment of members of the armed forces reflect the policies set forth in subsection (b).

"(2) The documents used to effectuate the enlistment or appointment of a person as a member of the armed forces shall set forth the provisions of subsection (b).

"(d) REQUIRED BRIEFINGS.—The briefings that members of the armed forces receive upon entry into the armed forces and periodically thereafter under section 937 of this title (article 137 of the Uniform Code of Military Justice) shall include a detailed explanation of the applicable laws and regulations governing sexual conduct by members of the armed forces, including the policies prescribed under subsection (b).

"(e) RULE OF CONSTRUCTION.—Nothing in subsection (b) shall be construed to require that a member of the armed forces be processed for separation from the armed forces when a determination is made in accordance with regulations prescribed by the Secretary of Defense that—

"(1) the member engaged in conduct or made statements for the purpose of avoiding or terminating military service; and

"(2) separation of the member would not be in the best interest of the armed forces."

"(f) DEFINITIONS.—In this section:

"(1) The term 'homosexual' means a person, regardless of sex, who engages in, attempts to engage in, has a propensity to engage in, or intends to engage in homosexual acts, and includes the terms 'gay' and 'lesbian.'

"(2) The term 'bisexual' means a person who engages in, attempts to engage in, has a propensity to engage in, or intends to engage in homosexual and heterosexual acts.

"(3) The term 'homosexual act' means—

"(A) any bodily contact, actively undertaken or passively permitted, between members of the same sex for the purpose of satisfying sexual desires; and

"(B) any bodily contact which a reasonable person would understand to demonstrate a propensity or intent to engage in an act described in subparagraph (A)."

(2) The table of sections at the beginning of each chapter is amended by adding at the end the following:

"664. Policy concerning homosexuality in the armed forces."

(b) REGULATIONS.—Not later than 90 days after the date of enactment of this Act, the Secretary of Defense shall revise Department of Defense regulations, and issue such new regulations as may be necessary to implement section 654 of title 10, United States Code, as added by subsection (a).

(c) SAVINGS PROVISION.—Nothing in this section or section 654 of title 10, United States Code, as added by subsection (a), may be construed to invalidate any inquiry, investigation, administrative action or proceeding, court-martial, or judicial proceeding conducted before the effective date of regulations issued by the Secretary of Defense to implement such section 654.

(d) SENSE OF CONGRESS.—It is the sense of Congress that—

(1) the suspension of questioning concerning homosexuality as a part of the processing of individuals for accession in the Armed Forces under the interim policy of January 29, 1993, should be continued, but the Secretary of Defense may reinstate that questioning with such questions or such revised questions as he considers appropriate if the Secretary determines that it is necessary to do so in order to effectuate the policy set forth in section 654 of title 10, United States Code, as added by subsection (a); and

(2) the Secretary of Defense should consider issuing guidance governing the circumstances under which members of the Armed Forces questioned about homosexuality for administrative purposes should be afforded warnings similar to the warnings under section 831 (b) of title 10, United States Code (article 31 [b] of the Uniform Code of Military Justice).

Source: Belkin and Bateman 2003, 177–181.

Appendix 3: Lesbian, Gay, Bisexual, Transgender, and Christian Right Organizations

Lesbian, Gay, Bisexual, and Transgender Organizations

ACT UP
http://www.critpath.org/actup

AIDS ACTION
http://www.aidsaction.org.au

American Foundation for Equal Rights
http://www.afer.org

Astraea Lesbian Foundation for Justice
http://www.astraea.org

Basic Rights Oregon
http://www.basicrights.org

Beyond Marriage
http://www.beyondmarriage.org

Bisexual Rights Center
http://www.biresource.org

Campus Pride
http://www.campuspride.org

Children of Lesbians and Gays Everywhere
http://www.colage.org

Family Pride
http://www.familypride.org

Freedom to Marry
http://www.freedomtomarry.org

Gay, Lesbian, and Straight Education Network
http://www.glsen.org

Gay and Lesbian Alliance Against Discrimination
http://www.glaad.org

Gay and Lesbian Medical Association
http://www.glma.org

Gay Asian Pacific Support Network
http://www.gapsn.org

Gay Men's Health Crisis
http://www.gmhc.org

GetEQUAL
http://www.getequal.org

GOProud
www.goproud.org

Hetrick-Martin Institute
http://www.hmi.org

HIV Hero
http://www.hivhero.org

Human Rights Campaign
http://www.hrc.org

Immigration Equality
http://www.immigrationequality.org

International Lesbian, Gay, Bisexual, Trans and Intersex Organization
http://www.ilga.org

Lambda Legal Defense and Education Fund
http://www.lambdalegal.org

Log Cabin Republicans
http://www/logcabin.org

The Movement Advancement Project
http://lgbtmap.org

National Association of Lesbian, Gay, Bisexual, and Transgender Community Centers
http://www.lgbtcenters.org

National Black Justice Coalition
http://www.nbjcoalition.org

The National Center for Lesbian Rights
http:www.nclrights.org

The National Gay and Lesbian Task Force
http://www.thetaskforce.org

The National Center for Transgender Equality
http://nctequality.org

National Minority AIDS Council
http://www.nmac.org

National Stonewall Democrats
http://www.change.org

National Youth Advocacy Coalition
http://www.nyacyouth.org

OutServe
http://www.sldn.org

Parents, Families, and Friends of Lesbians and Gays
http://www.pflag.org

People for the American Way
http://www.pfaw.org

Servicemembers Legal Defense Network
http://www.sldn.org

Service Women's Action Network
http://www.servicewomen.org

Soulforce
http://www.soulforce.org

Sylvia Rivera Law Project
http://www.srlp.org

The Trevor Project
http://www.thetrevorproject.org

Universal Fellowship of Metropolitan Community Churches
http://www.mcchurch.org

Urban Improv
http://urbanimprov.org

Christian Right Organizations

Alliance Defense Fund
http://www.alliancedefensefund.org

American Center for Law and Justice
http://www.aclj.org

American Family Association
http://www.afa.net

Christian Broadcasting Network—Pat Robertson's *700 Club*
http://www.cbn.com

Christian Coalition of America
http://www.cc.org

Concerned Women for America
http://www.cwfa.org

Eagle Forum
http://www.eagleforum.org

Family Research Council
http://www.frc.org

Focus on the Family
http://www.family.org

Moral Majority
http://www.moralmajority.com

The National Organization for Marriage
http://www.nationalorganizationformarriage.com

Traditional Values Coalition
http://www.traditionalvalues.org

Discussion Questions

Chapter 2

1. How have the assimilationist and liberationist strategies developed over time? In answering this question, be sure to discuss the specific tensions that have emerged between the two perspectives, as well as the ways that they have worked well together.
2. Describe specific examples of political organizing by the lesbian and gay movements prior to the Stonewall Rebellion of June 1969.
3. In what specific ways did the homophile movement provide a foundation for contemporary lesbian and gay movements' political organizing?
4. What connections can be made between the African American civil rights movement and the lesbian and gay movements?
5. What was the impact of the 1969 Stonewall Rebellion for the larger lesbian and gay movements?
6. Discuss the specific ways the Gay Liberation Front reflected a liberationist approach to political, social, and policy change.
7. Discuss the specific ways the Gay Activists Alliance reflected an assimilationist approach to political, social, and policy change.
8. How did the Christian Right emerge as a formidable opponent to the lesbian and gay movements during the 1970s?

Chapter 3

1. How did the onset of AIDS in the United States during the early 1980s affect the lesbian and gay movements' political organizing strategies?
2. How have the lesbian and gay movements intersected with the policy process over time as AIDS has developed in the United States and throughout the world?
3. What direct-action organizations grew out of the HIV/AIDS movements, and how specifically did they reinforce the liberationist approach to political and policy change?

4. What role has ACT UP played over time in the AIDS political and policy debates? To what extent has its role been an effective one? Be sure to define what you mean by *effective* as you answer this question.
5. Why has HIV/AIDS receded as a priority for the lesbian and gay movements' political organizing agenda? What might inspire the lesbian and gay movements to increase its visibility and importance?
6. How has the Christian Right intersected with the AIDS policy arena over time?
7. Discuss and evaluate how various presidents (Reagan, Bush, Clinton, Bush, and Obama) have responded to HIV/AIDS in the United States and on a global scale. What do you perceive to be the strengths and weaknesses of each of their policy responses?
8. In what specific ways is the Ryan White CARE Act an important policy initiative in response to HIV/AIDS? Why do you think that there continue to be debates over fully funding the legislation when it is up for renewal?
9. How have the boundaries between the lesbian and gay movements and the AIDS activist movement grown more rigid as AIDS has receded from public and policy attention and other issues have become more prominent on the lesbian and gay movements' agenda?
10. In what specific ways does the HIV/AIDS policy area reflect the underlying dilemma of this book—the tension between the assimilationist and liberationist approaches to political and policy change?

Chapter 4

1. How precisely does the debate over lesbians and gays in the military reflect the underlying dilemma of this book—the tension between the assimilationist and liberationist approaches to political and policy change?
2. Why did the lesbian and gay movements perceive that the Clinton presidency offered them political opportunities?
3. Discuss the treatment of lesbians and gays in the military over time.
4. Why did the military ban emerge on the national policy agenda in late 1992 and 1993?
5. Could President Bill Clinton have avoided the DADT compromise? If so, how?
6. What might the lesbian and gay movements have done differently in 1993 as the military ban emerged on the national policymaking agenda?
7. Why did President Obama support overturning the military ban?
8. What are the broader implications of how the military ban issue has been resolved for the larger lesbian and gay movements?

9. How has the Christian Right responded to the military ban debate over time?
10. What are the most persuasive arguments in the case for the military ban? What are the most persuasive arguments in the case against the military ban?
11. What comparisons can be drawn between the integration of African Americans in the military during the 1940s and the contemporary debate over the military ban?

Chapter 5

1. How, why, and when did same-sex marriage emerge on the national policy agenda?
2. How, why, and when did same-sex marriage emerge on the lesbian and gay movements' policy agenda?
3. Why do you think that same-sex marriage has emerged as a wedge issue in political campaigns? To what extent do you think that it is effective? In answering this question, be sure to define what you mean by *effective*.
4. What role have the courts played in the debate over same-sex marriage? What role do you think that they should play?
5. How has the Christian Right responded to the same-sex marriage debate? Do you believe that their response has been effective? In answering this question, be sure to identify your criteria for *effective*.
6. Why do you think President Clinton signed DOMA in September 1996?
7. In what ways has the United States Supreme Court's 2003 *Lawrence v. Texas* decision impinged upon the same-sex marriage debate?
8. Discuss the Obama administration's response to same-sex marriage during his two terms in office.
9. What are the most persuasive arguments for same-sex marriage? What are the least-persuasive arguments?
10. In what ways does the campaign for same-sex marriage reflect an assimilationist approach to political and policy change? In what ways does it reflect the liberationist approach?
11. What strategy should same-sex marriage proponents pursue in future? Should it be a state-by-state electoral strategy, a national strategy, or both?

Chapter 6

1. Discuss the implications of the analysis presented here regarding the assimilationist and liberationist approaches to political and policy change for social-movement theory.

2. Can the tensions between the assimilationist and liberationist perspectives be resolved over time? If so, how? If not, why not? To what extent are these tensions a healthy part of any social movement?
3. In what specific policy areas do you think the lesbian and gay movements have made progress over time? In answering this question, be sure to define what you mean by *progress*.
4. What are the sources of the possible lesbian and gay movements' progress in the future? What are the barriers? How might the barriers be overcome?
5. Do you believe it is possible for the lesbian and gay movements to embrace the assimilationist and liberationist approaches at the same time? If so, how? If not, why not?
6. Construct a political organizing strategy for the lesbian and gay movements. In doing so, be sure to identity what political strategies you would use and why, and identify what policy issues you would emphasize (and which ones you would de-emphasize) and why. Be sure to discuss the role that you think conventional insider, work-within-the-system political organizing strategies would play. Discuss as well the role that you think unconventional outsider organizing strategies would play.
7. Is there a way to build political coalitions across identities within the lesbian and gay movements? If so, how? If not, why not? And is there a way to build political coalitions between the lesbian and gay movements and other social movements? If so, how? If not, why not?

Glossary

ACT UP, the commonly used acronym for the AIDS Coalition to Unleash Power, is a grassroots AIDS organization associated with nonviolent civil disobedience. In the late 1980s and early 1990s, ACT UP became the standard-bearer for protest against governmental and societal indifference to the AIDS epidemic. The group is part of a long tradition of grassroots organizations in American politics, especially those of the African American civil rights movement, which were committed to political and social change through the practice of unconventional politics. ACT UP was founded in March 1987 by playwright and AIDS activist Larry Kramer.

The Campaign for Military Service is an organization created by prominent gay Democrats, including David Mixner, David Geffen, and Barry Diller, all of whom had ties to President Bill Clinton. The goal was to counteract the Christian Right's organizing efforts against President Clinton's attempt to overturn the military ban. The founders believed that the lesbian and gay movements needed to do much more in the way of grassroots organizing, and this organization was created with that goal in mind.

The Christian Right is a political alliance of evangelical Protestants and conservative Roman Catholics who argue against any form of equality for gay people. Antigay activism is central to their political organizing strategy, though they have also been on the forefront in the antiabortion movement as well. In addition, the Christian Right opposes teaching evolution in schools, affirmative action, and women in combat. The Christian Right opposed funding for HIV/AIDS education initiatives and the distribution of condoms in the 1980s, and since the mid-1990s, it has organized against same-sex marriage. Some of the most important Christian Right groups include Concerned Women for America, Focus on the Family, the Family Research Council, and the Traditional Values Coalition. The Christian Right has been particularly effective in using grassroots organizing over the years.

Classical liberalism is the underlying ideology in the United States, one that promotes such values as individualism, equality of opportunity, liberty and freedom, the rule of law, and limited government. The constitutional framers, influenced by eighteenth-century theorists John Locke and Adam Smith, embraced classical liberal principles from the outset.

Compassionate conservatism is a governing philosophy introduced by George W. Bush prior to the 2000 presidential election. Bush has used compassionate conservatism as his chief governing and campaign philosophy with respect to education, poverty, and global AIDS policy. It is rooted in the notion that government at all levels of society can help fellow citizens who are in need, but there must also be the required accompanying responsibility on the part of the individual and social service agencies and demonstrated results.

The Daughters of Bilitis was the first lesbian organization in the United States. Founded in San Francisco in September 1955, the group's name came from Pierre Louys's Song of Bilitis, a book of poetry that had been written by a man. Two of its founders—Del Martin and Phyllis Lyon—chose the name because they perceived it would be safe during the repressive environment of the 1950s. The organization was originally formed as a social and discussion group, and it eventually published the *Ladder*, a monthly magazine that first appeared in 1956, with Barbara Gittings as its first editor.

The Defense of Marriage Act was introduced by Senator Bob Dole (R-KS) in 1996, and President Bill Clinton signed it into law on September 21, 1996. The law defined marriage as the union of one man and one woman and also prevented states from being forced to recognize same-sex marriages that were viewed as valid in other states.

The degaying of AIDS refers to the period of the mid-1980s when AIDS activists made a crucial decision to publicize the message that "AIDS is not a gay disease." The goal was to gain greater funding and public support, and to convey the importance of AIDS prevention to all sectors of the population. The assumption was that the public and politicians would be more receptive if gay men were not the targeted beneficiaries of increased AIDS-related funding.

Distributive justice is a form of justice based on normative principles concerning what is the just allocation of rewards and goods in a society. Egalitarianism is at the core of this approach to the distribution of resources.

Domestic partnerships are composed of individuals of the same or opposite sex, who often live in committed relationships together but are not joined together in a traditional civil union or marriage.

Executive orders are presidential directives that become law. Congress allows presidents to issue executive orders to lessen its overwhelming legislative load, thus contributing to the president's legislative power.

The ex-gay movement refers to religious-based organizations and groups that purport to represent mental health interests. The movement claims that it can change the sexual orientations of those who identify as lesbian, gay, bisexual, or transgender by using a combination of strategies: Bible study, religious commitment, repentance, and reparative therapy. Organizations associated with the ex-gay movement include Exodus International, Love in Action, and Parents and Friends of Ex-Gays.

Focus on the Family is a Christian Right organization, headed by fundamentalist James Dobson, that has been on the forefront of antigay activity in the United States. It has engaged in aggressive education and grassroots campaigns to thwart the contemporary lesbian and gay movements' organizing efforts.

The Gay Activists Alliance was founded by former GLF members Jim Owles and Marty Robinson in New York City in December 1969. The GAA attempted to focus on the single issue of gay rights while avoiding issue fragmentation and anarchic organization. The GAA eschewed more radical liberationist change and instead embraced a more assimilationist approach to organizing. The GAA membership thought that meaningful reform would occur only if lesbians and gays organized politically for clearly defined demands (the repeal of New York State's sodomy and solicitation laws, an end to police entrapment of gay men, and employment discrimination protection) and exercised their political muscle to force positive legislative change.

The Gay Liberation Front was formed by gay and lesbian activists in the wake of the Stonewall Riots of late June 1969. Unabashedly celebrating liberationist approaches to change, the GLF drew on the principles and rhetoric of the more radical strands of the student, women's, and civil rights movements of the 1960s. Its goal was to dismantle and rebuild existing institutions—heterosexual marriage, the family, and relationships at all levels of society—according to liberationist principles.

Heteronormativity refers to the prevailing heterosexual standards by which people are judged and expected to conform in terms of their identities and as they interact with the world.

The homophile movement is the name given to the broad movement that emerged in the early 1950s. In its early stages, it embraced liberationist principles through the Mattachine Society. But by the 1960s, the homophile movement embraced more mainstream assimilationist goals. Mainstream homophile organizations were thrown on the defensive in the wake of the Stonewall Rebellion, as a new style of political organizing and leadership was demanded by newly energized lesbian and gay activists, many of whom were veterans of the various social and political movements of the 1960s.

Insider political strategies work within the formal channels of the US political system (voting and interest-group politics) to effect policy change. This approach to political organizing is often associated with assimilationist political strategies.

Lawrence v. Texas is a 2003 Supreme Court decision that overturned the 1996 *Bowers v. Hardwick* ruling permitting states to regulate sodomy. Writing for the 6-3 majority, Justice Anthony Kennedy celebrated the freedom of gay people to come together and to form relationships. The decision is viewed as a landmark decision because it essentially ruled state sodomy laws unconstitutional. In a bitter dissent, Justice Antonin Scalia (joined by Chief Justice William Rehnquist) warned of the dangers to the institution of marriage that might result from the Lawrence decision.

The Lesbian Avengers was founded in the fall of 1992 by six lesbian friends, most of whom had been active in AIDS, feminist, and other forms of progressive politics. They came together to create this new organization because they believed that more lesbians needed to engage in direct street action on their own terms, and they were frustrated with the unwillingness of gay men to address sexism in meaningful ways. Like ACT UP, they embraced unconventional politics in an effort to secure media attention.

The Mattachine Society was an organization founded in Los Angeles in 1951 and a key element of the early homophile movement's liberationist strategies. Based on an idea by Harry Hay, then working at the Los Angeles People's Education Center as a music teacher, the Mattachine Society was founded by Hay and several of his colleagues. Hay and his coorganizers built the Mattachine Society based on communist principles of organizing and social change, a model that would soon lead to considerable controversy within the organization. In 1953, the organizational structure and militant ideology of the Mattachine Society were challenged by rank-and-file organization members who favored a more assimilationist approach. The organization published the magazine *One* soon after its founding. The name Mattachine was first used by medieval masked singers. Hay and his cofounders used this name to suggest that homosexuals were also invisible.

The military-industrial complex is a term that was first used by President Dwight Eisenhower in his farewell address. It refers to the enormous political and economic power that is associated with the military and industry that work together under capitalism.

The Mississippi Freedom Summer was the summer of 1964, when 1,000 college student volunteers, many from prominent northern white families, went to Mississippi in an organized effort to highlight white violence against blacks. Civil rights activists, including Robert Moses, believed that attacks on white college students would receive national attention and more likely prompt federal action than the continuing and long-standing beatings of African Americans in Mississippi and elsewhere in the South.

Outsider political strategies are political organizing strategies that are often referred to as unconventional politics. They require participants to go outside the formal channels of the U.S. political system and policy process to embrace the politics of protest, direct action, and mass involvement.

Patriarchy refers to the societal dominance of men over women in all political, social, and economic institutions.

Pluralist democracy is a model of democracy that has, as its central tenet, the view that power is not concentrated in the hands of any one element in society; it is widely distributed among a host of competing groups. This broad distribution of power means that the political system is open and responsive to a wide array of competing claims.

Protease inhibitors were developed in the mid-1990s and are a class of anti-HIV drugs. They are often used in combination with other anti-HIV drugs, usually three or more. The drugs work together as combination therapy to block the replication of HIV in a person's blood.

Queer Nation was a short-lived radical lesbian and gay organization. It appeared in June 1991 with a goal of radicalizing the broader AIDS movement by reclaiming the word queer and embracing confrontational politics. "Queer" politics rejected the politics of assimilation and the labels "lesbian" and "gay."

The regaying of AIDS is a movement that began in 1992. At its core, the regaying of AIDS requires that gay men and lesbians play a much larger role in rethinking and restructuring community-based organizations' responses to AIDS. Those who support the regaying of AIDS argue that gay and bisexual men are far more at risk of HIV than anyone else and that public policy needs to reflect this reality.

Reparative therapy is a controversial therapeutic technique, one that is closely associated with the ex-gay movement. It is also often referred to as conversion therapy or reorientation therapy. The goal is to change the sexual orientations of people who identify as lesbian, gay, bisexual, or transgender to heterosexual.

Social movements are movements that have the following characteristics: an ideology, multiple leaders, group consciousness, and social group identity. In addition, they are decentralized and made up of an array of organizations. Finally, social movements typically represent those at the margins of American society, as defined by class, race, gender, or sexual orientation.

The Stonewall Rebellion of 1969 helped to usher in what is regarded as the contemporary lesbian and gay rights movements, though it is important to recognize that there were considerable political organizing and individual and group acts of courage for many years before in the United States and around the world. The Stonewall Rebellion (or Stonewall Riots) occurred at the Stonewall Inn in Greenwich Village, New York, over a period of several days beginning on the evening of June 27, 1969. When police raided the bar, many of the patrons decided to fight back, culminating in violent clashes between New York City police officers, patrons, and others in the area who were angered by the police action. By the time order was finally restored, the incident had received national and international media attention.

The Treatment Action Group is an organization that grew out of ACT UP/New York and was founded in 1992 by activists committed to a political strategy emphasizing the treatment of individuals with HIV/AIDS. Unlike ACT UP, which had a democratic organizational structure, TAG accepted members by invitation only, and membership could be revoked by the board. In addition, TAG members received salaries, and the group accepted a $1 million check from the pharmaceutical company Burroughs Wellcome, the manufacturer of AZT, in the summer of 1992. TAG used this money to finance members' travels to AIDS conferences throughout the world, pay salaries, hire professional lobbyists, and lobby government officials.

Unconventional politics is a form of politics that requires participants to go outside the formal channels of the U.S. political system (voting and interest-group politics) and embrace the politics of protest and mass involvement. Unconventional politics was employed with great success by the civil rights movement and has been used in contemporary American politics by groups across the ideological spectrum, including Earth First! ACT UP, Operation Rescue, and the militias.

Virtual equality is a concept coined by political activist Urvashi Vaid, former director of the National Gay and Lesbian Task Force, who argued that the assimilationist perspective should be rejected because it is far too accommodationist and too likely to be co-opted by more conservative elements in the lesbian and gay movements and society writ large. She worried that the lesbian and gay movements are more likely to accept the illusion of equality with straight people rather than to fight for true equality that would require a more liberationist political organizing strategy.

Wedge issues are highly salient issues, those that rally a candidate's supporters and divide his or her political opponents. Same-sex marriage has been used as a wedge issue in political campaigns at all levels of the political process.

Notes

Chapter 1

1. As this book will make clear, the so-called lesbian and gay movements are composed of a diversity of groups and individuals, and in them we see the convergence of a wide range of identities, including bisexuals and transgender individuals. Judging it inappropriate to collapse this rich diversity into a unitary discussion, I will refer to the lesbian and gay *movements* in the plural throughout this book. I place *lesbian* first in acknowledgment of the reality that women continue to occupy a position of structural inequality in the larger society.

Chapter 3

1. On May 30, 2007, President Bush requested that Congress double the funding of his U.S. global AIDS program to "30 billion over five years, which sets goals of helping support AIDS treatment of 2.5 million people" (Donnelly 2007, A15). This announcement was made at a White House Rose Garden ceremony and was part of the president's plan to secure at least one lasting, meaningful policy accomplishment as part of his legacy.

Chapter 4

1. Countries that allow out lesbians and gays to serve are: Albania, Argentina, Australia, Austria, the Bahamas, Belgium, Bermuda, Brazil, Canada, Colombia, Croatia, the Czech Republic, Denmark, Estonia, Finland, France, Germany, Greece, Ireland, Israel, Italy, Japan, Lithuania, Luxembourg, Malta, the Netherlands, New Zealand, Norway, Peru, Philippines, Poland, Portugal, Romania, Russia, Serbia, Slovenia, South Africa, Spain, Sweden, Switzerland, Taiwan, Thailand, United Kingdom, United States, and Uruguay (SLDN 2005, 1; and updated by author).

Chapter 6

1. As of August 2013, twenty-one states and the District of Columbia permitted lesbian and gay "partners to adopt children as couples instead of restricting parental rights to one partner" (Padgett 2007, 51). These states are Arkansas, California, Colorado, Connecticut, Delaware, Hawaii, Illinois, Indiana, Iowa, Maine, Maryland, Massachusetts, Minnesota, Nevada, New Hampshire, New Jersey, New Mexico, New York, Oregon, Rhode Island, Vermont, and Washington.

2. The Gay, Lesbian, and Straight Education Network (GLSEN) has collected survey data regarding the lesbian and gay experience in schools. These data provide empirical evidence to support the claim that lesbian and gay students (and those suspected of being so) face hostile environments in many of the nation's schools:

- 97 percent of students in public high schools in Massachusetts reported regularly hearing homophobic remarks from their peers in a 1993 report of the Massachusetts Governor's Commission on Gay and Lesbian Youth.
- 53 percent of the students reported hearing antigay remarks made by school staff.
- 46 percent of gay, lesbian, and bisexual students reported in a 1997 Massachusetts Youth Risk Behavior Study they attempted suicide in the past year, compared to 9 percent of their peers.
- 22 percent were in a fight that resulted in receiving medical attention, compared to 3 percent of their peers.
- Gay students are three times as likely to have been threatened with a weapon at school than their peers during the previous twelve months, according to Youth Risk Behavior surveys done in Massachusetts and Vermont.
- 28 percent of gay youths drop out of high school altogether, according to a US Department of Health and Human Services study. (Bronski 1999, 16)

References

Adam, Barry D. 1995. *The Rise of a Gay and Lesbian Movement*. Rev. ed. New York: Twayne.

Adams, Patrick. 2013. "In One Simple Tool, Hope for H.I.V. Prevention." *New York Times*, March 20.

Allyn, David. 2000. *Make Love, Not War: The Sexual Revolution, an Unfettered History*. New York: Little, Brown.

Alvarez, Lizette. 2006. "Gay Groups Renew Drive Against 'Don't Ask, Don't Tell.'" *New York Times*, September 14.

Alwood, Edward. 1996. *Straight News: Gays, Lesbians, and the News Media*. New York: Columbia University Press.

"Analysis: Supreme Court in No Rush to Grant National Gay-Marriage Right." 2013. *New York Times*, June 26.

Andriote, John-Manuel. 1999. *Victory Deferred: How AIDS Changed Gay Life in* America. Chicago: University of Chicago Press.

_______. 2011. *Victory Deferred: How AIDS Changed Gay Life in America*. 2nd ed., updated and expanded.

______. 2012. "Reclaiming HIV As a 'Gay' Disease." *Gay and Lesbian Review*, September/October.

Archer, Jesse. 2013. "Mid-Life Crisis, Squared: For Middle-Aged Men, an HIV Diagnosis Comes with an Extra Burden of Shame." *Out*, August, 44.

"The Armchair Activist." 2006. *Advocate*, October 10, 34.

Armstrong, Anthony. 2013. "Head's Up! ACA Could Jolt HIV Funding." *Gay and Lesbian Review*, May/June, 5.

Armstrong, Elizabeth A. 2002. *Forging Gay Identities: Organizing Sexuality in San Francisco, 1950–1994*. Chicago: University of Chicago Press.

"Army Dismisses Gay Arabic Linguist." 2006. *New York Times*, July 27.

Aronowitz, Stanley. 1996. *The Death and Rebirth of American Radicalism*. New York: Routledge.

Baer, Denise L., and David A. Bositis. 1993. *Politics and Linkage in a Democratic Society*. Upper Saddle River, NJ: Pearson Education.

Bailey, Robert W. 1999. *Gay Politics, Urban Politics: Identity and Economics in the Urban Setting*. New York: Columbia University Press.

Baldwin, Peter. 2005. *Disease and Democracy: The Industrialized World Faces AIDS*. Berkeley: University of California Press.

Bawer, Bruce. 1993. *Place at the Table: The Gay Individual in American Society*. New York: Poseidon Press.

Beam, Cris. 2007. *Transparent: Love, Family, and Living the T with Transgender Teenagers*. New York: Harcourt.

Behrman, Greg. 2004. *The Invisible People: How the U.S. Has Slept Through the Global Epidemic, the Greatest Humanitarian Catastrophe of Our Time*. New York: Free Press.

Belkin, Aaron. 2011. "Victory Found, Opportunity Lost." *Advocate*, February, 16–17.

Belkin, Aaron, and Geoffrey Bateman, eds. 2003. *Don't Ask, Don't Tell: Debating the Gay Ban in the Military*. Boulder, CO: Lynne Rienner.

Benecke, Michelle M., and Kristin S. Dodge. 1996. "Military Women: Casualties of the Armed Forces' War on Lesbians and Gay Men." In *Gay Rights, Military Wrongs: Political Perspectives on Lesbians and Gays in the Military*, edited by Craig A. Rimmerman, 71–108. New York: Garland.

Bereznai, Steven. 2006. *Gay and Single . . . Forever?* New York: Marlowe.

Bernard, Tara Siegel. 2013. "How the Court's Ruling Will Affect Same-Sex Spouses." *New York Times*, June 26.

Bernstein, David S. 2012. "A More Perfect Union." *Boston Phoenix*, May 18, 10.

Berubé, Allan. 1990. *Coming Out Under Fire*. New York: Free Press.

Besen, Wayne. 2011. "Top Ten GLBT Events of 2010." *Gay and Lesbian Review*, March/April, 5.

Bianco, David Ari. 1996. "Echoes of Prejudice: The Debates over Race and Sexuality in the Armed Forces." In *Gay Rights, Military Wrongs: Political Perspectives on Lesbians and Gays in the Military*, edited by Craig A. Rimmerman, 47–70. New York: Garland.

Biegel, Stuart. 2010. *The Right to Be Out: Sexual Orientation and Gender Identity in America's Public Schools*. Minneapolis: University of Minnesota Press.

Blasius, Mark, and Shane Phelan, eds. 1997. *We Are Everywhere: A Historical Sourcebook of Gay and Lesbian Politics*. New York: Routledge.

Bolcer, Julie, and Andrew Harmon. 2011. "Obama Steps Up Fight Against HIV." *Advocate.com*, December 1. www.advocate.com.

Boyd, Danah, and Alice Marwick. 2011. "Bullying as True Drama." *New York Times*, September 22.

Bram, Christopher. 2012. *Eminent Outlaws: The Gay Writers Who Changed America*. New York: Twelve.

Brier, Jennifer. 2009. *Infectious Ideas: U.S. Political Responses to the AIDS Crisis*. Chapel Hill: University of North Carolina Press.

Broder, John M. 2004. "Groups Debate Slower Strategy and Gay Rights." *New York Times,* December 9, A1.

Brody, Jane E. 2011. "Gay or Straight, Youths Aren't So Different." *New York Times,* January 3.

Bronski, Michael. 1998. *The Pleasure Principle: Sex, Backlash, and the Struggle for Gay Freedom.* New York: St. Martin's Press.

______. 1999. "Littleton, Movies, and Gay KIDS." *Z Magazine,* July–August, 12–16.

______. 2006. "Is the Gay Rights Movement Doomed to Fail?" *Z Magazine,* July–August, 18–20.

______. 2011. *A Queer History of the United States.* Boston: Beacon Press.

______. 2013. "A Note from the Series Editor." In *Family Pride: What LGBT Families Should Know About Navigating Home, School, and Society in their Schools,* edited by Michael Shelton, ix–x. Boston: Beacon Press.

Bull, Chris. 1993a. "Broken Promise." *Advocate,* August 27, 24.

______. 1993b. "No Frankness." *Advocate,* June 29, 24–27.

______. 1999. "Still Angry After All These Years." *Advocate,* June 19, 18–19.

______. 2001. "Uncharted Waters." *Advocate,* January 30, 24–26.

______. 2003. "Justice Served." *Advocate,* August 19, 36.

Burkett, Elinor. 1995. *The Gravest Show on Earth: America in the Age of AIDS.* Boston: Houghton Mifflin.

Burns, Robert. 2010. "With Gay Ban Debate Over, Military Impact in Doubt." *USA Today,* December 12.

Button, James, Barbara Rienzo, and Kenneth D. Wald. 1997. *Private Lives, Public Conflicts: Battles over Gay Rights in American Communities.* Washington, DC: Congressional Quarterly Press.

Cahill, Sean. 2003. "Public Policy Issues Affecting Gay, Lesbian, Bisexual, and Transgender People: Envisioning a GLBT-Inclusive Introductory American Political Science Textbook." Prepared for delivery at the 2003 annual meeting of the American Political Science Association, August 28–31.

______. 2004. *Same-Sex Marriage in the United States: Focus on the Facts.* New York: Lexington.

______. 2007. "The Anti–Gay Marriage Movement." In *The Politics of Same-Sex Marriage,* edited by Craig A. Rimmerman and Clyde Wilcox, 155–191. Chicago: University of Chicago Press.

______. 2010. "A Burst of Progress on HIV Policy." *Gay and Lesbian Review,* March/April.

Calmes, Jackie, and Peter Baker. 2012. "Obama Says Same-Sex Marriage Should Be Legal." *New York Times,* May 9.

Campbell, David C., and Carin Robinson. 2007. "Religious Conservatives for and Against Gay Marriage: The Culture War Wages On." In *The Politics of Same-Sex Marriage,* edited by Craig A. Rimmerman and Clyde Wilcox, 131–154. Chicago: University of Chicago Press.

Canaday, Margot. 2009. *The Straight State: Sexuality and Citizenship in Twentieth-Century America.* Princeton, NJ: Princeton University Press.

Cannon, Lou. 1991. *President Reagan: The Role of a Lifetime.* New York: Simon and Schuster.

Carpenter, Dale. 2012. *Flagrant Conduct: The Story of "Lawrence v. Texas."* New York: Norton.

Carter, David. 2004. *Stonewall: The Riots That Sparked the Revolution.* New York: St. Martin's Press.

Chait, Jonathan. 2013. "Gay-Marriage Foes Going Through Stages of Grief." *nymag.com.* June 26.

Chambers, David L. 2000. "Couples: Marriage, Civil Union, and Domestic Partnership." In *Creating Change: Sexuality, Public Policy, and Civil Rights,* edited by John D'Emilio, William B. Turner, and Urvashi Vaid. New York: St. Martin's Press.

Chauncey, George. 1994. *Gay New York.* New York: Basic Books.

______. 2004. *Why Marriage? The History Shaping Today's Debate over Gay Equality.* New York: Basic Books.

______. 2010. "Last Ban Standing." *New York Times,* December 20.

______. 2013. "The Long Road to Marriage Equality." *New York Times,* June 26.

Cianciotto, Jason, and Sean Cahill, 2012. *LGBT Youth in America's Schools.* Ann Arbor: University of Michigan Press.

Clendinen, Dudley, and Adam Nagourney. 1999. *Out for Good: The Struggle to Build a Gay Rights Movement in America.* New York: Simon and Schuster.

Clinton, Bill. 2013. "It's Time to Overturn DOMA." *Washington Post,* March 7.

Cohen, Cathy J. 1999. *The Boundaries of Blackness: AIDS and the Breakdown of Black Politics.* Chicago: University of Chicago Press.

Cohen, Peter F. 1998. *Love and Anger: Essays on AIDS, Activism, and Politics.* New York: Harrington Park Press.

Cole, David. 2013. "Equality and the Roberts Court: Four Decisions." *New York Review of Books,* August 15, 28–30.

Colegrove, James. 2011. *Epidemic City: The Politics of Public Health in New York.* New York: Russell Sage.

Connelly, Marjorie. 2012. "Support for Gay Marriage Growing, but U.S. Remains Divided." *New York Times,* December 7.

Crary, David. 2006. "Gay Marriage Ban Rejected in Arizona." http://news.yahoo.com/.

Crea, Joe. 2003. "Frist Supports Gay Marriage Ban." *Washington Blade,* July 4. http://www.washblade.com.

______. 2004. "'Austin 12' Divided on Bush: One Feels Bush-Whacked." *Washington Blade,* September 17. http://www.washblade.com.

Cruikshank, Margaret. 1992. *The Gay and Lesbian Movement.* New York: Routledge.

D'Amico, Francine. 1996. "Race-ing and Gendering the Military Closet." In *Gay Rights, Military Wrongs: Political Perspectives on Lesbians and Gays in the Military,* edited by Craig A. Rimmerman, 3–46. New York: Garland.

______. 2000. "Sex/uality and Military Service." In *The Politics of Gay Rights,* edited by Craig A. Rimmerman, Kenneth D. Wald, and Clyde Wilcox, 249–265. Chicago: University of Chicago Press.

"Declaration of Intolerance." 2003. *Advocate,* February 27, 15.

D'Emilio, John. 1983. *Sexual Politics, Sexual Communities: The Making of a Homosexual Minority in the United States, 1940–1970.* Chicago: University of Chicago Press.

______. 1992. *Making Trouble: Essays on Gay History, Policies, and the University.* New York: Routledge.

______. 2000. "Cycles of Change, Questions of Strategy: The Gay and Lesbian Movement After Fifty Years." In *The Politics of Gay Rights,* edited by Craig A. Rimmerman, Kenneth D. Wald, and Clyde Wilcox, 31–53. Chicago: University of Chicago Press.

______. 2002. *The World Turned: Essays on Gay History, Politics, and Culture.* Durham: Duke University Press.

______. 2006. "The Marriage Fight Is Setting Us Back." *Gay and Lesbian Review,* November–December, 10–11.

______. 2007. "Will the Courts Set Us Free? Reflections on the Campaign for Same-Sex Marriage." In *The Politics of Same-Sex Marriage,* edited by Craig A. Rimmerman and Clyde Wilcox, 39–64. Chicago: University of Chicago Press.

D'Emilio, John D., William B. Turner, and Urvashi Vaid, eds. 2000. *Creating Change: Sexuality, Public Policy, and Civil Rights.* New York: St. Martin's Press.

DiMascio, Jen. 2011. "GAO Reports High Cost of 'don't ask.'" *Politico,* January 20.

Dolkart, Jane. 1998. "Law." In *St. James Press Gay and Lesbian Almanac,* edited by Neil Schlager, 301–321. Detroit: St. James Press.

Donnelly, John. 2007. "With AIDS Funding Proposal, Bush Looks to His Legacy." *Boston Globe,* May 31, A15.

"Don't Ask, Don't Tell." *Wikipedia.* Accessed February 17, 2014, http://wikipedia.org.

Duberman, Martin. 2009. *Waiting to Land: A (Mostly) Political Memoir, 1985–2008.* New York: New Press.

Duggan, Lisa. 2003. *The Twilight of Equality? Neoliberalism, Cultural Politics, and the Attack on Democracy.* Boston: Beacon Press.

Eckholm, Erik. 2010. "In Efforts to End Bullying, Some See Agenda." *New York Times*, November 6.

______. 2013. "Boy Scouts End Longtime Ban on Openly Gay Youths." *New York Times*, May 23, A1.

Edsall, Nicholas. 2003. *Toward Stonewall: Homosexuals and Society in the Modern Western World*. Charlottesville: University Press of Virginia.

Eisenbach, David. 2006. *Gay Power: An American Revolution*. New York: Carroll and Graf.

Engel, Jonathan. 2006. *The Epidemic: A Global History of AIDS*. New York: HarperCollins.

Ephron, Dan. 2007. "General Comment." *Newsweek*, March 26, 34.

Epstein, Steven. 1996. *Impure Science: AIDS, Activism, and the Politics of Knowledge*. Berkeley: University of California Press.

Escoffier, Jeffrey. 1980. *American Home: Community and Perversity*. Berkeley: University of California Press.

Eskridge, William. 1999. *Gaylaw: Challenging the Apartheid of the Closet*. Cambridge, MA: Harvard University Press.

Ettlebrick, Paula. 1997. "Since When Is Marriage a Path to Liberation?" In *We Are Everywhere: A Historical Sourcebook of Gay and Lesbian Politics*, edited by Mark Blasius and Shane Phelan, 757–761. New York: Routledge.

Faderman, Lillian, and Stuart Timmons. 2006. *Gay LA: A History of Sexual Outlaws, Power Politics, and Lipstick Lesbians*. New York: Basic Books.

Feldblum, Chai. 2009. "The Selling of Proposition 8." *Gay and Lesbian Review*, January–February. 34–36.

Foreman, Christopher. 1994. *Plagues, Products, and Politics: Emergent Public Health Hazards and National Policymaking*. Washington, DC: Brookings Institution.

Foust, Michael. 2003. "Ruling Highlights Need for Marriage Amendment, Leaders Say." *SBC Baptist Press*, November 18.

Frank, Nathaniel. 2009. *Unfriendly Fire: How the Gay Ban Undermines the Military and Weakens America*. New York: Thomas Dunne Books.

Gallagher, John. 1993. "Terrible Timing." *Advocate*, October 5, 28.

______. 1996. "Speak Now." *Advocate*, November 11, 21.

Gallo, Marcia M. 2006. *Different Daughters: A History of the Daughters of Bilitis and the Rise of the Lesbian Rights Movement*. New York: Carroll and Graf.

GLSEN Fundraising and Information Newsletter. 2000. New York: Gay, Lesbian, and Straight Education Network.

Gogolak, E.C. 2013. "Windsor, Lead Plaintiff in Marriage Case, Responds." *New York Times*, June 26.

Goldstone, Jack A. 2003. Introduction to *States, Parties, and Social Movements*, edited by Jack A. Goldstone, 1–26. Cambridge: Cambridge University Press.

Goodstein, Laurie. 2013. "Opponents Say Decisions Have Strengthened Their Resolve." *New York Times*, June 26.

Gould, Deborah. 2009. *Moving Politics: Emotion and ACT UP's Fight Against AIDS*. Chicago: University of Chicago Press.

Gregory, Nancy. 2001. "The Gay and Lesbian Movement in the United States." In *Doing Democracy: The MAP Model for Organizing Social Movements*, edited by Bill Moyer, Joann McAllister, Mary Lou Finley, and Steven Soifer. Vancouver: New Society.

Guerriero, Patrick. 2004. "Gay Republicans Not for Bush." *Washington Blade*, October 8. http://www.washblade.com.

Haggerty, Timothy. 2003. "History Repeating Itself: A Historical Overview of Gay Men and Lesbians in the Military Before 'Don't Ask, Don't Tell.'" In *Don't Ask, Don't Tell: Debating the Gay Ban in the Military*, edited by Aaron Belkin and Geoffrey Bateman, 9–50. Boulder: Lynne Rienner.

Hamilton, Nigel. 2007. *Bill Clinton: Masking the Presidency*. New York: Public Affairs.

Harden, Victoria A. 2012. *AIDS at 30: A History*. Washington, DC: Potomac Books.

Harmon, Andrew. 2009/2010. "The Gender Identity Divide." *Advocate*, December/January, 50–52.

Herek, Gregory M. 1996. "Social Science, Sexual Orientation, and Military Personnel Policy." In *Out in Force: Sexual Orientation and the Military*, edited by Gregory M. Herek, Jared B. Jobe, and Ralph M. Carney, 3–14. Chicago: University of Chicago Press.

Hertzberg, Hendrick. 2003. "Comment: Dog Bites Man." *New Yorker*, May 5, 33.

Hertzog, Mark. 1996. *The Lavender Vote: Lesbians, Gay Men, and Bisexuals in American Electoral Politics*. New York: New York University Press.

Highleyman, Liz. 2002. "Radical Queers or Queer Radicals? Queer Activism and the Global Justice Movement." In *From ACT UP to the WTO: Urban Protest and Community Building in the Era of Globalization*, edited by Benjamin Shepard and Ronald Hayduk, 106–120. New York: Verso.

Hirsch, H. N. 2005. Introduction to *The Future of Gay Rights in America*, edited by H. N. Hirsch, ix–xiii. New York: Routledge.

Hirshman, Linda. 2012. *Victory: The Triumphant Gay Revolution*. New York: Harper Collins.

Hofmann, Regan. 2010. "Oh, Yes, He Did." *POZ*, June 9.

Hulse, Carl. 2004. "Backers Revise Amendment on Marriage." *New York Times*, March 23. http://www.nytimes.com/2004/03/23/politics/23AMEN.html.

Hunt, Ronald J. 1999. *Historical Dictionary of the Gay Liberation Movement: Gay Men and the Quest for Social Justice*. Lanham, MD: Scarecrow Press.

Hunter, Susan. 2006. *AIDS in America*. New York: Palgrave Macmillan.

Ireland, John. 2007. "Defining Hate in the United States." *In These Times*, May, 18–19.

Jacklin, Brad. 2012. "How LGBT People Benefit Under the Affordable Care Act." *Huffington Post.* March 19.

Jay, Karla. 1999. *Tales of the Lavender Menace.* New York: Basic Books.

Johnson, David K. 2004. *The Lavender Scare: The Cold War Persecution of Gays and Lesbians in the Federal Government.* Chicago: University of Chicago Press.

Kaiser, Charles. 1997. *The Gay Metropolis, 1940–1996.* New York: Houghton Mifflin.

Kaplan, Esther. 2004. *With God on Their Side: How Christian Fundamentalists Trampled Science, Policy, and Democracy in George W. Bush's White House.* New York: New Press.

Keck, Kristi. 2009. *"Gay Critics Say 'Too Little, Too Late.'" cnn.com,* June 18.

Keen, Lisa. 1999. "Vermont's 'Step Forward.'" *Washington Blade,* December 24, 1. http://www.washblade.com.

______. 2004. "Did 'Moral Values' Tip the Scale?" *Bay Windows,* November 11.

Kim, Richard. 2011. "Coming Out for Change." *Nation,* July/August, 5–6.

King, Mike. 1996. "Suicide Watch." *Advocate,* November 12, 41–44.

Klarman, Michael J. 2013. *From the Closet to the Altar: Courts, Backlash, and the Struggle for Same-Sex Marriage.* New York: Oxford University Press.

Knowlton, Brian. 2012. "Biden Comfortable with Gay Marriage." *New York Times,* May 6.

Koop, C. Everett. 1991. *Koop: The Memoirs of America's Family Doctor.* New York: Random House.

Kristof, Nicholas D. 2006. "The Deep Roots of AIDS." Op-ed. *New York Times,* September 19.

Landau, Elizabeth. 2013. "HIV May Be 'Functionally Cured' in Some." *CNN,* March 18.

Lee, Ryan. 2006a. "Experts Debate the 'New' Face of AIDS: Gay Men, African Americans Hardest Hit by Disease." *Washington Blade,* December 1, 1, 22. http://www.washblade.com.

______. 2006b. "25 Years of AIDS." *Washington Blade,* June 2. http://www.washblade.com.

"The Legislative Word on Gays." 1993. *Congressional Quarterly Weekly Report,* July 31, 2076.

Lehmkuhl, Reichen. 2006. *Here's What We'll Say: Growing Up, Coming Out, and the U.S. Air Force Academy.* New York: Carroll and Graf.

Lehring, Gary. 1996. "Constructing the 'Other' Soldier: Gay Identity's Military Threat." In *Gay Rights, Military Wrongs: Political Perspectives on Lesbians and Gays in the Military,* edited by Craig A. Rimmerman, 269–293. New York: Garland.

Levenson, Jacob. 2003. *The Secret Epidemic: The Story of AIDS and Black America.* New York: Pantheon.

Lewis, Gregory B., and Marc A. Rogers. 1999. "Does the Public Support Equal Rights for

Gays and Lesbians?" In *Gays and Lesbians in the Democratic Process,* edited by Ellen D. B. Riggle and Barry L. Tadlock, 118–145. New York: Columbia University Press.

Lewis, John, and Michael D'Orso. 1998. *Walking with the Wind: A Memoir of the Civil Rights Movement.* New York: Simon and Schuster.

Liptak, Adam. 2013. "Supreme Court Bolsters Gay Marriage with Two Major Rulings." *New York Times,* June 26.

Loffreda, Beth. 2000. *Losing Matt Shepard: Life and Politics in the Aftermath of Anti-Gay Murder.* New York: Columbia University Press.

Lofton, Katie, and Donald P. Haider-Markel. 2007. "The Politics of Same-Sex Marriage Versus the Politics of Gay Civil Rights." In *The Politics of Same-Sex Marriage,* edited by Craig A. Rimmerman and Clyde Wilcox, 313–340. Chicago: University of Chicago Press.

Lorde, Audre. 1984. *Sister Outsider: Essays and Speeches.* Freedom, CA: Crossing Press.

Loughery, John. 1998. *The Other Side of Silence: Men's Lives and Gay Identities: A Twentieth Century History.* New York: Henry Holt.

McFeeley, Tim. 2002. "Getting It Straight: A Review of the 'Gays in the Military' Debate." In *Creating Change: Sexuality, Public Policy, and Civil Rights,* edited by John D'Emilio, William B. Turner, and Urvashi Vaid, 236–250. New York: St. Martin's Press.

McGowan, Jeffrey. 2005. *Major Conflict: One Gay Man's Life in the Don't-Ask-Don't-Tell Military.* New York: Broadway Books.

Medina, Jennifer. 2013. "Anticipation Turns to Acceptance as California Awaits Marriage Ruling." *New York Times,* June 23.

Micklethwait, John, and Adrian Wooldridge. 2004. *The Right Nation: Conservative Power in America.* New York: Penguin Press.

Miller, Neil. 1995. *Out of the Past: Gay and Lesbian History from 1869 to the Present.* New York: Vintage Books.

Mixner, David. 2011. *A Home with Myself: Stories from the Hills of Turkey Hollow.* New York: Magnus Books.

Mohr, Richard. 1993. *A More Perfect Union: Why Straight America Must Stand Up for Gay Rights.* Boston: Beacon Press.

Moyer, Bill, Joann McAllister, Mary Lou Finley, and Steven Soifer. 2001. *Doing Democracy: The MAP Model for Organizing Social Movements.* Vancouver: New Society.

Mucciaroni, Gary. 2008. *Same-Sex, Different Politics: Success and Failure in the Struggles over Gay Rights.* Chicago: University of Chicago Press.

O'Connor, Karen, and Alixandra B. Yanus. 2007. "'Til Death—or the Supreme Court—Do Us Part: Litigating Gay Marriage." In *The Politics of Same-Sex Marriage,* edited by Craig A. Rimmerman and Clyde Wilcox, 291–312. Chicago: University of Chicago Press.

Odets, Walt. 1995. *In the Shadow of the Epidemic: Being HIV-Negative in the Age of AIDS.* Durham, NC: Duke University Press.

Office of the Press Secretary. 2003. "Marriage Protection Week, 2003." http://www.whitehouse.gov/briefing-room/.

Olson, Laura R., Paul A. Djupe, and Wendy Cadge. 2011. "American Mainline Protestantism and Deliberation about Homosexuality." In *Faith, Politics, and Sexual Diversity in Canada and the United States,* edited by David Rayside and Clyde Wilcox, 189–204. Vancouver: University of British Columbia Press.

Osborne, Duncan. 1994. "Military." *Advocate,* January 25, 53.

Padgett, Tim. 2007. "Gay Friendly Values." *Time,* July 16, 51–52.

Pascoe, C. J. 2012. Preface to the 2012 edition of *Dude, You're a Fag: Masculinity and Sexuality in High School,* vii–xvi. Berkeley: University of California Press.

Perine, Keith. 2004. "House Conservatives Seek Voters' Attention with Action on Gay Marriage Amendment." *CQ Weekly,* October 2.

Perine, Keith, and Jennifer A. Dlouhy. 2004. "Parties Worry About Political Risk in Stands on Gay Marriage." *CQ Weekly,* January 10.

Phelan, Shane. 2001. *Sexual Strangers: Gays, Lesbians, and Dilemmas of Citizenship.* Philadelphia: Temple University Press.

Pinello, Daniel R. 2006. *America's Struggle for Same-Sex Marriage.* New York: Cambridge University Press.

Radnofsky, Louise. 2010. "Policy's Progress: Key Milestones in the Rules over the Past 17 Years." *Wall Street Journal,* March 26, A5.

Radosh, Ronald. 1996. *Divided They Fell: The Demise of the Democratic Party, 1964–1996.* New York: Free Press.

Rauch, Jonathan. 2004. *Gay Marriage: Why It Is Good for Gays, Good for Straights, and Good for America.* New York: Times Books.

Rayside, David. 2007. "The United States in Comparative Context." In *The Politics of Same-Sex Marriage,* edited by Craig A. Rimmerman and Clyde Wilcox, 341–364. Chicago: University of Chicago Press.

Reed, T. V. 2005. *The Art of Protest: Culture and Activism from the Civil Rights Movement to the Streets of Seattle.* Minneapolis: University of Minnesota Press.

Riggle, Ellen D. B., and Barry L. Tadlock, eds. *Gays and Lesbians in the Democratic Process.* New York: Columbia University Press.

Rimmerman, Craig A., ed. 1996a. *Gay Rights, Military Wrongs: Political Perspectives on Lesbians and Gays in the Military.* New York: Garland.

______. 1996b. Introduction to *Gay Rights, Military Wrongs: Political Perspectives on Lesbians and Gays in the Military,* edited by Craig A. Rimmerman, xix–xxvii. New York: Garland.

______. 1996c. "Promise Unfulfilled: Clinton's Failure to Overturn the Military Ban on Lesbians and Gays." In *Gay Rights, Military Wrongs: Political Perspectives on Lesbians and Gays in the Military,* edited by Craig A. Rimmerman, 111–126. New York: Garland.

______. 1998a. "Military." In *St. James Press Gay and Lesbian Almanac,* edited by Neil Schlager, 253–272. Detroit: St. James Press.

______. 1998b. "U.S. Presidency." In *Encyclopedia of AIDS,* edited by Raymond A. Smith, 399–403. Chicago: Fitzroy Dearborn.

______. 2000. "A 'Friend' in the White House? Reflections on the Clinton Presidency." In *Creating Change: Sexuality, Public Policy, and Civil Rights,* edited by John D'Emilio, William B. Turner, and Urvashi Vaid, 43–56. New York: St. Martin's Press.

______. 2002. *From Identity to Politics: The Lesbian and Gay Movements in the United States.* Philadelphia: Temple University Press.

______. 2007. "The Presidency, Congress, and Same-Sex Marriage." In *The Politics of Same-Sex Marriage,* edited by Craig A. Rimmerman and Clyde Wilcox, 273–290. Chicago: University of Chicago Press.

Rimmerman, Craig A., Kenneth D. Wald, and Clyde Wilcox, eds. 2000. *The Politics of Gay Rights.* Chicago: University of Chicago Press.

Rimmerman, Craig A., and Clyde Wilcox, eds. 2007. *The Politics of Same-Sex Marriage.* Chicago: University of Chicago Press.

Robinson, Gene. 2012. *God Believes in Love: Straight Talk About Gay Marriage.* New York: Alfred A. Knopf.

Robinson, Paul. 2005. *Queer Wars: The New Gay Right and Its Critics.* Chicago: University of Chicago Press.

Rofes, Eric. 1990. "Gay Lib vs. AIDS: Averting Civil War." *Outlook,* no. 8 (Spring).

Rogers, Thomas. 2010. "Explaining American Schools' Gay Bullying Epidemic." *Salon.com,* December 12.

Rom, Mark Carl. 2000. "Gays and AIDS: Democratizing Disease?" In *The Politics of Gay Rights,* edited by Craig A. Rimmerman, 217–248. Chicago: University of Chicago Press.

Rosenberg, Debra. 2006. "A Renewed War over 'Don't Ask, Don't Tell.'" *Newsweek,* November 27, 8.

Rosenthal, Andrew. 2013. "The Court's Same-Sex Marriage Rulings." *New York Times,* June 26.

Ross, Alex. 2012. "Love on the March." *New Yorker,* November.

"The Same-Sex Marriage Rulings." 2013. *New York Times,* June 26.

Savage, Dan, and Terry Miller, eds. 2011. *It Gets Better: Coming Out, Overcoming Bullying and Creating a Life Worth Living.* New York: Baltimore.

Schiavi, Michael. 2011. *Celluloid Activist: The Life and Times of Vito Russo.* Madison: University of Wisconsin Press.

Schlager, Neil, ed. 1998. *St. James Press Gay and Lesbian Almanac*. Detroit: St. James Press.

Schmitt, Eric. 1994. "Gay Troops Say the Revised Policy Is Often Misused." *New York Times*, May 9, A1.

Schwartz, John. 2012. *Oddly Normal: One Family's Struggle to Help Their Teenage Son Come to Terms with His Sexuality*. New York: Gotham.

Scott, James. 1990. *Domination and the Arts of Resistance: Hidden Transcripts*. New Haven, CT: Yale University Press.

Seidman, Steven. 2002. *Beyond the Closet: The Transformation of Gay and Lesbian Life*. New York: Routledge.

Servicemembers Legal Defense Network. 2005. *Fact Sheet*, August 30, 1. http://www.sldn.org.

Shalikashvili, John M. 2007. "Second Thoughts on Gays in the Military." *New York Times*, January 2.

Shepard, Benjamin, and Ronald Hayduk, eds. 2002. *From ACT UP to the WTO: Urban Protest and Community Building in the Era of Globalization*. London: Verso.

Sherrill, Kenneth. 1996. "The Political Power of Lesbians, Gays, and Bisexuals." *PS: Political Science and Politics* 29, no. 3 (September): 469–473.

Shilts, Randy. 1993. *Conduct Unbecoming: Gays and Lesbians in the U.S. Military*. New York: St. Martin's Press.

Signorile, Michelangelo. 2011. "Rewriting History." *Advocate*, March, 26–27.

Silver, Nate. 2012. "Support for Gay Marriage Outweighs Opposition in Polls." *New York Times*, May 9.

______. 2013. "Same-Sex Marriage Availability Set to Double in One-Year Span." *New York Times*, June 26.

Siplon, Patricia. 2002. *AIDS and the Policy Struggle in the United States*. Washington, DC: Georgetown University Press.

Snyder, R. Claire. 2006. *Gay Marriage and Democracy: Equality for All*. Boulder, CO: Rowman and Littlefield.

Sokolove, Michael. 2004. "Can This Marriage Be Saved?" *New York Times Magazine*, April.

Solomon, Andrew. 2012. *Far from the Tree: Parents, Children, and the Search for Identity*. New York: Scribner.

Spade, Dean. 2011. *Normal Life: Administrative Violence, Critical Trans Politics, and the Limits of Law*. Brooklyn, NY: South End Press.

Stein, Rob. 2010. "Obama Administration Launches a Sex-Ed Program." *Washington Post*, A3.

Stoddard, Thomas B. 1989. "Why Gay People Should Seek the Right to Marry." In *We Are Everywhere: A Historical Sourcebook of Gay and Lesbian Politics*, edited by Mark Blasius and Shane Phelan, 753–757. New York: Routledge.

Stolberg, Sheryl Gay. 2009. "On Gay Issues, Obama Asks to Be Judged on Vows Kept." *New York Times,* June 30.

Strasser, Mark. 1997. *Legally Wed: Same-Sex Marriage and the Constitution.* Ithaca, NY: Cornell University Press.

Strub, Sean. 2014. *Body Counts: A Memoir of Politics, Sex, AIDS, and Survival.* New York: Simon and Schuster.

Sullivan, Andrew. 2004. *Virtually Normal: An Argument About Homosexuality.* New York: Alfred A. Knopf.

Talbot, Margaret. 2013. "Game Change." *New Yorker,* May 13, 21–22.

Tarrow, Sidney. 1994. *Power in Movement: Social Movements, Collective Action, and Politics.* Cambridge: Cambridge University Press.

Teal, Donn. 1995. *The Gay Mandates.* New York: St. Martin's Press.

Terkel, Amanda. 2013. "Tom Carper Signs On as 51st ENDA Cosponsor." *Huffington Post,* June 17.

"The Thirty Years' War: As AIDS Enters Its Fourth Decade, We Look Back at the Events That Changed the Course of History." 2011. *Out,* June/July 2011.

Tiemeyer, Phil. 2013. *Plane Queer: Labor, Sexuality, and AIDS in the History of Male Flight Attendants.* Berkeley: University of California Press.

Toobin, Jeffrey. 2013a. "Adieu, DOMA!" *New Yorker,* July 8 and 15, 27–28.

______. 2013b. "Wedding Bells." *New Yorker*, April 1, 21–22.

Vaid, Urvashi. 1995. *Virtual Equality: The Mainstreaming of Gay and Lesbian Liberation.* New York: Anchor Books.

______. 1997. "Coalition as Goal, Not Process." *Gay Community News* 22, no. 4 (Spring): 6–9.

______. 2012. *Irresistible Revolution: Confronting Race, Class and the Assumptions of LGBT Politics.* New York: Magnus Books.

Vick, Karl, and Ashley Surdin. 2008. "Most of California's Black Voters Backed Gay Marriage Ban." *Washington Post,* November 6.

Von Drehle, David. 2013. "How Gay Marriage Was Won." *Time,* April 8, 16–24.

Wald, Kenneth D. 2000. "The Context of Gay Politics." In *The Politics of Gay Rights,* edited by Craig A. Rimmerman, Kenneth D. Wald, and Clyde Wilcox, 1–28. Chicago: University of Chicago Press.

Wald, Kenneth D., and Graham B. Glover. 2007. "Theological Perspectives on Gay Unions: The Uneasy Marriage of Religion and Politics." In *The Politics of Same-Sex Marriage,* edited by Craig A. Rimmerman and Clyde Wilcox, 105–129. Chicago: University of Chicago Press.

Wallsten, Peter, and Scott Wilson. 2012. "For Obama, Gay Marriage Stance Born of a Long Evolution." *Washington Post,* May 11.

Warner, Michael. 1999. *The Trouble with Normal: Sex, Politics, and the Ethics of Queer Life*. New York: Free Press.

Welsh, Jennifer. 2011. "Homosexual Teen Suicide Rates Raised in Bad Environments." *www.livescience.com*, April 18.

Whitman, Christine Todd. 2005. *It's My Party Too: The Battle for the Heart of the GOP and the Future of America*. New York: Penguin Press.

Wieseltier, Leon. 1993. "Covenant and Burling." *New Republic*, February 1, 77.

Wilcox, Clyde. 2007. Preface to *The Politics of Same-Sex Marriage*, edited by Craig A. Rimmerman and Clyde Wilcox, ix–xi. Chicago: University of Chicago Press.

Wilcox, Clyde, Paul R. Brewer, Shauna Shames, and Celinda Lake. 2007. "If I Bend This Far I Will Break? Public Opinion About Same-Sex Marriage." In *The Politics of Same-Sex Marriage*, edited by Craig A. Rimmerman and Clyde Wilcox, 215–242. Chicago: University of Chicago Press.

Wilson, Cintra. 2011 and 2012. "Active Duty: Reviewing the Repeal of 'Don't Ask, Don't Tell.'" *Out*, December and January, 62, 64.

Wolfson, Evan. 2004. *Why Marriage Matters: American Equality and Gay People's Right to Marry*. New York: Simon and Schuster.

______. 2012. "For Marriage Equality, the Work's Not Just in Court." *New York Times*, December 10.

"The World at a Glance." 2007. *Week*, June 29, 7.

Wortman, James, with Maggie Francis and Robert Greenwald. 2010. "Health Care Reform Checkup." *POZ*, June, 44–47.

Yoshino, Kenji. 2012. "For Obama, It's About the Children." *New York Times*, May 12.

Index

CPSIA information can be obtained
at www.ICGtesting.com
Printed in the USA
LVOW10s0235060717
540360LV00014B/1725/P